THE MASKS
OF TRAGEDY

The Masks of Tragedy

ESSAYS ON SIX GREEK DRAMAS

THOMAS G. ROSENMEYER

decorations by Donald L. Weismann

UNIVERSITY OF TEXAS PRESS • AUSTIN

Library of Congress Catalog Card No. 63–7436
Copyright © 1963 by Thomas G. Rosenmeyer
All rights reserved
Printed in the United States of America

FOREWORD

IT MAY BE ASKED whether there is room for yet another study of Greek drama. If it is true that the ancient dramas have to be interpreted anew for each succeeding generation and for each cultural group, has this not been done with eminent success? A continuing stream of books and articles dealing with one phase or another of the subject testifies to its lasting popularity. Many of them are works of scholarship, designed for the benefit of the specialist; of these there can never be too many. The present volume does not claim to be one of them. As for the more popular publications, they fall roughly into two classes. The majority are devoted to the study of an author or a period. That is to say, the plays are analyzed under the auspices of a literary biography. This is important; if through an examination of the plays we can gain a greater insight into the personality or the purposes of a Sophocles, we are the beneficiaries. The same is true of the type of study in which a number of dramas are discussed for the sake of arriving at an understanding of the specific "laws" or the "idea" of tragedy. Even for the iconoclastic playwright there is, one suspects, such a thing as the model play or the norm against which he fashions the product of the moment. The principal disadvantage of this approach, however, has been that sometimes it does not do full justice to a particular play. If the study of the playwright or of the dramatic form is to be exhaustive, the evidence must be complete. That means, a large number of plays have to be taken into consideration. This emphasis on wealth of evidence, along with the demands of the major thesis argued by the critic, makes it impossible to devote as much scope to each play as it deserves. Significantly, no more than eight or ten pages are often thought sufficient for saying what has to be said about a play to make its evidence felt.

But a play is not only evidence. Hence a dissatisfaction with this kind of analysis has recently increased the output of studies, both in the form of articles and latterly also in the form of full-length books, which are devoted to the analysis of a single play. Where these unifocal studies have permitted a fuller savoring of a single work of art, without sidetracking us into comparison, statistics, biography, or anthropology, they have been welcome. But even so it is natural that a critic who channels his interpretive acumen into the explication of one play may come to regard this play as the realization of a generic ideal. Though this was not his original intention, he may eventually adopt the same perspective which prevails in the other camp, and see his play as the approximation to a norm, as representative rather than autonomous. It is, of course, humanly impossible to do anything else. Criticism, like other cognitive activities, operates with models and paradigms. But I dare say that what matters about a play is not the extent to which it is like any other play, but the way in which it is itself and different. This is, I suggest, how the ancient audiences received the performances. The jokes of Aristophanes justify the presumption that each play was felt to have it own ethos and its own objective.

My purpose, then, in writing these essays is twofold. First, I wish to devote enough space to the discussion of each play to allow its special tone and texture to emerge without hindrance and at leisure. And, second, I want to include in one collection analyses of plays so different from one another that the accent will come to rest on the variety of the tragic experience rather than on any one narrowly defined norm. The purpose is not without its perils. What seems to me necessary by way of an unhurried inquiry may appear to some slow and fullsome; the stress on variety and difference may be regarded as a willful disregard of systematic connections. In actual fact I have not been able to proceed without occasionally reminding myself that this is a play by Aeschylus or Euripides rather than just a play. And the combined analysis of two plays attempted in the third essay should prove that I have not discarded the comparative method entirely. But I should like to insist that the comparison was undertaken to underscore a contrast. The fact that both the *Ion* and the *Bacchae* are concerned with cult divinities is made the occasion for separating the plays as widely as the common concern allows.

Given this approach, the choice of the plays to be discussed, and the order in which they were to be taken up, were matters of some initial uncertainty. Eventually I decided to include among the titles some that are bound to be well known to the readers—Aeschylus' *Prometheus*, Euripides' *Bacchae* and *Alcestis*—and some that may be less familiar—Aeschylus' *Seven Against Thebes*, Sophocles' *Ajax*, and Euripides' *Ion*. As for the order, I arbitrarily decided to start with an extreme example of what may be called hieratic lyricism, the *Seven;* to finish with a tragicomedy, the *Alcestis;* to put the comparative essay on the *Bacchae* and the *Ion* in the middle; and to put the two heroic plays, the *Prometheus* and the *Ajax*, in second and fourth place. The order is not chronological, nor does it follow any other prescribed canons. But it does seem to me best suited to convey the impression of diversity and flexibility which I am concerned to argue.

The diversity of tragic experiences invites a diversity of critical approaches. The critic who wants to emphasize the wealth of what is possible within the dramatic genre must expose himself to the charges of eclecticism and impressionism. The only tool which I have firmly excluded is that of the biographical interpretation. For the purposes of this book I am not interested in finding out—though it is an eminently legitimate interest—how the young Sophocles differed from the old, how his techniques shifted along with his sympathies or his ideologies, and how this may account for the handling of a certain scene or character. For the present I want to regard the plays as going somewhere rather than as evolving from somewhere. I suspect that an ancient audience, too, is more likely to have been impressed with what the play had to say to them, not with the conditions of its manufacture.

There is a further score on which I propose to be abstemious. Modern criticism often begins by trying to discover what is explicit or implicit in the smaller units of a work of art, in the images and tropes and turns of speech, before it permits itself the luxury of conceiving a more general response. But it may well be that ancient drama becomes meaningful in its fashion only if the larger response precedes the analysis of the subunits, both in the perception of it and in the critical formulation. A meticulous scrutiny of details and key-words is important, but it must be obedient to a larger *parti pris.* By itself it will fail to generate a plausible facsimile of the intended reaction. Close reading has its use chiefly for purposes of verification rather than interpretation. This is particularly true of the intensive study of imagery. A criticism which starts out by collecting and classifying images and then proceeds to develop an interpretation based on the results of the collection, defies the essential simplicity—one might almost say naïveté —of the projected impression. Tragic diction and tragic thought were destined for the theater; they were meant to provoke certain large and immediate feelings of which an immense audience, taken as a group, should be capable.

The end of tragedy, it may therefore be said with some trepidation, abhors subtlety. In a criticism of Greek drama it is impossible to avoid using the simple obvious words—man, nature, gods, good, bad, nobility, suffering—which are the hallmark of that writing. The temptation is to go far beyond these essentials, and to ferret out meanings and references and effects which may not be there. I have not myself completely resisted this temptation; I would not have enjoyed my work if I had not made myself here and there liable to the charge of overinterpretation or inconsistency. One is, for example, tempted to plot the progress of a play—take the *Prometheus,* or a play by Seneca —in terms of pure dynamics, the movement from turmoil to relative calm and back. But though this touches upon an important element in the experience released by the performance, the gain is comparatively small. For the significant thing about most of the plays is their appeal to the conscious verbal imagination, to the communal intellect, if I may use this phrase. Kinetic and structural aspects are helpful, but they do not determine the effect of a play as significantly as elements which lie closer to the rational understanding.

Above all, however, there must be no undue belaboring of single words. On the whole, I think, the ancient dramatists would have approved of Maimonides when he said: "Let not the meaning of your words be far removed from their literal sense; say not: 'If a person probe deeply, he will see that what I said is right.' Let not your words require farfetched interpretation and extraordinary perception before they can be understood."[1] An interpretation of Greek dramas for an English-speaking audience makes poor enough reading; either the Greek must be translated into literal English or it should perhaps not be cited at all. In any case, the thrill which comes from being exposed to great poetry in bits and snatches is missing. But a Greekless reader ought to be assured that in the vast majority of cases the sense of the words is tolerably clear and not nearly so complicated as some nineteenth-century translations may have led him to believe.

Obviously, then, I do not consider a predominantly formalist or a structuralist treatment adequate to the task of examining the nature of Greek dramatic writing. Greek criticism did not consider textual patterns, sound combinations, structures of rhythm, or syntax the principal objectives of the craft. The audience was expected to respond less to the way things are said than to *what* they conceive the poet is talking about. Hence if the criticism attempted in these pages appears somewhat old-fashioned, my excuse must be that the Greeks themselves seem to have looked at their literature with a conventional eye. In fact, if we wish to put ourselves in the place of a fifth-century audience, we should pretend to think that the play is an illusion of reality, to be appreciated as a self-contained slice of life and not as the contrived product of an artistic plan. No self-respecting critic would now admit that this is a perspective which promises new results. And it may, quite properly, be asked whether there is any real hope

[1] Judah Goldin (ed.), *The Living Talmud* (New York, The New American Library, 1957), p. 89.

of transcending our present critical position, or whether there is any profit in adopting what is perhaps an inferior position, and one about which we know so little. But now and then it will be useful to pass up some of the more intriguing modern perspectives and to look at a play as if it were an action meant to be observed with no more sophistication and no less sympathy than those which we encounter in "real life."

As we all know, there is in the Greek literary experience a greater attention to audience reaction than, say, in the writings of the late eighteenth or early nineteenth century. Greek tragedy is a species of oratory aimed at generating in a jury of peers the passions appropriate to a life fully lived. Hence criticism should not shy away from the words "we" and "us" and "I." Our direct responses are indeed worth talking about, because the play needs us in order to have its own life, precisely as the ancient epics needed their princely listeners. But the playwright, unlike the bard, is not in evidence. We are face to face with the characters and the issues of the play; it is, therefore, legitimate now and then to talk about the characters as if they were saying and doing things on their own instead of being manipulated by the author. More than that, it is proper to talk about the characters as if they had a future and a past beyond the immediate scope of the play. The question: "How many children had Lady Macbeth?" is not perhaps so very silly after all. Will Ion be happy in Athens? What is going to happen to Cadmus? Greek drama, compressed and narrowly focused as it is, raises a great many questions which the play itself, outside of prologue or epilogue, has no time or no business to answer. The emergence of the questions into the consciousness of the audience is part of the effect of the drama. Sometimes the writer does not want a particular question to be asked; he then tries by dramatic means to block its formation. But there is no reason why criticism should not explore some of the vistas opened up. For the greatness of a play can be measured in part by the questions, profound or superficial, which it provokes in the minds of those who love it.

In sum, then, what I have attempted to do in these essays is to jot

down some of the questions—and one or two tentative answers—
which occurred to me in reading the plays and in reflecting upon my
initial responses. The essays were first given in the form of addresses
to groups of laymen under the auspices of the extension program
of the University of Washington, and I am grateful to the administration of that program for giving me that opportunity of first trying
out some of my remarks on a live and inordinately patient audience.
I am grateful also to those friends, teachers, and students who over
the years have helped me to assemble and organize my thoughts on the
subject. My friends Arnold Stein and Paul Pascal have each read a
chapter of the manuscript and assisted me with a compelling mixture
of critique and charity. My debt to the great scholars and critics who
have worked in the field of ancient drama is enormous. Those who
know about these matters will have no difficulty in identifying my
various obligations. I thought it better, however, not to burden the
writing with the scholarly apparatus of learned footnotes, except on
the few occasions where textual problems made this necessary. Finally,
I owe a great debt of gratitude to two fund-dispensing bodies, the
American Council of Learned Societies and the Graduate School of
the University of Washington, which honored me with stipends that
allowed me to take off two summers and finish the book.

T. G. R.

University of Washington
Seattle, Washington

CONTENTS

THE MASKS
OF TRAGEDY

A Note on the Translations

Line references in the text are to the first line of the passage cited. The translations, unless marked otherwise, are my own. My objective has been to be literal; they are as close to the Greek as I dared to keep them without lapsing into downright ugliness or unintelligibility. Only in the translations from the *Alcestis* have I occasionally ventured to push the humor at the expense of literalness.

Acknowledgment is made to the following publishers for permission to use quoted material: University of Chicago Press, six lines from *Aeschylus I: Oresteia,* and seventeen lines from *The Iliad of Homer,* both translated by Richmond Lattimore; Penguin Books (Harmondsworth, England), fourteen lines from *Euripides: The Bacchae and Other Plays,* translated by Phillip Vellacott, and thirteen lines from *Sophocles: Electra and Other Plays,* translated by E. F. Watling; Harcourt, Brace & World, Inc., sixteen lines from T. S. Eliot, *The Complete Poems and Plays 1909–1950.*

Seven Against Thebes:
THE TRAGEDY OF WAR

THIS IS A PLAY ABOUT WAR, a play "full of Ares," as an ancient critic put it. Perhaps we should say: a play about *a* war, for the attack of the Argive champions on Thebes, the struggle of Greek against Greek, brother against brother, is a particular chapter in history. Aeschylus does all he can to remind us of the uniqueness of the event. But the nature of war is such that the chroniclers of particular wars always transcend their immediate focus and touch upon the archetype. War, "the father of all," is a more intrusive reality than other universals operating behind and through the events.

How, then, does one go about writing a play about war? One way is that of Shakespeare, in whose Histories war is presented as an extension of diplomacy, the busyness and chicanery of royal intercourse brought to a boil. Political intrigue, council sessions, duels, flourishes, and soldiers groping in darkness: the panoramic range of the Elizabethan stage delights us with the sheer beauty of effort, of vital force clashing with vital force. What tragedy there is, is almost forgotten over the bluster and the strainings on the field of battle. Homer provides us with the closest Greek analogue. Yet there is this difference that in the *Iliad* fighting is not only a thing of beauty, but carries its own tragic moral. For Shakespeare, war is an extension, a pinpointing, and also a catharsis of the tragedy of human relations; for Homer, war is the proof and authorization of life itself.

Another way is that of some recent playwrights who portray the fears and the miseries and the desperate gentleness of the common soldier. E. M. Remarque's *Im Westen Nichts Neues,* conceived as a novel, but experienced as drama, set the tone. The mood is unheroic, candid, lyrical, an Archilochian mixture of grossness and sensibility. In the film version of Remarque's book the hero dies while watching a butterfly. In this kind of play, life stands still and death takes control. That is to say, war shows itself as a protracted and endless numbing of life, an eraser of ambition and desire and privilege, an embalmer of Everyman. There are no heroes in this war, only sufferers; their pleasures are such as can be eked out from death, the small inglorious pleasures of men condemned to die. Of this perspective brief flashes are to be caught here and there in Greek drama. Take, for example, the herald's speech in the *Agamemnon* (555 ff., tr. Richmond Lattimore):

> Were I to tell you of the hard work done, the nights
> exposed, the cramped sea-quarters, the foul beds . . .
>   We lay
> against the ramparts of our enemies, and from
> the sky, and from the ground, the meadow dews came out
> to soak our clothes and fill our hair with lice.

The herald goes on to recall the dying of the birds, the sea paralyzed into wavelessness, the dead men fixed in their graves. Hopelessness, revulsion, and death are the keynotes of this formulation of war.

Then there is the war lampooned by Aristophanes. His thoughtful clowns are brothers in the flesh to the Achaean soldiers encamped below Troy and fighting against dew and vermin. But in comedy it becomes possible for the sufferers to change into scoffers, to turn back Death with a flick of the wrist and laugh him off the scene. Aristophanes achieves this by domesticating war; in the place of swords and helmets and breastplates, the paraphernalia of a heroic delusion, the comic heroes use cooking utensils to make battle. Thus war becomes both manageable and funny. Yet its horror continues to be felt, for the domestication remains a device, open for all to see. The device produces a moral, by posing a question: why not use the pots and pans for making porridge or soup? Why not use iron for ploughshares, atomic power for cancer research? It is the triumph of comedy that now and then, using the kind of material which informs tragedy, it can, by means of comic distortions and inversions, prompt the asking of specific questions and generate a directed response.

In most plays about war, it appears, the treatment is unified. War is visualized in a certain way, and the actions and responses of the characters are brought into line with that particular emphasis. It is not to be expected that Coriolanus feels about fighting as Virgilia does. For Agamemnon the Trojan War means one thing, to Clytemnestra it means something quite different. But within the imagination of the audience each play that deals with a war establishes a recognizable pattern, a unique impression of the specific quality and meaning of that war. This is as true of Shakespeare's Histories as it is of Goethe's *Götz* and of the political plays of Euripides. The status and the appeal of the war are clearly defined, for a very good reason. For war, in these plays, is to serve as a matrix for the action or inaction of the tragic hero. The brighter, the better defined the foil, the more mysterious and affecting is the individual heroism pictured against it.

The *Seven Against Thebes* of Aeschylus deviates from this norm, as it deviates from the attitudes toward war lightly sketched above. In this drama war and the hero are not related to each other as the field of action and the agent. There is between them a reciprocal relation, a mutually quickening involvement, which reduces the traditional schemes of free will, fate, and responsibility to irrelevance. The war shapes Eteocles, and Eteocles in turn shapes the war. What is more, the war itself is developed in terms of a daring counterpoint. Toward the beginning of the drama it is an impersonal mechanism, an irresistible brutal assault on the weakness of man, a senseless grinding pressure from abroad. Under its aegis beauty takes refuge in despair and heroism is cast out. Toward the end of the play, on the other hand, the machine aspect of war is long forgotten, beauty has re-entered with the engagement of the leader, and heroism saves the day. Between the beginning and the end there is much subtle manipulation of the contrapuntal themes of tanks versus bayonets, of logistics versus courage, of Ares versus the Curse. As against Shakespeare's panorama of blood and fuss and thunder, against Remarque's portrayal of human frailty sustaining senseless bombardment, Aeschylus' image of war in the *Seven* is more complex and more comprehensive. It is also more real because it partakes of the ambivalence and the mystery which attach to the heroic achievement.

It will be useful to recall the ancient legend, or, more specifically, the version of the legend which Aeschylus chose to adopt. Laius, king of Thebes, was told that Thebes would flourish only if he had no sons. He flouts the oracle, begets Oedipus, exposes him after his birth, and is ultimately killed by him. The flouting of the oracle in combination with the parricide produces a curse which settles heavily on the royal house. Oedipus himself, crushed by the curse, revitalizes the Fury by cursing his own sons before he dies. Against this compounded curse the brothers, Eteocles and Polynices, attempt the feeble protection of a political settlement. Eteocles, the older, is to remain and rule in Thebes; Polynices is to go south and seek a kingdom of his own. Polynices is lucky; on the strength of a dynastic marriage in Argos he gains influence and persuades Adrastus, king of Argos, to march against

Thebes and challenge his brother. As the play opens, the siege has begun. Eteocles selects seven leaders from the Theban army to engage seven champions of the Argive forces at the seven gates of Thebes, arranging for himself to take up the position opposite Polynices. The brothers kill each other, the city is saved, and the play ends with the sons of Oedipus being laid alongside their father in a holy grave.[1]

It is often said that Aeschylus delights in spectacle, in violent action on the stage, in vivid colors and extravagant gestures. The present play forms an exception to this rule also. The setting is simple. At the back of the stage stands a large stepped altar adorned with seven divine statues, each of them representing the divinity that presides over one of the seven gates of Thebes. It is these seven images, clearly characterized as belonging to Athena, Ares, Poseidon, and so forth, which determine the stage action. Both the chorus and the actors focus their attention, as the progress of the play requires, now on this divinity and now on that, or on all of them jointly. The choreography and the movements of the actors may be plotted as a continuous rite of worship, as a series of supplications, protests, and challenges directed to the Theban pantheon enshrined on the stage. In other words, there is no allowance for the acting out of personal relationships. The constant reference to the gods clothes the proceedings in severity. The public character and the grandeur of the issues, at least so we are led to believe from the beginning, rule out intimacy and sentiment. Apparently they also rule out flamboyance and baroqueness. The stage is simple, the movements on it deliberate and repetitious, masks and costumes purposely subdued in color and design. The reason for this intentional lack of variety and sprightliness will become clear later. For the present it is sufficient to note the fact.

[1] In spite of some recent objections, most scholars are today agreed that the play originally ended with line 1004. What follows in the traditional text is subsequent additions inspired by Sophocles' *Antigone*.

ii

As the play opens, we face a public situation. Thebes is under attack, and the question is whether and how the salvation of the city can be worked out. Eteocles, the king, is charged with finding a solution to the problem. In this task he is disturbed by the presence of the chorus of Theban women. They break in on his calm and reasoned dispositions with an almost prophetic fervor, born from fear. In their excitement they visualize the enemy spilling over the city walls although the battle has not yet begun. Eteocles, the confident organizer, manages to break the hysteria of the women. Actually, as we shall see in a moment, he strikes a compromise with them. He suggests that they go home, a time-honored suggestion wherever a tragic character comes upon an excited chorus. But of course they cannot take his advice, for a chorus must remain on the scene. As women imperiled by war they symbolize the endangered city as a whole; and in this capacity they must be present to frame the composure of the King, and to justify his decisions.

Eteocles, it appears, simultaneously faces two different fronts. On the one hand there are the attackers, beyond the stage, outside the city. They are the enemy, and his position as leader requires that he devote his undivided attention to counteracting that threat. At the same time, however, his mind is distracted, and his function complicated, by the women who are on the stage, within the city, visible to the audience. Standing between the two blocks he forms a connecting link between them; he finds out that he may have as much to fear from the one as from the other. In the end, in spite of some brave maneuvring to protect his rear, he is crushed between them. But this will not happen until the play has run its course. For the present we do not see the disaster, but take our visual cues from the King. By alternately focusing on the aggressors outside the city and on the sufferers within, Eteocles permits us to recognize the gulf which separates the two. In this we are helped along by the poetic elaboration of a network of crucial antinomies. On the stage we witness a segment of Greek culture, with its altars, its gods, and its demonstrations of freedom; beyond, there are barbaric rites, Titans invoked, and the threat of slavery. Here we see reasoned organization and responsible administration, only temporarily unbalanced by the cries of the women; out there we sense disordered, brutal impetus. On the stage we review solid fighters, relying on courage and modesty and little else; beyond, the instruments of action are beasts and emblems and idle boasts. Here, soft women conveying the suffering that comes with war; there, shields and chariots and brazen bells, the glossy impenetrable impersonal equipment of battle. In Thebes, a reliance on Earth, the great mother, the giver of food and the shaper of feelings; outside, blood and fire and rootless, barren monstrosity.

Let us look at some of the details of this antiphonal system of references. The conception that the Thebans are Greeks while their enemies are barbarians has of course no foundation in history or reason. What is more, for an Athenian playwright in the fifth century to intimate that an Argive army was less Greek than the Thebans is a diplomatic *faux pas* of the first order. And yet Aeschylus dares to fly in the face of familiar history, by unmistakably contrasting Thebes (71),

> a city which pours forth the speech of Greece

with (170)

> an army of another tongue.

For Aeschylus is a dramatist, not a historian. To point up the viciousness of war, and to deepen the gulf between the city and the forces beyond, he does not scruple to practice a patent deception and to paint his Argives with the colors of the Persians of recent historical memory. The result, at least to begin with, is a clearer drawing of the lines, a more crystalline hardening of opposites.

One reason why the enemies have to be barbarian in speech and character is their lack of a home. To be Greek, within the world of this play, means to be tied to the soil which your fathers have cultivated. In his speech from the throne at the beginning of the drama, Eteocles contemplates the beneficence of Earth (16),

> the mother, our own nurse.
> She reared the young crawling on her kindly lap,
> entertaining the full burden of your nurture . . .

The word for "nurture" is *paideia,* the sum total of everything physical and spiritual that makes a man a mature Greek. This culture is rooted in the soil; no immigrant or vagabond can have it. The loss of Thebes would mean, beyond all else, the loss of a living hoard of Greek tradition. The opponents do not share in this earth-bound culture; uprooted, uncommitted as they are, they are shown to practice a vain and vicious self-reliance, an autarky such as is exhibited by fools, villains, and barbarians.

When the messenger first tells us about the seven enemy champions we find them engaged in a bloody and uncivilized rite (43):

> . . . who cut a bull's throat into a black-rimmed shield,
> and dipped their hands into the gore of the bull,
> and swore their oaths to Ares, Enyo, and bloodthirsty
> Terror . . .

There is a reference here to the magic ordeal of tasting bull's blood, to put to the proof the validity of one's purpose. Pausanias tells of a priestess who is forced to prove her virginity by drinking bull's blood; the presumption is that if she does not speak the truth, the blood will kill her. Such magic is not part of the *paideia* espoused by Eteocles. By itself, however, this would not be enough. What finally stamps the enemies as barbarians is that they do not swear by the gods of their city. They have no city in which to anchor themselves, they live in a vacuum, unsupported by the values of an experienced past. Their lack of a mooring reduces them to the folly of taking their oaths by a god who happens to be a protector of Thebes. True, they call on Ares in his capacity as a war god. But this invocation of a glorified *Augenblicksgott* cannot be expected to hold its own against an invocation in which Ares figures as a beneficial deity of continuous force. Not only are the barbarians foot-loose and unorganized, their very tactics are self-defeating.

The Thebans have freedom, the opponents offer slavery. This constant theme, struck whenever the issue between Greeks and barbarians is raised, forms one of the major motifs developed in the choral songs. The women fear enslavement, ending in concubinage. With vivid and

pathetic colors they paint scene after scene of subjugation and humiliation. But at this point Aeschylus introduces a jarring note. Eteocles, at
pains to calm their fears, suggests to the women that it is they who, by
their own behavior, are liable to bring about their enslavement (254):

> It is you yourselves who enslave me and all the city!

Perhaps he means to say only that their lack of control is interfering
with an effective defense of Thebes. But I believe there is more in
this than the forecast of a dreaded outcome. The present tense of the
verb and the steady progression from "you" to "me" to "the city"
hint at a contagion spreading outward from the women. Their behavior shows that they are unfree, they are jettisoning the dignity and
the spiritual strength, the *sophrosyne,* which they should have absorbed with their *paideia.* Eteocles reminds them of their birthright
and their obligations as free citizens. For the members of the chorus
are citizens, whatever the status of women in Greek politics.

In this fashion Aeschylus averts what might have been a fatal flaw
in his design. There is nothing more dangerous to the successful
planning of a tragedy than a moral situation which is all black and all
white. The treatment by antinomies which pervades the play brings
it very close indeed to the line beyond which tragedy resolves into
melodrama and audiences may hiss in comfort. The names of the
brothers, Eteocles—the man of true fame—and Polynices—the man
of much strife—underscore the tendency toward moral naïveté.
Aeschylus is daring enough to exploit this onomastic antithesis when
it suits his purpose, as if it involved no element of risk at all (577).
But this is, after all, a tragedy, and it can be that only because the
antinomies are not allowed to stand without some subtle adjustment.
Hence the characterization of the women, who are not entirely free.
The absence of Polynices from the stage is a further touch to blunt
the edge of melodrama. It is true, of course, that he could have come
on the scene only under the protection of a truce; and that would
have meant proliferating the action in a way which Aeschylus, unlike Euripides, avoids. Polynices, at any rate, does not appear; and a
villain off stage can never be quite so effective in drawing upon him-

self the hatred of the audience as an adversary who faces the hero visibly and concretely.

But these are rather superficial measures. There are other, more incisive, means whereby Aeschylus arranges to prevent the set contrarieties from degenerating into a moral paradigm. They are, principally, the dynamics of the selection scene, and the gradual self-revelation, completely unexpected, of Eteocles, who in the end turns out to be, and to have been, quite different from what we had a right to expect. For, and this is part of the irony which restores to the action its tragic dimension, Eteocles winds up as one who "would seem rather than be."

The initial role of Eteocles is highlighted by one of those nautical metaphors which recur in many parts of the play (1):

> He must speak to the point
> who watches the course from the city's deck,
> his hand on the tiller and his eyes unsoothed by sleep.

Eteocles is the pilot of the State. There is no reason to doubt, during the first part of the play, that his chief business is to guide his crew. His speeches bear down significantly on his status as a public functionary, as a guarantor of order and safety. It is as an administrator that he clashes with the chorus. About his soul, his private feelings, his hopes and fears as a human being, we learn nothing at all. The public crisis requires a public official to cope with it according to the lights of his profession. He is the sort of professional whom the Sophists were soon to advocate as the promoter and chief instrument of human perfectibility. Eteocles calls to his fellow citizens (14):

> Help the city, help the altars of our native
> gods . . .
> and the children, and Earth, the mother, our nurse!

The premise of his command is that men are responsible and effective agents, that they are masters in their own houses. They have the power to protect the city and the altars—the two cannot be separated; they may even protect the gods, for is not Earth a goddess? The good city, the end of human ambition, is within the reach of man if only

he puts himself out and knows how to achieve it. Thus the administrator proudly appeals to the reasoned, orderly human achievement
which the optimism of the age proclaims to be both feasible and
necessary.

The language of political authority has a ring all its own. It makes
statements, it shouts commands, it never hedges or wavers or falters.
Above all, it works through speech. Eteocles has no lyrics. His iambic
trimeters consistently reflect the rational calm of his public commitment. The King, as king, has no music. Contrast the women; their
utterance exhausts itself in exclamations and interjections and rhetorical questions. Theirs is the language of despair, of terror, of the
imagination. Except for a short passage (245 ff.) when Eteocles seemingly succeeds in abating their frenzy and the chorus respond to his
advice through the mouth of their leader, the choral communication is lyrical. They sing and dance out their experiences, and the
varying curve of their passions finds audible expression in the intricate texture of their musical rhythms. It is almost as if we could read
the precise quality of each momentary feeling from the "beat"—
dochmiac or some variety of Aeolic—to which it is sung. It is only
toward the end, when Eteocles reverses himself, that the shock causes
the chorus to interrupt the continuity of this musical pattern and to
lapse into speech. But this is a deviation which proves the rule. The
antithetical positions of the leader and his flock are acted out through
the antithesis between music and the spoken word. Particularly when
they turn toward each other, to persuade or beseech, the "epirrhematic"
alternation of song and speech (203 ff.) carries an obvious moral.

We have noted that the mind of Eteocles works on the level of
reason, while the women give themselves over to their emotions and
their violent fancies. This is only another way of saying that it is
Eteocles' role to think of others and for others, whereas the members
of the chorus are wrapped up in their own fears and specters. At any
rate this is true of the Eteocles and the chorus who are presented to
us in the first half of the play. That the women should be so concerned about their own fate and their own sufferings, instead of helping to support high strategy, is only to be expected. It is not for noth-

ing that this chorus consists of women. This is a play about war, and war's destructive power is felt most sharply by women. Men brave war, they enter into a partnership with it, the terms of the partnership being that if they win, they have the glory, and if they are killed, they have neither shame nor suffering. But women are the losers whatever the outcome. Driven by restless fancies the chorus contemplate only the worst, and some of Aeschylus' formulations have the keen edge of collective memories of pain (326):

> . . . and that the women be corralled and herded,
> young and old,
> dragged by the hair as horses by the mane,
> with their dresses torn on their bodies . . .

Or (333):

> Weep upon girls freshly plucked who, even before
> the cruel harvest of marriage rites, leave
> their home on an odious path.
> Nay, I say that the dead
> have a fate better than this.

Or again (363):

> Slaves now, young, untrained in suffering,
> enduring a captive bed
> of a man in luck, an
> enemy superior.
> The only hope that the night runs its course,
> a steady surf
> of cries and pains.

The picture is one of women wasted, violently and at random. Aeschylus merges this with another picture, a vision of foodstuffs recklessly spilled (357):

> A wealth of fruits strewn on the ground
> where they fell
> vex the spirit and stab
> the housewife's eye.
> Again and again the gift of the earth
> in senseless confusion pours itself out
> in waves of nothingness.

This passage comes just before the description of the women entering the captor's bed. The housewifely concern for food wasted, for larders raided and provisions spilled, is mingled with sorrow for the shame and the hurt of the women's fate. As a portrayer of women's thoughts and feelings Aeschylus has few equals among the great writers of tragedy. He does not set out to create lifelike characters, to copy the bundle of significances and irrelevancies which constitute a specific personality. But he understands the important differences between the world of men and the world of women. This prevents him from ever designing his women as mere negations or parodies of masculinity, such as are occasionally found in the plays of Sophocles and Euripides. The dramatic situation is often contrived or abstract, but the variety of human responses which Aeschylus builds into his situations is drawn from a fountain of sympathy and discrimination.

The women suffer most in war. Their suffering is augmented by the acuteness with which each sense reacts to its stimuli. As a description of the fall of a city, the choral ode in which the women envisage the enemy bursting into their midst is very nearly perfect (338):

> When a city is conquered she
> suffers many ills.
> Man drives man, now this, now another,
> kills, or puts to the torch. The whole
> bastion is filmed with smoke.
> Raging Ares, man-destroyer, blows
> his breath, polluting sanctity.
> Rumblings throughout the city, the network of turrets
> inclines,
> man is killed
> by man with the spear.
> Bloodied wailings ring,
> just born, of
> babes at the breast.
> Pillage, kindred of random running.
> Plunderer settles with plunderer,
> calls him empty-handed, himself empty-handed,

wishes to have him for partner,
craving neither less nor an equal portion.
What sense could
be conjectured from this?

The impressionistic, not to say pointillistic, arrangement of wailing
babes—not experienced as babes but as wailings, as units made up
of blood and cries and fondling and death—of roaming plunderers,
fire and smoke, leaning battlements and calculating eagerness, is untranslatable. This is the quintessence of war, its terror and its incalcula-
bility, and also its inhuman nonchalance. For war, seen whole, de-
taches itself from the feelings and motives of individual souls and
turns into a distant machine, dealing out wounds and shocks on so
vast a scale that the net effect, even in Aeschylus' powerful verse, is
one of remoteness and ease, and almost of beauty.

When the chorus, in their characteristic hallucinations, see the
enemy vaulting the wall, the objects on which their inner eye dwells
are many: horses, chariots, helmets, plumes, spears, bridles, shields
small and large, and disembodied crashes and thunderings (100):

> Listen to the clang of the shields—
> do you hear it? . . .
> My eyes are on it—the crash of many spears.

Behind this imposing front of armor and equipment the men themselves are barely noticed.[2] The concentration on the war machine, on
the gear and the artillery, is deliberate. For it communicates the hard
impersonality of war which Aeschylus wishes us to accept as the initial
thesis of the play. Above all, there is the accent on the shields. The
symbolic function of the shields in the selection sequence will be discussed directly. But long before that phase of the play, beginning with
the pouring of bull's blood into a "black-rimmed shield," the shield asserts itself as the principal image of the vision of war we have been
discussing: war as a meaningless mechanism, as crude physical necessity and violence, as the impact of mass on mass. We need not rely
on our own sense of metaphor to see how fitting the image is; archaic

_____
[2] In line 92 Buecheler's *poda* must, for this reason, be rejected.

vase painting furnishes us with independent evidence. When the artist paints a duel, the contortions of the limbs, the tautness of the facial muscles, are sharply individualized. Each fighter has his own posture and his own momentum; the contest is one in which two souls meet and clash. The arms, though an important part of the artistic design, are largely decorative, or at any rate subordinate to the contours of the heroic physique. But then there are the vases with serried ranks of fighters moving into battle or engaging an enemy host. In such scenes of mass fighting the soldiers are, as a rule, barely differentiated as men; their movements and their facial expressions form a repetitive design. Only their shields, reaching from chin to knee and allowing only the smallest margin to heads and extremities, are grandly distinguished, by their blazons. These blazons—snakes and eagles and bulls' heads and Gorgons and boars—form the real personalities, the true entities engaged in the battle. It is a battle of shields, not of men.

This is the formulation which Aeschylus uses in the first half of his play. The conception is essentially visual, invented by painters for their panels of mass war. Because it appeals to the eye, its use by Aeschylus is particularly effective. For it is important that a playwright should, at the beginning of a tragic action, supply his audience with a firm visual anchoring. The image of the shield permits us to follow the development of the theme with a full perception of the distance we are travelling. More particularly we shall be able to appreciate the achievement of Eteocles, who, in spite of the seemingly impervious harshness of war symbolized by the shield, succeeds in imposing his organic, unmechanical, purposeful will upon it. But I must not anticipate. For the present let us merely acknowledge the objective of the design: a picture of war as a destructive machine, crushing anonymous human existences, blotting men from sight. Even the soldiers seen plundering and burning and entering into mock partnerships are tentacles of the mechanized monster. Their roaming is a compulsive thing, spasmodic jerks of the complex, but in its way perfectly coordinated, robot.

Eteocles begins his career as a strategist. That is to say, he intends to accept the machine at its face value and to meet it with counter-measures channeled through the line of command. His position vis-à-vis the chorus is typical of his policy. There are, as I have said, two areas of activity, the field of action outside the city walls, and the community within. The two are, from the point of view of naïve realism, separate, and the King, with his rational, organizational approach to the task, would like to keep them separate. But the women confuse the two worlds; they have their vision of the machine rolling over the walls. It is this visionary muddling of realities, this sacrifice of the tidy distinctions set up by the rational mind, which provided Plato with one of his chief objections to the psychological effect of tragedy. The women fail to distinguish between the present and the future, sense experience and hallucinations, the here and the there. Eteocles is a Platonist; he wants to keep the two worlds distinct and to assign the appropriate value to each.

The same proto-Platonism also characterizes the religious stand of Eteocles. Over against the self-surrendering enthusiasm of the chorus he puts the emphasis in worship on discipline and decorum. In his view service to the gods takes its cue from reasons of State. There is no conflict between Church and State; rather, the city is all, and the gods are a part of its political life (236):

> I do not mind your honoring the race of gods.
> But lest you turn your citizens' hearts to baseness,
> be calm, do not indulge your fears!

In their exchange—the chorus singing and dancing and Eteocles countering with speech—the women insist on imploring and embracing their gods, whereas the King feels that ritual must not interfere with preparations for defense. His attack on orgiastic cult practices borders on downright secularity (217):

> It is said
> that when a city falls the gods desert.

The Aeschylean hero stands alone, unaided by the gods, sometimes obstructed by their wills. In the present circumstances the unnatural fervor of the gods' worshippers blocks his administrative progress. As

a general and tactician, he cannot allow religious commitment to endanger his planning. He seems to believe that good generalship is
all that is needed. The efforts of the citizens must be directed toward
one goal only: to turn back and perhaps destroy, by means of a reasoned campaign and with only nominal help from the gods, the
machine rumbling beyond the walls.

iii

At the end of the stretta which concludes the
exchange between the King and his people (245 ff.) there is a momentary reconciliation. It marks the end of the exposition, of the setting of the stage for the tragic action that is to follow. The women
are impressed with the warnings of Eteocles; they promise to control
themselves, to subject their anxieties to the military-political-philo-
sophical discipline recommended by him (263):

I hold my tongue; and bear the general fortune.

From here on, the women are launched on their slow road to political
and personal salvation. There will be lapses into their old nervous-
ness and trepidation, notably in the ode which follows immediately
upon their apparent adjustment to the policy of Eteocles, after the
King quits the stage and leaves them to themselves. The metrical patterns of the ode, and of the brief choral interludes which follow,
testify to a continuing undercurrent of fear and self-concern. But the
first flash of a new spirit has been glimpsed, a token of the strength
and the freedom which the women are to achieve before the play
comes to an end.

More important, Eteocles, at precisely the same moment, begins to
travel in the opposite direction. The reconciliation is no one-sided affair. To pacify the chorus and give them the confidence they need
for their conversion, the King promises to relinquish his generalship
and to become a fighting soldier. This decision to fight—though
Adrastus, the leader of the opposition, does not—is a concession won
from Eteocles in his contest with the women. Ostensibly the move is
not out of keeping with the military preparedness for which he

stands. In reality it is in the nature of an abdication. Earlier, before the
force of the choral frenzy exacted its toll, he had asked (208):

> How now, does the skipper, when his ship
> wearies against the sea swell, find a means
> of safety by leaving the stern for the bow?

With his announcement that he will share in the fighting (282):

> I shall range six men, and I shall be the seventh,
> to ply our oars against the enemy . . .

he himself turns into a skipper who leaves the stern, who gives up his
post of command and joins the sailors in their undirected efforts
throughout the length of the ship. The detached leader, the organizer,
begins to be personally involved. At first the involvement is only on
the surface; his fighting is to be primarily for show, to convince the
women that there is nothing to fear. Even in the thick of the battle
he intends to remain clear-sighted, to keep the reins of the strategy
in his hands. He continues to regard himself as the pilot of the city,
as if such doubling in brass were possible in the world of the city-
state. But administrative discipline is not the stuff from which
heroes are made.

The chorus calmed, Eteocles leaves. Now we expect the battle.
But Greek drama shows no battles on the stage, just as it is reluctant
to show deaths. Perhaps the writers feel that an enactment of dying,
particularly of blood and wounds, would strain the nice tension between truth and illusion which is demanded in the theater. An imitation of feelings or of certain actions causes the audience to feel
sympathy or joy or horror as the occasion warrants. An imitation of
death is likely to provoke disbelief or, worse, laughter. There may be
other reasons, beyond good taste and a sense of what is proper and
effective, to account for the reluctance to dramatize death, especially
violent death. Some suggest that the religious setting of the performance, the Dionysiac background, must be held partly responsible.
Whatever the reason, the battle cannot be staged. It must be reshaped
to fit the bounds of the tragedy.

Now what is a heroic battle? It is the measuring up of two men against each other. What counts is the comparative standing of the two contenders, the reserves and intentions they bring into the fight, the robustness or lack of robustness with which they impress their opponents. Significantly in Homer the great duels are fought through the medium of oratory before they are decided by means of arms. Often we are made to feel that the fight is won when one of the heroes has managed to deflate the ego of his opponent through his superior art of boasting. The wounds inflicted afterward are merely the natural consequence of the power arrangement which the speeches of the men have rehearsed before our eyes. Thus, if we could look into the hearts of the people as they confront each other, instead of having our eyes distracted by the haphazard noise and smoke and physical pain of the battle, we might perhaps be able to catch the quintessence of the duel. We should perceive the form or idea rather than the phenomenon, which is stunted and disfigured by accidental detail. The confrontation of vital components is to be found already in the antiphonal symbolism discussed earlier. But now we need more than a thematic counterpoint. We need a concrete clash, the full shock value of the sight of solid bodies meeting head on. To furnish this is the purpose of the selection sequence. We cannot have the paltry reality of a genuine battle; so the formal organization of speeches and counter-speeches, stately and deliberate and richly colored, gives us what we need to know about each of the fighters, to judge or to applaud. The sequence permits us not only to *see* the duels, as we might in a proper war, but to assess their worth and to reflect on the rights and wrongs of the fighters. Above all, it saves the duels from appearing either ludicrous or obscure.

It is easy to be put off by the severe symmetry of the selection sequence. Its length also might give us pause, for, if we include the choral odes which frame it at beginning and end, the sequence constitutes more than half of the play. But the formal severity is a basic feature of the plan. We are reminded of analogous structural designs on archaic vases and temple friezes. The visual arts of Aeschylus' time are committed to the principles of symmetry and repetitive patterns. In the present case, however, the formalism of the art has more than tradition to commend it. It serves to dramatize a sort of ritual, a consecration of the spirit of war, in which each initiative, each thrust and counterthrust, is granted equal time and a matching benediction. There is no haste about this ceremony; a sacred service is expected to be deliberate, exhaustive, canonical. Above all else it must satisfy the participants' sense of continuity, their feeling that what is taking place has happened before and will happen again. Recurrence and repetition are of the essence of the ritual event.

The sequence consists of seven double panels, each separated from its neighbor by a brief choral interlude in which the enduring fears of the women continue to be voiced. Each of the seven panels consists of two speeches; in the first the messenger describes the preparations of an attacker; in the second Eteocles arranges for a defendant to repel the enemy. At the end of Eteocles' final rejoinder the chorus do not add their usual sung comment but adopt the blank verse of the speakers. For once they respond with a remonstrance rather than a sentiment or apprehension. This suggests that the last panel is different from the others, and that perhaps the others are meant to prepare for this one. Indeed, just before the choral ode which concludes the sequence there is an exchange between Eteocles and the chorus, parallel to the exchange which prompted the earlier reconciliation and obviously conceived as a complement to it. By purely formal means, therefore, we are given to understand that at the end of the selection sequence the King and the chorus once more find themselves at opposite poles, but in reverse, and that a new solution of their difference must be worked out. The reason for the new constellation of attitudes is supplied by the sequence itself. It turns out to be the dramatist's chief instrument for refashioning our vista of war, for guiding us from the impersonal horror of the machine and its extensions to the moral and spiritual substance of the heroic encounter.

If we compare the attackers named by the messenger with the defenders sent against them by Eteocles, the Thebans are, for the most part, a colorless lot. They have to be, for color in this play is linked with wrong. The colorfulness of the enemies is part of their barbarism,

their Orientalism; it is the visual confirmation of their boastful preen-
ing. Color is, as it were, the accompaniment of emptiness. Solidity
and substance are persuasive enough without the surface thrill of an
optic illusion. This also explains why, as mentioned earlier, there is a
notable lack of color in the Theban setting. The throne of modesty
worshipped by several of the defenders is no glossy façade. The fiery
spirit of Polyphontes, though superior in power to the flaming fire-
brand in the hands of his adversary Capaneus, cannot compare with
it for visual magnificence.[3]

The aggressors are all the more interesting. First there is Tydeus.
Aeschylus' audience knew that he killed the Theban champion and
drank his brain, for which deed he was himself struck down by the
gods. Aeschylus does not refer explicitly to this extraordinary tale,
but the characterization of Tydeus keeps close to the tradition. He is
a beast; more particularly he is the proverbially roaring beast. He
roars like a serpent—the context suggests that the bellow of a dragon
rather than the hiss of a snake is intended; a little later (392)

> . . . he neighs
> like a horse that pants against the bridle's might,
> the blare of the trumpet driving him ahead.

He is all animal sound, and bells attached to his shield furnish a
continuous obligato to the "mad noonday brayings" of his voice. The
beast imagery and the impression of vocal compulsiveness carry us
beyond the limits of good and evil. Tydeus lacks the moral dimension
which makes of a man a responsible human agent. He is part of the
animated machine; through the turbulence of Aeschylus' verse we
experience some of the terror spread by the inhuman howl of the
monster.

Capaneus, the next man from Argos, though differently conceived,
is of the same stuff. Like Tydeus and all the other attackers but one
he is a blasphemer (427):

[3] The underplaying of color, the emphasis on the unspectacular, may explain
Eteocles' curious remark early in the play (24) that the Theban prophet has found
his knowledge from the birds, through an effort of ears and mind, "rather than from
the flame." Physical fire is to be associated with the enemy camp.

He says he will destroy the city whether the god
grant it or not . . .

But with him blasphemy is not merely an attitude, a partial symptom
of his villainy; it is his very nature. His "gigantic" frame brooks
no commerce with the gods; the lightning bolts of Zeus are to him
only a mild discomfort to be shrugged off along with the midday
heat. He is, or fancies himself, an irresistible and unfeeling bulk,
an engine destined to hurl firebolts of its own and burn the city. Like
Tydeus, then, Capaneus perpetuates the vision of war as a compulsive mechanical threat, which is the play's point of departure.

Roughly the same is true also of the portrait of the third Argive
warrior, Eteoclus, except that in his case the emphasis is less on the
unfeeling mechanism than on the irrational nature of the monster
(461):

> He wheels his mares snorting in their muzzle
> straps, eager to dash against the gate.
> The muzzles whistle with a barbaric ring,
> filled with a nostril-sniffing insolence.

This is all we learn about the person of Eteoclus (the embarrassing
closeness of the name to that of Eteocles must mean that the myth
on which Aeschylus draws is based on historical memories, however
dim). A picture of savagely gyrating horses kicking against the re-
pressive control of muzzles and reins with unearthly and—more important—un-Greek neighing, may not be adequate as the sketch of a
man. But if the lines are meant to delineate the untamed and un-
tamable fury of mass war, they are appropriate. The personality of
Eteoclus disappears behind the vicious energy of his horses. Once
more we find ourselves stationed in a moral desert, in a fierce devilish
stamping ground where good and evil have no meaning.

The horses of Eteoclus duplicate, with an increase in the brutality
of it, the neighing of Tydeus. Similarly Hippomedon, the next aggressor to be described, may be called a doublet of Capaneus. But now
the governing idea of automatic bulk is fully realized; the description comes to be completely divorced from the anatomy of the human

body. To be sure, the first few lines seem to say that he too is a giant (488). But from the sequel we gather that the eyes of the messenger are not fixed on the person of the man, or even on his "frame and huge design" (488), but on the shield. The shield, the symbol of mechanical war, has come to cover and hide the lineaments of the fighter behind it. It usurps the space theoretically saved for the soldier, and grows to unmanageable size. This enlargement and self-assertion of what should be an instrument in human hands contains an element of humor. Bergson reminds us that human beings who are shown behaving like machines are funny. Aeschylus, with characteristic courage and with a minimum of subterfuge, exploits the humor where it presents itself (489):

> I shuddered as he wheeled his vast threshing-floor—
> I mean, the round of his shield.

It is this type of humor about sartorial idiosyncrasy to which we owe the expression "ten-gallon hat." Aeschylus follows this up with a phrase which is tantamount to "pardon the expression." The robot-like nature of mass war is here fixed in a pattern so simple, so naïve, that the messenger himself, the selfless reporter, shrinks from the truth and seeks refuge from the obvious in a joke. The fact remains that the shield has now become an autonomous substance. As an image it is no longer merely basic, but also terminal. No further development of the initial conception of war is possible, unless the drama is to bog down in the species of humor which feeds on insistence and hyperbole. A continuation of the present argument and the present imagery would carry us farther and farther away from the complexities of the tragic perception. The joke of the messenger, therefore, heralds a turn.

The first thing to be noted about the messenger's description of Parthenopaeus is its anonymity. He withholds the name till almost the end of his speech, which is a little longer than the earlier descriptions. True, near the beginning of the passage there are certain pointers— "mountain-dwelling mother," "man-boy," and others—which an audience learned in mythology will interpret correctly. But it is a mat-

ter of interpretation, and for most of us, as for the majority of the
ancient audience, the speech is a protracted riddle, whose solution, in
this case the name, is held off until the personality has been cast in full
relief. For now, and for the first time, the messenger gives us a man, a
complex human being, rather than a monster or a machine. Like the
others he is a blasphemer (529) :

> He swears by the spear he holds, prizing it more
> than a god, nay, higher than his eyes . . .

The terms of the comparison are revealing. The enemy worships his
spear; in that he resembles the others. But in his vanity he makes
reference to his eyes, and it so happens that these eyes belong to an
unusually pretty face. The warrior has, we are told, an adolescent,
girlish look—and in fact that is the meaning of the name as yet unannounced. But his spirit is by no means girlish, and his eye, set in a
lovely, ephebic face, is a true mirror of his spirit: a grim Gorgon eye.
In short, Parthenopaeus is an angelic miscreant; charming without
and rotten within, he exhibits a gross disparity between character and
looks.

His thoughts about the war are equally remarkable (545) :

> Nor is he likely to dole out the fight,
> to dishonor the funds provided for the journey,
> the Arcadian Parthenopaeus. An Argive immigrant,
> he means to pay them back for his welcome there.

It is clear that with the appearance of this man we have entered a new
arena. He is not a beast, or a colossus, or a shield, or one of the other
unnatural concretions which take us beyond the pale of pity and fear.
He interests us as a person, for we know his type. But he is more than
that. A type, even if familiar, would not mark the break with the
preceding characters quite so radically as this mercenary, this non-
Argive who has enjoyed the fruits of Argos and who has decided to
pay back his keep by not acting as a thrifty businessman would, but
by confusing the accounts of battle and giving war away gratis. The
notion itself is striking enough. We are reminded of

> War, the money-changer of dead bodies,

that illustrious and significant image in the *Agamemnon* (437).
Parthenopaeus is less calculating than Ares, for he has recognized that
war offers no accounts (357). He has intuited the nature of war, and
he models his own actions to conform with the setting in which they
are performed. But what matters most is that Parthenopaeus is a
man, a difficult, riddling figure of a man who reflects on his function
and acts accordingly. His reflection may not be profound; his decision
not to pinch the pennies of battle may be prompted by the chain reaction of killing as much as it is a conscious resolve. Still, we have left
the machines and the beasts behind us; from now on we shall be
looking at men.

With the next messenger-report, which is even longer than the
preceding and complicated further by the introduction of direct
speech, the leap is complete. The sixth aggressor is Amphiaraus, a
prophet. We have briefly met him in the first messenger-speech as
the seer who tries to prevent Tydeus from crossing the Ismenus River
and becomes the butt of Tydeus' abuse (378). As a prophet Amphiaraus stands above factional and tribal differences. But the tradition
suggested an even greater incentive for him to turn against his com-
rades-in-arms (587):

> Look at me; I shall enrich this country's soil,
> a prophet bedded in an enemy land.

He knows that the expedition will fail and that he himself will, by
his death, enhance the power of Thebes. In the great heroic tales of
the Greeks it has always been the function of the prophet to serve as
a warner, to channel the energies of the kings into divinely acceptable
patterns, to obstruct the chances of *hubris*. Amphiaraus, however, is
more than a warner. He opposes the whole war and along with it
the men who have carried it to the gates of Thebes. This is what we
would expect from a hero who resembles Eteocles in being temperate
and controlled (568), who holds his shield quietly instead of whirling
it (590), and who carries no design on the shield. For (592)

He means not to seem best, but to be,
and gathers fruit from the deep furrow ploughed
in his mind where noble counsels grow and thrive.

His opposition to the other Argives and the cast of his mind mark him as a second Eteocles, a doublet of the protagonist built into the army of the attackers. He is a good man, substantial and colorless. His judgment of his companions permits us to see them as they are, from close up, in the perspective of one who is not a partisan but an insider.

Amphiaraus is not easy to understand. The unorthodoxy of his position answers to the tension in his mind. His name-calling of Polynices, drawn out into a veritable catalogue of denunciations, points to a harsh sense of frustration. We should remember also that he is a prophet, a "man of curses," as his name says. His abuse has the force of crushing souls. After he has finished with Polynices we can no longer believe that Polynices has any justice on his side, or that he will be victorious. A good man who curses the aggressors; an enemy who helps to secure the salvation of Thebes: no wonder Eteocles bursts out in sorrow and perplexity at the spectacle of Amphiaraus conjured up by the messenger. For the anomalousness of the position of Amphiaraus closely resembles his own: he also has found himself at odds with his friends; he also is in danger of being (614)

pulled down and smashed along with the rest, God willing.

Amphiaraus does not deserve to die; he is (610)

a temperate man, just, good, and reverent.

The catalogue of the ancient virtues gives us the background against which to judge the deeds of Polynices. It is dramatically significant that Amphiaraus, at this point, levels his criticism against Polynices rather than anyone else. With the nature of Amphiaraus clearly defined, the position of Polynices becomes more untenable than ever before. But the curses also show us that the wickedness of Polynices differs from the monstrosity of a Tydeus or a Hippomedon. It is a matter of morals rather than of brute dynamics. The moral uprightness of Amphiaraus doubly ensures the ethical tenor of the scene which follows.

The goodness of Amphiaraus does something else. Earlier I commented on the artistic precariousness of a dramatic situation which is morally all white and all black. The presence of the prophet among the villains is yet another means of mitigating the risk. It appears that the attackers are wicked but not unexceptionally so. Eteocles, under another name, has been inserted into the ranks of the aggressors, to redistribute the light and the shade, and to save the tragedy from becoming an open book. At the same time the device cannot fail to suggest that the comparison works also the other way round. Because Eteocles is like Amphiaraus we must be prepared for the possibility of the King's defeat. For the doom of the prophet shows that the good are not necessarily victorious.

But, to turn now to the last panel, Polynices is a moral agent, a man, not part of the machine. He prays to Justice, and carries her image on his shield. To be sure, she is *his* justice, a fragmentary portion of justice of which Heraclitus would say that it is illusory like a dream. It is worse than illusory; being a relativist distortion of true justice it is more evil than moral indifference. There is a similarity between the power invoked by Polynices and the barbarous, vengeful spirit of retribution exorcized in the *Eumenides*. But the Furies prior to their conversion have a real complaint, for they have suffered an injury. Polynices, on the other hand, has no case. The author means us to understand that his departure from Thebes was voluntary and sanctioned by usage. Polynices is in the wrong; but instead of simply drawing him as a villain Aeschylus has him indulge in a flight of ethical fancy which prompts us to reflect on the justice or injustice of his enterprise. Through his person, as through that of the prophet, we are enabled to view the war as a contest of right and wrong, as an *agon*, that is, a collision of energies *between* men, rather than as a ruthless force unleashing itself *over* men. And finally, the moral complexion of his character, itself prefigured by the virtues of Amphiaraus, helps to prepare for the eventual shift of Eteocles. Thus the selection sequence turns out to have an important function in shifting our focus from mass war to personal engagement and the question of right and wrong, and in setting the stage for Eteocles' liberation from his role as detached manipulator.

iv

Through most of the selection sequence, Eteocles remains the master strategist. Each of the attackers, we are told, carries a shield with a telling blazon, all except Amphiaraus, who prefers being to seeming. That is to say, the shields are conceived as outgrowths and manifestations of the hollowness of the aggressors. They need shields, and colorful and articulate shields at that, to conceal their own lack of substance and to frighten their opponents. Such shield magic, like the boasting speeches that precede a duel, serve the purpose of psychological warfare. It is up to Eteocles, in his capacity of general, to oppose the magic and to devise countercharms. The answers of Eteocles to the messenger's descriptions, therefore, constitute a display of magic at work. But this particular magic, unlike that exercised by the shields, is a magic of words, a protective wall of remedial oratory raised up in the face of monstrous shapes and blasphemous images. Modern civilized rhetoric here overcomes the ancient power of grimacing. In the drama, to be sure, the visual magic is itself cast in the form of speech. There are, in this play, no violent spectacles such as crimson carpets or rocks hurled underground. But the speech conjures up vistas of massive bucklers and garish blazons calculated to deflate the will and paralyze the mind. Eteocles' rejoinders, on the other hand, are in the nature of arguments, of philosophical rebuttals.

The shield of Tydeus carries a flaming sky with stars and a bright full moon. Eteocles' answer (403):

> If he should die, and night descend on his eyes,
> this arrogant device would rightly prove
> its nature and its name for him who bears it.

Note the high-toned emphasis on "nature" and "name," the pivots of a rational dialectic. If the intention were to meet force with force, this sort of procedure would be awkward and ineffectual. In the person of the Theban general, traditionalism and abstract reflection are joined in a competent mixture which defeats the cruder ventures of the enemies at every turn. Capaneus displays a naked man with a lighted torch in his hands and the legend: "I shall burn the city." Eteocles contrasts this torch with its divine counterpart (444):

> I believe he will be struck, inescapably,
> by the burning thunderbolt.

The answer is particularly appropriate as Capaneus had likened thunder and lightning to the petty discomfort of the midday sun. Eteoclus' shield shows a fully armed man ascending the rungs of a ladder toward an enemy battlement, with the legend: "Not even Ares will cast me from the ramparts." Eteocles' answer has the ring of a Socratic whimsy (478): the device will enable the defender Megareus to capture two men and a citadel. Hippomedon, the fourth attacker, has on his shield a picture of Typhon spewing black smoke from a fiery mouth. On this occasion Eteocles' rebuttal is ready-made: Father Zeus, flaming weapon in hand, will fight on the side of Hyperbius and win his ancient victory all over again. The refutation is so obvious that for once, and perhaps also for the sake of variety, rhetoric descends to the level of iconography, and Zeus is shown enthroned on the defender's shield (512). But the next adversary, Parthenopaeus, is once more neutralized with the proper refinement and wit. His device, ever more baroque than those of the others, is the voracious Sphinx holding in her talons a single Theban man (544),

> for most of the missiles hurled to hit this man.

The notion is that the Theban soldiers, faced with the prospect of injuring one of their own, would be reluctant to fight. Eteocles deftly exposes the ambivalence of the implied argument (560): it is the Sphinx herself, the archenemy of Thebes, who will have cause to complain, for she will be much buffeted when she gets close to the citadel.

And so the battle is dramatized as a series of magic pretensions on one side and counterarguments on the other. Both the magic and the dialectic are used toward an artistic objective, to let us see the power and the limits of the personalities posted for battle, to create and in turn unmake the characters participating in the attack. The sequence may be termed an experiment in character construction. H. D. F. Kitto has recently reminded us that the characters in a Greek tragedy are constructive; that is to say, the Greek dramatic writers, instead of aiming at the flexible naturalism usually found on the modern stage, conceived of their characters as aggregates of significant features and behavior patterns required by the action of the play. The selection sequence grants us a glimpse into a workshop in which such characters are manufactured. Because the characters of the attackers are secondary, geared to this one scene only, the process of construction is even more radical than usual. The characters are built up only to be removed again immediately, and all this is done by means of words, for though we are made to see their clothing and the rest of their external trappings, they do not appear on the stage. They do not confuse us with their gestures, their mannerisms, the solid but opaque appeals of souls revealed in the flesh. We see their essences, without the accidents. Thus the selection sequence realizes a tendency inherent in all tragic art; for tragic costume, mask and buskin serve the same goal of minimizing accident. The impact of such raw constructiveness as is attempted here is very powerful indeed.

Amphiaraus carries no shield design, hence no rebuttal is needed, only an expression of sorrow which comes from the reflection that good men perish indiscriminately with the bad (597):

> Alas, the luck which does associate
> the just man with the impious.

Here, just before the curse begins to move him, in the very teeth of war, Eteocles injects a last and most emphatic note of human sympathy. He cuts short his dialectic, his tactical argumentation, and falls back on an elegiac mood, on pathos, self-inquiry, and reproach. As suggested earlier, he senses in the fate of Amphiaraus a parallel to his own. The elegiac mood, and especially the initial apostrophe to luck—or, literally, to "omen"—is not the kind of thing we should have expected from the confident leader of the earlier part of the play. We should sooner have looked to the chorus to supply this strain of mournful resignation. In fact the whole speech of Eteocles, with its somber contemplation on the fate of man and with its formal division into general examples and specific application, has a decidedly choral quality. Eteocles has undergone a change. By itself the present scene is not sufficient to reveal the precise nature of the change. This much is clear, however, that the public function of the general has become overshadowed by the private ponderings of the man, and that his former sanguine assurance has given way to a new humor, to worry and despair. From a leader manipulating war he is turning into a man experiencing the war in himself. The progression which we have noted in the catalogue of the aggressors, the change-over from tanks to bayonets, the transition from the machine war to the personal combat, is beginning to tell also in the figure of Eteocles.

But there is one more shield-carrying enemy: Polynices. His device is not symbolic in the same way as those of his associates. Rather it conforms more closely to the reality with which we are already familiar. The image shows a woman decently leading a man in full armor (644); the legend says that she is Justice conducting her champion back to regain his native city and to enjoy the freedom of his home. This is not magic; the image is too "realistic" to have a share in sorcery. By putting himself into the picture Polynices shows it for what it is, a pictorial design which directly communicates the spoken announcement which it is meant to convey. Let us call it a campaign poster, informing all and sundry: "I shall return." Far from intending to frighten the defenders into insensibility, the motto is designed to appeal to their moral intelligence, to convert them. In the eyes of Eteocles this type of blazon must be the most dangerous of all. He has no countermagic, no deflecting whimsy, no refutation. All he can do is deny the claim. Simple negation is the only instrument left to him when an ethical claim takes the place of brute force. As it will turn out, negation is not enough.

In the case of Amphiaraus no magic was necessary because the prophet already knew his destruction; he had no need to have it invoked against him. In the case of Polynices magic is equally out of place, if only because the relationship between the brothers would render any such extravagancy petty and irrelevant. For now, at the end of the sequence, the contest is between two moral agents locked in meaningful combat. The stress is no longer on the device but on the men themselves and on their intentions. The men are seen as products of a development, as characters with a past; each has his upbringing and his achievements, almost in the Sophoclean manner. We note the biographical dimension of Eteocles' answer (622):

> If Justice, the maiden child of Zeus, had stood
> by him, in his deeds and thoughts, this might well be.
> But no, not when he escaped from his mother's darkness
> nor in his childhood nor in later youth
> nor even when his chin collected down
> did Justice glance on him or judge him just.

We cannot miss the undertone of regret and disappointment at a life of promise steered in the wrong path. Eteocles is not only a general or a soldier; he is also an older brother who still, as it were, considers himself his brother's keeper. With the other aggressors, from Tydeus to Parthenopaeus, he has nothing in common. With Amphiaraus he is connected only by the tenuous link of a moral understanding. With Polynices he shares a life, and a curse.

v

> Alas, the god-crazed towering hatred of heaven;
> alas, my clan, the tear-drenched clan of Oedipus;
> alas, my father's curses now fulfilled!

This is Eteocles' reformulation of the curse, of the divine hatred under which his family has labored for generations (653). A curse is something constant, a stain which cannot be expunged except under the most unusual circumstances. And yet, so that it may retain its full force in the hearts of men, it has to be re-evoked periodically from generation to generation. This, at any rate, is what we find in Aeschylean and Sophoclean tragedy. A curse once pronounced goes into effect unto the third and fourth generation; the men affected by it turn into spontaneous victims, reasserting at crucial junctures their commitment to the curse. That is the reason Oedipus cursed his sons, though various other more or less frivolous motives were later substituted by an uncomprehending posterity. Similarly now, with Eteocles' outburst, we are thrust back into the living domain of the curse. No longer does the city occupy his thoughts; the war machine has vanished from the scene. Eteocles has ceased to be a general, sovereign and efficient, and has turned into a hero, involved, committed, obsessed. To be a hero, whether on the Homeric battlefield or in Attic tragedy, means to be unreasoning, self-centered, surrendering oneself headlong to the needs and demands of an engrossing mission. The hero listens to a call from within himself; he does not weigh alternatives, he does not regulate, he obeys. For such a man a curse presents a challenge and a scope.

The chorus recognizes the shift (677):

> Do not, child of Oedipus, break our hearts
> by raving like an evil-spoken zealot.

Here we have an extraordinary development. The mention of Oedipus shows that the chorus perceive the workings of the curse. Moreover, in their judgment the brothers are now as one, for there can be little doubt that Polynices is precisely such an "evil-spoken zealot." Eteocles' evocation of the curse has eliminated the tenuous boundary which previously separated him from his brother. Finally, as Eteocles rejects his public status and concentrates on his own person, on his needs and his fate, the chorus give up their own self-centeredness and begin to take thought of the hero. By a radical crossing of lines the chorus assume the earlier role of Eteocles, the role of the unselfish warner. Formally also they authenticate their new position, for these lines are spoken rather than sung. Each of the preceding six tableaux of the selection sequence is terminated by a choral lyric; now, at the end of the final tableau and (not counting stage directions) for the

first time in the play, the leader of the chorus takes over with a small
speech of her own.

> Let not madness, filling the heart,
> spear-crazed, carry you away!

So sing the chorus, resuming their traditional lyric medium (686).
And Eteocles answers (689):

> Since it is the god who activates the event,
> let it sail before the wind, straight to Cocytus,
> the whole Apollo-hated clan of Laius.

Such subservience to the gods, such willingness to be carried in whatever direction pleases the divine powers, had once been the preserve
of the chorus. Now Eteocles has adopted the perspective for his
own. There is more yet. A few moments before he rushes into the
battle he states (710):

> Too true the visions of nightmarish dreams . . .

We had hardly dared to suspect that Eteocles, like the chorus, might
have his own hallucinations. His Platonizing homage to the intellect,
his strictures on the women's turmoil, have proven a sham. Given the
proper setting, in this case the catalyzing effect of war, man, whatever
his position, will betray himself as the simple, raw, vulnerable organism that he is, without the spurious protection of public status or
a body of philosophical beliefs. And vulnerability is the first condition of heroism. The administrator cannot be heroic, only an undisguised and unsheltered human being can, a man reduced to his
essential condition by the curse.

The liveliness of the action has perhaps caused us to forget that
there is a curse. A commander in chief issuing orders is not likely
to remind us of the Furies hovering over the clan. And yet Aeschylus,
in his own careful manner, does not mean us to forget. In Eteocles'
second speech, near the beginning of the play, when the King calls
on his divinities to protect the land and the city—he does not refer
to himself as requiring protection—he prays to Zeus, Earth, the city's
gods, and the (70)

Omnipotent Curse, the Fury of my father.

This first appeal to the curse is contemplative, almost gentle, quietly edged in. From then on, each mention of Oedipus, each mention of the family of which Eteocles is a member, should prepare the audience with cumulative explicitness for the final explosion. Nothing else is to be expected in this third play of the Theban trilogy. A king is tied to his community; it glories and suffers with him. Laius had failed to do his duty and thereby brought ruin on city and house. The city remains in danger; she cannot be saved except by deflecting the curse so that it will come to rest entirely on the house. Only by meeting the curse head on, by identifying his fate with it, and incidentally thereby affirming the power and dignity of his manhood, can Eteocles hope to eliminate it. This is not to say that Eteocles recognizes the need for saving the city as he prepares to meet his brother. With the cessation of his role as administrator, all forethought, all planning and reasoning, are sacrificed. But by allowing the curse to operate at full strength, by challenging its potency into the limited area of the fratricide, he makes possible the survival of the city. The achievement remains his, no matter that his original perspective, his concern for the community, has been cut off.

Sophocles, a generation or so later, was to show in his *Oedipus Tyrannus* that the evasion of a curse makes for an intensification of the doom. Conversely he demonstrated, yet another generation later, in his *Oedipus Coloneus,* that a man could, by submitting to the curse and uniting it to himself and his career, bring about an eventual release. Just so Eteocles, by rekindling and embracing the curse, brings about the great cleansing and liberation with which the trilogy ends. Even with the fragmentary evidence available to us it is quite apparent that the proper ending of a trilogy is one in which conflicts are resolved and passion stories terminated. It does not matter whether the resolution is profound or superficial, whether it is achieved by reconciliation or adjudication or, as in our case, sacrifice. Sometimes, as in the *Oresteia,* the ending is happy; sometimes it hinges on a death. The important thing is that by the end of the third play the tensions and conflicts which are set up and manipulated in the trilogy have ceased to operate. That is not to say that all questions, philosophical or otherwise, that may have been stimulated by the action will have been answered. On the contrary, the cancellation of the immediate conflict often raises as many questions as it purports to answer, and more. Perhaps a tragedy, like a Socratic dialogue, should do precisely this. But looking at the play as a self-contained unit, as a unitary aesthetic experience, the abolition of the governing conflict is the principal business of the ending. This resolution is usually climactic; it coincides with an act of heroism or a similarly impressive event underscoring the power or the littleness of man. In the present play the curse has produced a war, and both curse and war are terminated when Eteocles allows the Fury to seize him up and deliver him to certain death.

The curse is the theme of the choral song which follows the exit of Eteocles. The ode begins and ends with the picture of hardened steel in the hands of the brothers (727):

> A stranger-friend allots the shares,
> newly arrived from Scythia,
> a sharp divider of property rights,
> raw-spirited steel.

And again (788):

> And they with steel-wielding
> hand will yet divide their
> property.

The iron is the special tool and substance of the curse, now fully materialized after more than a lifetime of hints and threats. More particularly the iron succeeds to the shield. Before personal involvement and private impulse undermined the relentless workings of the machine, the shield had served as the chief image of the war and of the attitudes taken toward the war. As such, characteristically, the shield was visualized as an autonomous entity, not suspended from the shoulder or held on the lower arm, but, as it were, dwarfing the bearer and obeying an action or motion of its own. By way of contrast the steel rests in the brothers' hands. We can watch the physical effort, the specific turn of the body which gives to the weapon its aim and success. Thus once more the imagery helps us to follow the shift from the machine to the soul.

It is strange that a curse, ostensibly a pollution coming in from the outside, should enable or force men to reflect on their selves, to recognize in their fate a challenge to their minds and hearts. But this is a thoroughly Greek concept for which modern ideas concerning freedom of will and the like make no allowance. Perhaps it is because the Aeschylean and the Sophoclean hero is often primarily a political man, a person who takes his administrative obligations seriously, that he needs the shattering blow of a curse to train his eyes on himself and see himself as he is. Once the curse has struck, the hero finds himself less powerful and less happy but more purposefully alive than ever. In real life a curse, such as that pronounced over the Alcmaeonids, is likely to paralyze the individual and cripple his initiative; on the stage the effect is the opposite.

The king is killed, but the city is saved. The two outcomes are reported and accepted side by side, in the order of their importance to the reporter and his audience. Both the messenger who enters to announce the events and the chorus who respond to the news first emphasize the salvation of the city (792):

> Take courage, nurslings of your mothers' care;
> our city has fled the yoke of slavery!

And (822):

> Great Zeus, and gods of the city,
> you who stand ready to protect
> the ramparts of Cadmus;
> shall I rejoice, shall I cry out
> in triumph at the city's day of grace?

Only after this first spontaneous cry of happiness over the deliverance of the city do messenger and chorus turn to consider the death of the brothers, and to allow grief a place beside their joy. This grief, an unintricate, noble, calming grief is not for Eteocles alone but jointly for the brothers. With their death the curse has fulfilled itself and

the community is restored to health. Hence their death emerges as
a beneficent thing, and the question of justice or injustice pales before the simple act of self-sacrifice in which both brothers share to an
equal degree, no matter what the intentions that lay behind it. The
curse had set the brothers at each other's throats; the curse had drawn
forth Eteocles from his isolation and made him come to grips with
the war on terms of intimacy and wrath. Now the curse has bound
the brothers together in a new union and wiped out the scores of
guilt and resentment.

In their great hymn to the curse, the women predict (734):

> When they die killing their own,
> their own victims,
> and the Earth's dust drinks
> black-clotted murder-blood . . .

Earth, the giver of life and freedom and culture, is to be the arena of
the final torture, the recipient of the sacrifice. But Earth is to be
something more than that. By an old magical Greek tradition the
burial of a sinner, of a polluted man, makes for a hallowed spot.
Oedipus and others like him had broken the basic laws of decent
society; in their lifetime they represented a serious threat to the
communities with which they were associated. But once they were
dead it was thought that the same vitality which previously endangered
the public peace would now, from the sepulcher underground, work
for the benefit of the people. Just so the fratricide, in itself a monstrous act, is now absorbed by Earth and metamorphosed into an
asset (947):

> They have their share, unhappy beneficiaries,
> of god-given lots;
> and below, in the body of the Earth,
> there will be fathomless wealth.

In this manner Earth, "the demon having ceased" (960), contributes
her own time-honored magic to help along with the "happy ending,"
the restoration of balance and the cleansing which we expect at the
end of the play and the trilogy.

The exorcizing of the curse is above all the result of Eteocles' conversion. This is a fact; but the fact needs to be confirmed, ritually
and aesthetically. Hence the dirge. The curse is rescinded once and
for all by the lament of the chorus which follows upon the first shout
of triumph for the delivery of the city, and which stretches over more
than 150 lines to the end of the play. Its inordinate length and its
lack of poetic interest have caused much dismay. It will help to
remember, however, that the dirge was sung and danced, that the
ritual exigencies of a funeral song rule out poetic venturesomeness,
that the lament is designed to conclude the whole trilogy rather than
merely one play, and, finally, that it serves a special function: it is a
kind of binding song, analogous to the sorcerers' chant with which
the Furies in the *Eumenides* try to overcome the resistance of Orestes.
The burying of the brothers, vicariously enacted in the dirge, also
becomes a burial of the curse, and thereby a storing up of pregnant
treasure. To ensure all this the dirge must allow liberally for the
repetitive formulas native to prayer. One might even say that the
dirge imitates, on a grander scale, the patterns of the curse it is laying
to rest. Without an appreciation of the religious cast of the lament
we cannot hope to understand the emphatic terminalism of the last
scene.

Still, we cannot be entirely persuaded that the curse has been neutralized. In the course of the play we have seen the terror and grue-
someness and unintelligibility of war subjected to a process of refinement and subversion until only heroism and tragedy and finally
sacred blessings remain. Aeschylus asks us to pay tribute to war and
to carry away the illusion—for that is all a dramatic solution can give
us—that war is manageable, that even at its worst it allows a man
to exercise his most personal aspirations, to struggle for heroism
and glory. But the terror, the brutal shock of the barbaric shield, the
desolation of the sacked city, are not completely muted. In spite of
the resolution and of the allaying of the family curse, the antiphonal
arrangement of the theme of war continues to echo in our ears and
to release its ration of fear and disgust. The satyr play which followed—it is no longer extant but we know that it dealt with the

Sphinx—would of course erase this echo, or cushion it with a soothing dose of harmless laughter. But the palliative is short-lived. When
the whole tetralogy has been played through, the sanguine finale is
soon forgotten, and the tragic mood of the earlier plays is recalled in
full. That this mood is not all terror and futility, that the dramatization of war which the play gives us leaves room for glory and dignity as well as horror: this is the special achievement of Aeschylus,
an achievement equaled only perhaps by Homer's *Iliad*.

It is tempting to suggest that in mood, style, and objective the
Seven Against Thebes is cast in the epic mold. Homer made it the
business of the epic to formulate the manifold nature of war, to
point up its beauty and its ugliness, its significance and its pettiness,
its grandeur and its bestiality. But in the *Iliad* the complexity of the
experience emerges from the successive highlighting of various isolated perspectives. Now we see the war through the eyes of Priam,
now through the eyes of Achilles, now of Hector. Each one of the
key figures catches the meaning and the spirit of the war from a
specific angle which, despite minor variations depending on the
situation in which the witness finds himself, is on the whole constant.
For Hector the war is a defensive operation, to be organized along
lines of tactical responsibility. Occasionally he forgets the necessity of tactical considerations; then he lives to regret the blunders.
For Achilles the war starts out as the legitimate occupation of the
class of which he is a member, and takes on special meaning after
the death of his closest friend. He is turned from a businesslike
knight into an avenging fury. But even this change indicates not so
much a shifting of his perspective as rather an intensification of his
energies. About the nature and the justice of the war to be fought and
about his own particular role in it Achilles has few doubts, his specious rebuttals in Book 9 notwithstanding. Everyone in the *Iliad* takes
the war for granted and accepts the part in it which destiny has allotted
him.

In the *Seven* the relation between men and war is not similarly
fixed. For one thing, war is not seen as a necessary or normal thing,

to be dealt with as best one can. It is an enormity, an aberration from the settled ideals of peace and culture and domesticity. More important, however, the view of war is not, as in the epic, a totality of singular views each of which admits of some sort of definition by itself. Instead of the perspective of the father and the perspective of the defender and the perspective of the knight and so forth, our play develops a portrait of war which is not a composite of perspectives at all, but an organic experience, growing under our very eyes. From the moment when Eteocles begins his address to the citizenry, with his cool appraisal of the military contingencies, to the point when the chorus lyrically re-enact the fratricidal duel, the picture of war undergoes a constant shifting. Its outlines never grow sufficiently firm to allow the picture to harden into a set of perspectives. E. Staiger has said about the lyric that in contrast to the drama and the epic it does not deal with "objects" and therefore does not operate with perspective. The poet and his world are not sufficiently distinct to require the help of a perspective. Aeschylus' tragedy verges upon the lyric mood; the picture of war which it distills into us, to use a term of Staiger's, is a feeling rather than an image, an experience rather than the fruit of an illumination.

Neither Eteocles nor the chorus can be said to offer us a single identifiable formulation of what war means to them. Above all, the gradual incubus-like growth of war in the soul of Eteocles, the transformation of the planner into the enthusiast, permits us to focus on war in its full extent through the lens of a single life and a single commitment. This is an act of compression which cannot but enhance the power of the communication. In the epic, the understanding of war is fragmented; the audience is asked to bring the fragments together and weld them into a response of its own. In the *Seven* the representation of war is whole, evolving, natural. Driven by the vigor of Aeschylus' verse the audience must surrender itself to the comprehensive truth generated on the stage. To this extent, then, the play goes far beyond the epic, in spite of the epic touches of its language, and in spite of its echoes of the Homeric world of heroes. Unlike the

Iliad it does not describe a succession of battles, it creates a war. It plants its disharmonies into our very hearts, with an urgency and a pathos which only tragedy can accomplish, and which are the special hallmark of the art of Aeschylus.

Prometheus Bound:
TRAGEDY OR TREATISE?

First let us note some peculiarities of the *Prometheus*, some features which distinguish it from the other Aeschylean dramas that have come down to us. The differences are striking, and some scholars have, not without cause, concluded regretfully that the play as we have it could not possibly have been written by the author of the *Oresteia* and the *Suppliants*. The question of authorship will not concern us here. But the singularity of the play merits detailed comment.

The most apparent characteristic of the *Prometheus* when compared with almost any other Greek drama is the prominence of iambic speech. Spoken orations seem to have encroached on the territory usually held by the lyric element and to have relegated the music to a position of entr'acte decorativeness. To be sure, Prometheus and Hermes do some chanting, and Io has an aria whose musical texture resembles that of choral songs in other Aeschylean plays. But the choral odes themselves are infrequent, brief, and seemingly undistinguished, as if the composer felt that the iambic medium ought not to be interrupted beyond the minimum claims of the tradition. In the spoken passages the language and the versification have little of the gnarled compactness or of the sheer joy of muscle which marks Aeschylus' iambics elsewhere. Mostly the verse is restrained, dry, subtle, sometimes prosaic. If a comparison is in order, the simplicity of the *Prometheus* contrasts with the exuberance of the *Persians* as the brittleness of the *Tempest* does with the turbulence of *Lear*. The *Prometheus* shows the same containment, the same deliberate rejection of baroque expansiveness and bulky metaphor, the same delicate control of the rhythmic patterns. Whether all this means that the *Prometheus* is written in the style of old age, must be left to future epigraphic discoveries to determine. We do not know the date of the performance, and in fact we do not know whether it was ever performed.

The play is not without its share of full-throated passages. The description of the monster Typhon (355),

> who hisses panic from terrifying jaws
> and strikes a Gorgon lightning from his eyes,

is a forceful reminder of the Aeschylean flair for color and bigness. On the whole, however, there is an obvious avoidance of purple patches and full orchestration. The speech tends to be simple, direct, almost colloquial; some of the lines read like quotations from comic dialogue or anticipations of Hellenistic genre writing. The imagery also, though of considerable interest as we shall see later, is much reduced in tension and scope, as if the Aristophanic Euripides had, after all, won his case. Sometimes, indeed, the imagery seems trite or pale and even thoughtless, but such first impressions can be deceptive. In any case, it is apparent that on the several levels of style and diction the play lives up to its special character of moderation, of recoiling from poetry and pomp.

So much for matters of style. When we turn to the action our attention is pre-empted by the figure of Prometheus himself. He is more than a hero or a central figure; of all known characters in Greek tragedy he alone is on stage all the time. The play is about him and no one else; he is the play. Moreover, once he has been placed in position against the rock in the center of the stage he remains motionless. This rigid fixity, as unique as it must have been uncomfortable to the actor, reads like a protest against excessive motions on the tragic stage, against the Ajaxes and the Lycurguses, who express the violence of their feelings through extravagant gesturing and savage stridings. Like Nero Wolfe, Prometheus achieves a special effect by the contrast between his own stillness and the unimpeded comings and goings that surround him. And like that celebrated investigator he seems to supervise and perhaps originate much of that motion. It will, I suspect, be of some importance to keep track of the purely kinetic relationships, of the interplay between various kinds of motion and rest which structures the play, from its halting, almost sluggish beginning to its cyclonic end.

The constant presence of the chief character on the stage should, it may be expected, furnish a modicum of unity. The assumption is that the longer a man is with us and the longer we know him, the more we are likely to find out about him, and this progressive familiarity will make us see more and more clearly the end toward which the drama aims. This expectation, of an experience both unified and rising in intensity, is plausible enough. Unfortunately the *Prometheus* does not fulfill it. There is in it no unity, no consistency, no interlocking of event with event toward the steady building up to a climax such as we have in the *Oedipus Tyrannus*. In spite of the staggering of the interlocutors there seems to be no perceptible growth in intensity. Contrary to the Aristotelian axiom, the play is no living unit with beginning, middle, and end conditioning one another. Rather it may be called a series of scenes or tableaux, more or less artfully joined together but ostensibly independent of one another. The connecting statements are often bald, not to say ungainly. After Io's great introductory aria, for instance, the author wishes to supply an explanation, again by Io, of her sufferings. The transition from song to speech may be summarized as follows (604): Io, *singing:* Tell me my future. Prometheus, *speaking:* I shall tell you whatever you wish to know. Io, *speaking:* Why are you suffering? Prometheus: I shall not repeat what I have just finished telling. Io: How long will I continue my wanderings? Prometheus: I had better not tell you. Io: Please do. Prometheus: All right, I will. Chorus-leader: No; first we want her to tell us more about her troubles. Prometheus: Yes, that is a better idea. And then follows Io's speech. It should be added that this summary reproduces a conversation which extends over thirty-six lines of text.

In a radio studio this laborious plotting of who is to speak next and about what, is called "traffic." The present passage is by no means the only traffic sheet in the play, though it may well be the most explicit. Other examples of a meticulous conferring regarding spots on the program are to be found in lines 696 ff., 778 ff., and 816 ff. Once the assigning is organized as a children's game (778):

> PROMETHEUS: Of two orations I shall give you one.
> Io: What kind? Hold out your hands and let me choose.

Each of the traffic sheets has the function of separating two major speeches, or at any rate of introducing a new speech. They are mechanical introductions which mark the speeches as lectures or performances rather than spontaneous outflowings of organically conceived characters. On this score also, therefore, it is clear that we are not dealing with a drama of character, featuring a probable or a significant life, and presenting a combination of causes and results which make for a meaningful continuity. That there *are* characters on the stage will, of course, not be denied. Even a superficial reading of the play produces a strong feeling of the basic differences in thought and temperament and tone between Prometheus and Io and Ocean and Hermes. But the presence of distinguishable characters does not necessarily give us a play whose plot and meaning derive principally from the purposeful interaction of its agents. It is symptomatic of the sort of drama *Prometheus Bound* is that it contains comparatively little dialogue, and that what dialogue there is turns out in most cases to be the trafficking which connects the speeches. In substance, the play consists of revelations and self-revelations, the paratactic unfolding of issues and feelings and historical fact, instead of the interlacing and merging of lines of thought and the pooling of sensations which a true drama of character would seem to demand.

At the end of the play the advance of the action over what is found at the beginning is nil. There has been no enlargement of themes, no energetic expansion to sustain our imagination toward climax and resolution. It may well be asked whether this leaves us with a static mass, a symposium of speeches organized without regard for what Kenneth Burke has termed the sense of crescendo. The answer to this question is No. There are some elements of movement and articulation and even of tension. But they are artificial, or at least imposed from outside; they do not correspond to any intrinsic direction or purpose. One such adventitious device calculated to infuse a sense of mystery and anticipation into the proceedings is the motif of the secret. Prometheus knows the identity of the lady destined to bear a son whose status will exceed that of his father; Zeus, who is about to choose a bride from a large group of candidates, does not, and is in fact close to selecting the very girl whose ominous gifts Prometheus alone divines. Between Prometheus' first and second speeches to Io there is a reference to this secret, and also to another enigma concerning a future deliverer of Prometheus. On the surface these dark hints have the purpose of breaking up into two separate speeches what otherwise might have been a single interminable oration. In other words, the remarks about the secret are analogous to the regulatory passages preceding the speeches, and indeed the two are often combined. But there is something else. As the secret is touched upon again and again the references become less and less veiled until in the end it is felt that Prometheus is ready to divulge the full contents of the secret to the enemy. He does not do so; but this frustration of our legitimate

hopes—or fears—becomes the crowning touch of Aeschylus' use of
the riddle as a creator of suspense and crescendo. A minor mythological detail generates a tension which the subject matter as such does not
rightfully carry, and produces the illusion that in the end Prometheus
might barter a piece of knowledge for his liberation. For an illusion
it is, at any rate within the limits of the play we have. Thus the secret
of Zeus' marriage is a device, we might almost call it a gimmick,
to extend pace and momentum to an otherwise static mass. Later we
shall see that it is much more than that.

Mythology once more provides yet another extrinsic means of introducing suspense. From Hesiod and from vase paintings we know
that the audience associated the impaled Prometheus with his eagle.
In the present play, when Prometheus is dragged in and nailed against
the rock, the eagle is absent. Prometheus chants his great apostrophe
to Nature, at the end of which he announces (124):

> Alas, what is it I hear? The fluttering
> of birds near by? The air hums
> with the volatile strokes of wings.

It is not the expected eagle that enters, but the members of the
chorus. We cannot here discuss the vexed question of the means of
transportation by which the girls make their entry. I for one consider
it most likely that they come in on a ship-cart. They do, after all, come
from the ocean, and the analogy between oars and wings is familiar
from the Homeric epic down. What matters is that their appearance
is heralded by an announcement designed to mislead the audience
into expecting the eagle. Some time later, after the chorus have established themselves on the stage, there is another rustle of wings.
This time there is no announcement; the winged creature advances
too rapidly. The mermaids scatter and hide behind the rock. But
again it is not the eagle, only a parody of that royal bird, a fanciful
hobby monster supporting the withered physique of Father Ocean.
Only toward the end of the play, when we have ceased to look for
the eagle, does Hermes schedule its arrival. On second thought it is
obvious that it would have been bad taste, a confusion of the genres,

to present the eagle on the stage. The tone of the play is perhaps not so far removed from the tone of comedy as one might wish. But the outlandishness of the animal figure could only have compromised the Titanic dignity of the hero. Hence we are shown only the domesticated variety, a whimsical plaything for an Ocean who has long lost his standing as a Titan.

Thus, though there is some suspense, it depends largely on externals, on spectacle and mythology and similar instruments of surface appeal. It would of course be wrong to suppose that there is no increase whatever in the emotional tempo of the play. Prometheus' anger, for one thing, is steadily intensified by the successive interviews with the gracious and timid mermaids, the sober and ineffectual Ocean, the tormented Io, and finally the malicious and crude Hermes. Each person elicits a different response from Prometheus, and, if nothing else, sheer momentum carries him to greater and greater heights of expostulation and wrath. The rising curve is intentional. This is proved by the way in which the writer arranges the beginning of the play. The initial absence of the chorus is nothing more than a debt owed to the tradition. But the silence of Prometheus as he is being hammered against his rock, his continued silence after the workmen have left the stage, and the feeling of isolation which speaks from the address to inanimate Nature into which he then launches, all indicate that the author knows the value of a slow start. But our first judgment remains unchanged all the same. If there is a development, it is not effected by converging lines of plot or revelation of character or the merciless unfolding of an embodied truth. The reason for this is very simple; the *Prometheus Bound* is not a tragedy of plot and character—the life and sufferings of Mr. X—but an entirely different species of dramatic composition. E. A. Havelock has, very properly, called it a masque. Like a Renaissance masque, it dramatizes issues and abstractions rather than the joys and sorrows of living men. A masque cannot be read as a tragedy proper is read, it must be translated and decoded before it can be understood. In the case of a Renaissance masque a tracing of classical models and conventions will often furnish the clue. But the *Prometheus* has no precedent, at

least not in the drama of the Greeks. Hence we must try to understand what the play has to say from within itself, with only occasional help from our knowledge of the intellectual climate of fifth-
century Athens. Because the play is an innovation, not firmly rooted
in a soil of conventions and rules, no solution of the enigma of its
meaning can be anything more than tentative. But some attempt at
giving an answer has to be made; that is what a masque is for. The
particular question before us is: Who is being punished, and for what?

ii

By rights the question should be answered
for us in the Prologue of the play. And in fact the Prologue is unusually informative, without appearing to lecture us. As we watch
Hephaestus and Might going about their lamentable business we
become acquainted with the ostensible issue, the punishment by Zeus
of a rebellious god; with the identity of the chief contestants, Zeus and
Prometheus; with the setting of the passion story, a mountainous
region at the very edge of the world; and, most important, with the
varied composition of the camp against which Prometheus is fighting.
For in the persons of Hephaestus, Might, and Violence we find the
enemy camp split into segments of contradictory intentions. Violence,
a mute, is but a Hesiodic doublet of Might. But between Might and
Hephaestus there is little sympathy. Might is the loyal, unthinking
executive, carrying out the wishes of a Zeus grown cruel in his wars.
Hephaestus does not similarly represent Zeus; he serves him but his
heart is not in the task, and he strains against the duty.

In his *Adventures of Ideas*, Whitehead[1] speaks of the struggle between "formulated aspirations" and "senseless agencies." His chief
examples of the former are Christianity and democracy; the latter are
conveniently represented by barbarians and steam. It is Whitehead's
contention that the career of human civilization has always been
marked by the interaction of solid hopes for happiness and peace with

---

[1] Alfred North Whitehead, *Adventures of Ideas* (Harmondsworth, England,
Penguin Books, 1942), p. 13.

an equally solid estate of frustration and ruin. As for the latter, the senseless agencies, the Greek writers "are apt to speak of compulsion (*ananke*) when these agencies appear with a general coordination among themselves, and of violence (*bia*) when they appear as a welter of sporadic outbursts." The distinction between two aspects of necessity—compulsion and violence—is of some importance to us, for they are both fully dramatized in our play. More generally Prometheus himself recognizes that his struggle is against the senseless agencies, and that it must be hopeless (514):

> Skill is far weaker than necessity.

But to say that a struggle is hopeless is not the same as saying that it is wasted. Necessity, the grim exclusiveness of the world enveloping cultured man, cannot be gainsaid, but it can be confronted and judged, and by way of dramatic illusion it can be made to render up its exclusiveness, almost. And in the struggle man will perhaps find the reward of his dignity.

Whitehead shows that as culture and civilization become conscious achievements, as beauty and obligation and all the other civilized values are worked out, necessity is felt more and more keenly. As life turns gentler, it creates its own harshnesses and points up the cruelty of its environs. Every increase in knowledge carries with it an expansion of the territory which is unknown and felt to be hostile. Every comfort gained is doubly compensated by the infliction of new cruelties. As we learn in the play, the civilizer is immobilized by the fruits of harshness reaped from the softness he has sown. Shelley is mistaken when he has his hero speak of the

> swift shapes and sounds which grow
> more fair and soft as man grows wise and kind
> and, veil by veil, evil and error fall.

Aeschylus understands the perils of progress; he knows that the sensitizing and refining of men can only serve to widen the gulf between them and a cosmos whose vastness and incomprehensibility grow in the same ratio as aspirations are fulfilled.

But in the play necessity is not all force and darkness. There is also Hephaestus, the reluctant executive, friend of Prometheus and bene- factor of men but indentured to Zeus and under orders to do his hammering. The violence of the cosmos is thus prismatically split. If the senseless agencies were one in their direction man might more easily cope with them. If they were hostile and nothing else, his role as adversary and protester would be relatively easy to sustain. But a violence tinged with hesitation and regret blurs the picture and makes it harder for the civilizer to keep up the fight and hold off despair. At the same time such mingling of feelings heightens the poignancy of the tragedy. In a world all gentle, heroism would cease to exist; in a world of untempered harshness there would be no room for sympathy; the result would be catastrophe rather than tragedy. It is imperative that the hero entertain some relations with the opposition. Hephaestus is the poet's first instrument for the establishing of such bonds. From the very beginning the hidden feelings and secret loyal- ties of members of the opposition are used to complicate and deepen the area of conflict.

It is a pity that we are not given Prometheus' response to the spe- cial pleading of Hephaestus. But a reply at this early stage in the play would have been premature. There will be enough time later to devel- op the various attitudes of the hero toward the enemy. The beginning is to be slow. When we first hear from Prometheus he is to be a man with a message, a demonstrator, perhaps a boaster or a complainer, but not an answerer. His failure to respond to the pitiful advances of Hephaestus reinforces our awareness of his isolation, both imposed and self-chosen. Thanks to the skill of Aeschylus—I assume that had he wanted to he could have employed a third actor and let Prometheus speak—we comprehend the two camps separately, through the in- transigence of Might and the silence of Prometheus, and the ineffec- tualness of Hephaestus' overtures, before there is a suggestion of con- tact and negotiation. Later, in a sense, Prometheus does answer Hephaestus, that is, Hephaestus revisiting: Ocean. Hephaestus is the agent who would prefer to be inactive but cannot (45):

O hated and accursed handicraft!

Ocean is the bystander who would rather be active but whose action will be useless and self-defeating (383),

> a foolish and redundant exercise.

Both gods, the enslaved smith and the side-lined river god, symbolize the same ineffectuality caught from two separate angles. Effective action is, for the time being, a prerogative of Zeus. There is no room for intermediaries, especially for those whose sympathies are more on the side of Prometheus than of Zeus. In terms of action and results Prometheus stands for frustration and failure, and this frustration cannot but affect also the purposes of those willing to work on his behalf.

The near-identity of the roles of Hephaestus and Ocean, with their kindliness and their abortive generosity, would be puzzling if this were a conventional play of character, where we should expect a certain economy and differentiation in character development. As it is, the doublet serves notice that the duality of harshness and gentleness will be continued through the play. The mood set by the juxtaposition of Hephaestus and Might will be extended, in a different manner of composition, by the succession of Ocean and Hermes. As Might opened the drama, so Hermes will close it, on a shriller and less assured note, which is in itself an indication of some sort of surface progression. As we shall see directly, the combination of harshness and gentleness is characteristic also of the physical world which Prometheus set out to remake for the betterment of man and which now holds him captive. Together, harshness and gentleness form a setting within which the hero must act and suffer, and with which he has to come to terms to remain a man and not merely be a hero. A comparison of Sophocles' *Ajax* with his *Philoctetes* shows how unresponsive Ajax is to the gentleness around him; in this respect, as in others, Philoctetes is more human, the more rounded character. Whether Prometheus manages to transcend his heroic status is a question to be answered later.

Wherein lies Prometheus' principal activity on the stage? Apart from his complaining, his chief business seems to be that of instructing. He is offering to instruct the chorus in the events of the future when he is interrupted by the entry of Ocean, and there are other offers of the same kind, some of them fulfilled. One might be tempted to think of him as a prophet; his mother, Themis, is nothing if not prophetic, and his knowledge of the secret stamps him as an expert in divination. But the form and the content of his pronouncements point in a different direction. Unlike most prophets he does not express himself in riddles, in dark, compressed conundrums. He is not concerned with the fate of an individual or a house or a single city; he does not warn or bully or mislead. His is the full explanation, the extended listing, the explicit argument. The whole of humanity, society as such, is his concern. He is a teacher, an intellectual, or, as the Greeks would call him, a *sophistes*. The fifth-century Sophists—and that includes Socrates, if we follow the lead of the comedians—claimed that the correct exercise of man's reason will make for a happier and more harmonious society. All Greek tragedy contains a measure of protest against this Sophistic naïveté. But the *Prometheus* occupies a special position in the series, stressing not only the falsity of the message but also the beauty and dignity of it, and the pity of its untruth.

The dream of man setting himself above the senseless agencies, above cosmic regularity and barbarians and steam, is encouraged by an old myth found in many parts of the world, the myth of the culture hero who separated heaven and earth and suffered in order that mortals could live their own life apart from the gods. "Suffering for our sins," as it was put by a later tradition which had its eyes fixed on Adam's fall. Prometheus, in myth, is a precursor of the last of the culture heroes, with his dual nature, human and divine. Like Jesus he sees his mission as that of a mediator; but unlike Jesus he is an encourager of man's equality. We may speculate that the culture hero himself is responsible for the tension existing between god and man. But in our first account of his activities, in Hesiod, the tension already exists, and Prometheus attempts to eliminate it by raising men to the level of the gods. Aeschylus went far beyond the version of the myth given by Hesiod. What had been a trickster, a secretive poltergeist, became in his formulation a Titan, a hero of majesty and wisdom, and of a directness which leaves no room for deception. This aggrandizing of Prometheus, and the cutting out of features of the folk tale which had come to be regarded as unsavory, set the pattern for all later versions. In modern parlance, "Promethean" equals "Titanic"; and this we owe to Aeschylus.

In the folk tale, Prometheus deceives the gods; in Aeschylus, he helps man, and in fact makes man what he is. Prometheus is a second creator, perhaps the only true creator. The change of emphasis is significant. The folk tale piously though with some obvious gratification stresses the misdemeanor; Aeschylus puts the accent on the accomplishments. The list is indeed an impressive one. Even a bare catalogue, and that is precisely what the play gives us, manages to convey the proud satisfaction with which homo sapiens regards the diversity of his triumphs. Among the benefits listed we find the building of houses, carpentry, astronomy, arithmetic, the art of writing, the taming of horses, navigation, medicine, and the interpretation of dreams and omens. The arrangement of the items in the catalogue does not obey any manifest system, in spite of the bundling together of certain related activities. The lack of system is not necessarily a disadvantage; better than a pedant's orderliness it communicates the richness of civilized experience. Above everything else we learn that all the crafts mentioned are derived from one fundamental art, the kindling of fire (109):

> . . . the stealthy spring of fire,
> bound in a hollow stalk, the first instructor
> and great resource of human industry.

Characteristically, however, the motif of the civilizing fire is underplayed. Fire is the visible embodiment, the always freshly experienced reminder of man's wisdom and man's perfectibility. But fire is also the pledge of a continued association between man and god. The culture hero separated the two, but at the same time he assured man of a permanent connection with the gods, of god-likeness, through his gift of the divine fire. If we scan the play we discover that, apart from the passage cited above and a fleeting reference in the dialogue between Prometheus and the chorus (252), there is no poetic development of the theme of Promethean fire. Where fire is mentioned it is ranged on the side of Zeus, in the form of a smoldering thunderbolt or a searing storm. It is as if the author shrank from enlarging on the one element of the human achievement which more than any other reflects its celestial origins. In spite of the entirely new conception of the ancient tale the Hesiodic theft remains embarrassing. The "stealthy spring of fire" is ambiguous, but the ambiguity is no mere oversight.

But more important than what the author does *not* say is his affirmation of what is singular in the human accomplishment. At the end of an elaborate speech for the defense which Prometheus addresses to the chorus, the god explains a further and more profound contribution to the new order. To save man he deprived him of the foreknowledge of death and gave him hope (248). The meaning of this is apparent; the life of society is based on ambition and industry, which an awareness of the finality of death would destroy. Men can be like gods only if they refuse to know death, that it comes and when, and if they hope for immortality, either in person or in the song of posterity. They can hope to equal the gods only through a delusion, granted by Prometheus as a boon. Civilized life is founded on an act of blindness. But it is some comfort to consider that this is the only delusion which a man needs for a rational existence. Hence Prometheus prides himself on having roused man from the dreamlike stupor which was his fate before he became blinded to the fact of death. In these speeches in which Prometheus details his benefactions we sense the full-blooded optimism rampant among the enlightened of the time. Man must be wide awake; only the examined life is worth living; had not Heraclitus said that only the waking know the true order of the world? And Prometheus, upright against the rock, never sleeps.

Now it will perhaps be possible to understand the function of Io in the play. She is a creature who lives most acutely in dreams and hallucinations. When she comes on stage she thinks the dead Argus is still with her (567):

> . . . Away, away! I am afraid
> at the sight of the herdsman's thousand eyes.
> He marches along, radiating deceit;
> he is dead, but the earth refuses to keep him.

She knows that Argus has died, and yet she cannot shake off the vision of his sly-eyed form. With her, reason and unreason are mingled in an indeterminate and sterile mixture. Later when she ceases her dancing and adopts iambic speech, the whole tale of Zeus wooing and hurting her is cast in the mold of a dream (645):

> Again and again night visions straying into
> my maiden chambers flattered me with smooth
> and slippery speeches . . .

The simplicity of Io's account has led many critics to assume without further ado that Aeschylus' account of Io is taken straight from the traditional story. The truth is that the playwright, contemporary of Hecataeus and other critics of myth, completely refashions the material handed to him. Like Herodotus he ostensibly accepts the ancient tale only to rework it until an entirely new production emerges. In Herodotus the mechanics of the transformation often derive from the historian's interest in clinical psychology. So here, what in the myth had been the amorous advances of Zeus toward a passive and ingenuous woman, is portrayed as the hallucinatory experience of an introverted adolescent. Io's speech contains no reference to an actual encounter with Zeus, or to the jealousy of Hera,[2] only to Zeus as the instigator of her exile and peregrinations. The emphasis is on the life of the mind, on dreams and fears and visionary horrors, rather than on the flesh-and-blood escapades of a divine libertine. Aeschylus took a wronged princess and made of her a mask for the soul of pre-

---

[2] I cannot accept Gottfried Hermann's restoration of *Hērās* in Io's initial aria, line 600. The only two references to Hera, once by Prometheus (704) and once by the chorus (900) come long after Io has conditioned us to view her suffering as inward rather than divinely imposed. Prometheus and the Oceanids give us the myth; Io communicates an experience.

Promethean man, for the terrors of human life prior to the advent
of cultural progress and enlightenment. Her words, her gestures, her
dance motions on the stage betoken man in his primeval wildness,
rootless, uncontrolled, tossed by constant apprehensions of his weakness and dependence. Unlike Prometheus she cannot plan or predict,
she can only suffer; and even in her prayers to the gods she can only
beg for more sufferings of the kind which befit wild beasts (577):

> O son of Cronus . . .
> scorch me with fire, or hide me in the earth,
> or throw me as food to the monsters of the sea!

It is hard to see how Goethe in 1799, in a note on staging the tale of
Prometheus, could have written: "Io's dreams, pleasant and light."
If a dream is acted out on the stage, as it must be in the ballet which
Goethe had in mind, the performance is of course likely to achieve an
air of lightness and buoyancy in spite of the material which has gone
into it. In Greek tragedy dreams are as a rule not dramatized, they
are reported. Only thus can the raw realities of the world of sleep
be rendered intact. In our play the report helps to produce the confrontation of the waker and the dreamer, of homo sapiens and the
human animal (complete with hoof and horns), of steadfast doer
and frantic sufferer, of intellectual masculinity and vegetative Eve.

There is considerable fascination in thus fixing the lines of contrast between the immobile hero and the girl-heifer whirling below
him. But is the contrast quite so simple as our allegory would seem
to demand? There are some few straws in the wind to suggest that
the relationship between Prometheus and Io, and the constellation of
forces for which they serve as masks, is rather more complex. The
question will be taken up when we begin to ask whether an allegory
pure and simple can ever be a tragedy. At this point it will be sufficient to mention one such indication. Io, as she tells us herself (663),
was exiled as the result of an oracle from the Delphic god. Her physical ordeal is thus directly due to the skill of men in searching out the
will of the gods. This happens to be a skill which Prometheus counts
among his major contributions to civilized life (484):

I staked out numerous ways of divination . . .

Here, through the puzzle of an almost frivolous incongruity, we catch a glimpse of a greater discordance within which Prometheus and Io are joined closely together. In this particular instance the meaning seems fairly simple. Man, through the institution of oracles and the art of soothsaying, aspires to gain some measure of control over the gods and necessity. But the oracles rebound and show him up for the puny slave he is. Further, they constantly remind him of the inborn savagery which he hopes he has left far behind him, and in the overcoming of which the founding of the oracles was designed to be an effective step. The concept of the means of civilization aborting their own objective is not explicitly stated, but it is a natural heirloom of all Greek tragedy, whether tragedy was Dionysiac in origin or not. More will be said about this in our discussion of the *Bacchae* of Euripides.

In the *Prometheus*, the idea of man's estate controlled and broken is conveyed by one of the principal images of the play, the image of the bridle. To be sure, the special quality of the diction which we noted above is borne out also in the use of metaphors. There are fewer of them than in any other Aeschylean dramas, and they are employed in the interest of discursive argument rather than poetic impact. They operate in the manner of slogans or newspaper cartoons, to clarify and summarize; only rarely do they appeal to the lyrical imagination. Such metaphors as there are will be found to derive from the program of disciplines instituted by Prometheus and promoting civilized intercourse: medicine, horse training, gymnastics, navigation, hunting. In various contexts in the play Prometheus is, respectively, a healer, a trainer, an athlete, a helmsman, or a hunter. But things are not left quite so simple. On the evidence of his crucifixion these competences refer rather to the past, perhaps to the future, at any rate to what Aristotle calls the events "outside the drama." On stage his achievement is not equally unambiguous: he is a patient as well as a healer, a broken horse as well as a trainer; the athlete is immobilized, the helmsman turns into a drowning sailor,

the hunter into the prey of the hunt. Mostly he is the wild colt reined
in and tamed. Both Io, through her father (671)—

> . . . the bridle of Zeus
> compelled him . . .

and Prometheus has suffered the bit of the god.

Thus even the images, in spite of their seeming barrenness, help
to underscore the paradoxical position of the hero. A Prometheus
who is both powerful and impotent mirrors the dual reign of harshness and gentleness which the intellectual must uncover. For, to repeat, it is the predicament of science that in serving to make the
world more convenient it makes it more complex and rarely gentler.
The greater the progress and the more acute the understanding, the
more threatening is the harshness released. That science, as the Greeks
regard it, man's use of waking reason for the betterment of the city,
is a dominant theme in the *Prometheus* has always been recognized.
The fact is clear from the language used and from the procedure followed. Take the Prologue. As we watch the piecemeal fastening of the
body to the rock (55 ff.)—now the hands, now the arm, now the
chest, now the sides, finally the legs—we are put in mind of analogous
cataloguings of parts of the body, in the Hippocratic corpus or in
Thucydides' analysis of the plague in Athens. The Prologue is symptomatic of the whole, for the slow consecutive listing of observable
data, the painstaking effort to achieve completeness, are among the
most marked features of the play. In science, stock-taking and ex-
haustiveness are the norm, not suggestion and allusion. The scheme
of the catalogue derives from epic literature, but when science takes
it over it is adapted to an entirely un-Homeric purpose. To put it
briefly, the epic catalogue fixes a rhythm, it underscores the stability
and the regularity of the world order. Through the near-monotony of
the Homeric catalogue the sensory world proves itself as a source of
delight and strength and as a solid springboard for heroic action. In
science the effect is more neutral; the scientific catalogue does not
savor and acclaim, it records. The items listed are not registered for
their own sake, but as preliminary entries which are needed for other

more abstract calculations. The spirit in which the details are collected is one of detached curiosity. The intention is not to attune oneself to a natural rhythm, but to defy time and isolate pieces of evidence for the sake of a timeless truth. This is the spirit which we find in the *Prometheus*. Its catalogues, along with the comparative dearth of metaphor, the restraint of the diction, and the emphasis on lecturing techniques, are scientific in nature and intent.

The scientific cast is particularly obvious in the geographical speeches, the symmetrically balanced orations in which Prometheus details the future and past wanderings of Io among Scythians, Chalybians, Caucasians, Amazons, Cimmerians, Maeotians, Graeae, Gorgons, Arimaspians, Aethiopians, Aegyptians, Dodonians. Perhaps we had better speak of mock science, for this travelogue is a horrendous mixture of fact, myth, and free association. The division into Asia and Europe which allegedly gives the account its proper coordination is downright unintelligible. No one could hope to duplicate the journey here outlined without running into a maze of impossibilities. But the manner of presentation is scientific. Instead of the marvelous visions of a Marlowe, instead of the pregnant adjectives of epic folklore, Prometheus asks us to consider a sober collection of names, unexcited, devoid of pomp, without a climax to thrill to or a periphrasis to crack. The effect is that of a geographical dictionary, of a world map in words, rather than of an escapist mirage.

What is the purpose of these barren rehearsals? We cannot learn the answer to this question from Io, for she does not register a response. After the termination of the lectures Io merely relapses into her unhappy dervishism. It is evident, however, that one effect of the catalogues—and their deliberate mystifications may stem from this —is to call attention to the vastness and unfamiliarity of the world around us. The approach is not that of the lyricist or the prophet, but of the scientist who is compelled by his own sanity and tidiness to recognize the limits of his capacity. Man-scientist finds himself in a world which he tries to analyze and describe, but there comes a point at which analysis turns into wonder or, at best, guesswork. Then the catalogue, despite its ostensible function, which is to organize and make more manageable, by the stateliness and monotony peculiar to it underscores the stubborn and prodigious power of what it sets out to catch. Thus the geographical "digressions" point up our old ambiguity. Prometheus seems to have, or thinks he has, some control over his environment: he catalogues. But the strangeness of the material, the swirl of the unknown beyond the visible horizon, re-establishes the natural proportions, however sober and deceptively factual the speech in which it is put. The untrodden and ungentle wastes of the world rise to swallow up the civilizers and the knowers. Prometheus is surrounded by them; the travels of Io provide the rude impetus and the vertigo with which the vastness beyond checks the proud motionlessness of Prometheus.

But that is only one side of the picture. Prometheus needs Io; Io the itinerant completes Prometheus the thinker. Her movement symbolically brings into the scope of the action the world outside, the waste land as well as the paradises, but especially the waste land. Through her the deserts and mountains and armed savages and "the jagged jaws of the sea" (726) come to life in stiff and disciplined and speciously masterful speech. By the end of the play Prometheus is no longer alone; we see him encircled by all the specters conjured up by Io's fate. And these specters, harsh and militant as they are, aggrandize the stature of the hero whose keenness has brought them to life; their existence is a measure of his achievement. Without the Scythians, Gorgons, and Arimaspians, Prometheus could not be himself.

What is the status of the thinker vis-à-vis the nature he wants to control? In the first choral ode the mermaids applaud Prometheus' undertaking to transform nature into more than nature, and regret its partial failure. As they put it, Asia—i.e., as commonly in this play, uncultured land—and the watery elements had put their hopes in Prometheus and now mourn his frustration (434):

> The springs of sacred streams lament
> and pity the grievous pain.

The Colchians, Scythians, Arabians, along with Earth, springs, and, above all, the Oceanids themselves, the waves personified, sympathize and sorrow with Prometheus. For nature is not only hard but also pliant, otherwise man would never have been able to shape it. Man's work upon nature is in one sense nothing but an eliciting of nature's destiny. Ocean, the embracer of land, wishes to be embraced and confined and covered with keels in turn. Asia wishes to be made into Europe; hence the sorrow of the Arabians. There is a readiness in nature, a potential in barbarism, for what the thinker has in mind for it, for progress and humanization. It is the mission of Prometheus to put gardens in the mountains, to bend the iron into spears and pruning hooks. This mission coincides, to an extent, with a tendency rooted in nature itself. So when the hammer blows are stilled, nature sends out its delegates, the chorus, to offer its condolences.

But it is impossible to overlook the undercurrent in the opening section of the play of that other side of nature which resists man's encroachment, of the wave not lapping in harmony but crashing discordantly, of the waste land persisting in its fruitless isolation. Nature delights in the tortures of the fallen intellectual who must forever, by a Dantesque dispensation, stand cruelly exposed to the elements which he attempted to soften, ever upright, sleepless, unbending: a fiendish perpetuation of his role as civilizer and creator. He whose role had been to transmute the raw and inhuman into a structure of sensibility and meaning, is now himself incarcerated in a landscape without meaning, sterile and raw. Nature rendering its benefits to man and nature attempting to preserve and enlarge its identity against man; the Chalybians desiring to be civilized and rejecting civilization: a notorious ambivalence, shipwrecking missionaries and engineers, which constitutes the testing ground for the hero of the play and is tested in its turn. Nature's dual status and man's dual identity are linked to one another by a network of mutual harmonies and antagonisms. Prometheus is cousin to the Oceanids and uncle to Zeus. Shelley's

> This bleak ravine, these unrepentant plains

draws too simple a picture, as if nature were only an adversary of the human soul. They are indeed antagonists, and yet they inform and quicken one another because they are part of a larger cosmic division. The dyarchy of harshness and gentleness does not respect the boundaries which human isolation has tried to establish around itself. The formulated aspirations of which Whitehead speaks may well be found embodied in the natural world, just as the senseless agencies are not unknown in human shape.

iii

In the eternal struggle of kinship between man and his world, what is the role of Zeus? We learn something about the manner of his rule in the second choral song, just before Io runs on stage. The Oceanids, irresolute and retiring in the traditional choral style, pray that (526)

> omnipotent Zeus may never
> strike back at any position we hold . . .

They are more than willing to extend to the god the recognition which is the path of least resistance. In contrast, they suggest (543), Prometheus overindulges in his unconventional position of honoring mortals too much. They deprecate (548)

> the weak-willed, dream-like
> impotence of the human race . . .

By a twist of irony, man facing Zeus permits himself the same broad alternative as nature in its relation to civilizing man. He may submit to the authority of the god, as the Oceanids, representative of the plastic potential of nature, appear to recommend. Or he may rebel and try to achieve his proper destiny by blocking the tyranny of heaven and annexing some of its prerogatives. But the situation is reversed, for the struggle is against harshness rather than gentleness. Zeus' dictatorial desires are to be taken as a symbol of raw necessity. He is "pitiless," as we learn in the first choral song and again and again in the course of the play. His pitilessness is the unfeeling stubbornness of the senseless agencies. Zeus is cruel and he is irresponsible; compulsion and violence are the natural modes of his operation.

This conception of the father of the gods has on occasion proved a disagreeable morsel to swallow. Usually, however, the difficulty is caused by a misconception, according to which the author decided to write a play in which Zeus would take a prominent role, and then proceeded to furnish Zeus with a character strangely unlike the character known to the earlier writers on mythology. This is getting hold of the wrong end of the stick. Nor again is Aeschylus at pains to construct a new theology, or to transform the traditional mythology. There is in this picture of Zeus no element of confession or commitment or moral philosophy. Rather, Zeus is in the play because Aeschylus needed a supreme and comprehensive focus for cruelty and irresponsibility, a focus so vast and incontrovertible that the rational imagination would boggle at it and refuse to question the existence of the force described. For this purpose, only Zeus would do. In Athens his majesty was as great as his popular standing was negligible. One told stories about him, and worshipped him in unreflected civic rites; but no one would have thought of making the Homeric divinity his personal god, a deity to ply with fervent supplication and private queries. Thus, though all respected Zeus, nobody called him his own. By a happy coincidence it was this eminently useful divinity who was featured as the opponent of Prometheus in the traditional story. The dramatist took over the person though not the character of Hesiod's Zeus; but the meaning of the masque, the intellectual programme of the drama, was settled without reference to the god. It would of course be nonsense to say that the significant outlines of the action were fixed long before Aeschylus decided to turn to the figure of Zeus for the appropriate divine symbol. The act of literary creation presumably is not quite so mechanical as this. But it is fair to assume that it was the power of Zeus rather than any of his more domestic or ethical characteristics which the writer kept within his sights while designing his plan. Thus the image of the enthroned father came to stand for an entirely new complex of ideas, generated by the new conception of the role and personality of Prometheus. It may be asked whether an Athenian audience would have been willing to go along with this daring step, with the superimposition of a celebrated if little-felt name on a conception shaped largely independently of that name. The question is tied up with one to which I had occasion to refer earlier, namely, whether the play is likely to have been performed in the theater at all. Neither question can be answered definitively. It remains only to acknowledge that a masque must operate with known symbols, even if the content that is poured into the symbols is so new as to make likely misunderstanding and doubt.

Once all harshness, all compulsion and violence outside man, has been centered in the image of Zeus, the writer has a freer hand in portraying more concretely the sympathetic component in nature. Near the end of the play Hermes pictures for us, and Prometheus prophesies and then describes, the turmoils of nature which are to accompany his downfall. Because Zeus and, to a lesser degree, Hermes have attracted to their persons the obstructive and merciless aspects of the universe, the convulsions of Earth and winds and waters turn into expressions of grief rather than triumph. Even in his greatest suffering Prometheus has the comfort of knowing that brute nature, barring sheer necessity, is tormented as he goes down. The Oceanids underscore this compact, through their last-minute rejection of the appeal of Hermes and through their resolution to join the hero in his throes. In the end civilizer and nature move in unison, against the retarding force of cosmic lethargy: an auspicious message, in the spirit of the enlightenment which posed the problems of the play.

Can we go further in our attempt to read a precise meaning into the balanced symbols of the work? It might be suggested that Zeus is, in a manner of speaking, the creature of Prometheus. After all only a thinker is capable of recognizing and formulating the laws or the special quality of lawlessness which marks the obduracy of the cosmic automatism. Perhaps that is the notion which underlies the report, to which Prometheus reverts again and again, that he helped Zeus to power, for this is a feature of the myth of which there is hardly a trace in the tradition on which Aeschylus drew. Now the kingmaker has been discarded, and he dreams of seeing the downfall of the power he helped to create; an idle dream, but typical of the intellectual's malaise at recognizing and resenting the forces he has uncovered. The bonds and wedges fixing Prometheus to his rock are ultimately self-imposed; the anvil on which they were forged is of his own ambitious devising.

Man, civilized man, is impotent. But in his weakness he has one consolation which restores meaning to his life and sets him above the gods: he has his choice, his accountability, his moral freedom. The exercise of intelligence is, to be sure, ineffectual in its collision with the will of Zeus. But it is necessary and dignifying; it is founded on insights and liberties unknown to the god. When Prometheus says to Ocean, who at that moment acts as a spokesman for Zeus (330):

I envy you your chaste immunity,

he is being heavily ironical. The agent incurs a responsibility, and therein lies part of his satisfaction. Action is the end of life—at least this is what the Greeks seem to have felt prior to the advent of the Hellenistic philosophies—but action entails accountability. Mechanical nature, the irresponsible gods, those "who have no accounts to render," as the writer puts it with strong political emphasis, are victorious, but there is no substance in their victory. As in the Homeric epic, a god's triumph can only be frivolous or petty. It is won without a consciousness of effort, without the risk of defeat and death, and the god has no cause beyond the mere fact of his existence to give the triumph its meaning. Ocean has his griffin, Prometheus will have his eagle. The difference between the amusing, unessential plaything and the hurtful companion, deliberately elected, repeats in the visual realm what we learn from the speeches of the opponents.

It may be asked why Aeschylus does not put Zeus himself on the stage. A play about two antagonists in which one does not appear in his own person but is rather unenthusiastically represented by emissaries is an oddity on the Greek stage or any other stage. Analogies could perhaps be cited from the modern theater, plays in which a character struggles in vain against a code or a combination of forces which eludes his control. But the comparison is not quite proper, for in these modern tragedies—the works of Ibsen, Hauptmann, Arthur Miller come to mind—the unconquerable element is not seen as a personal adversary. Hence it is not expected to emerge into open view. In those plays—Goethe's *Faust* is an instance—in which the opposing force is visually caught in a specific mask, usually one taken from mythology, the mask is, as a rule, manifest on the stage. The Devil is a member of the cast. Why did Aeschylus avoid a similar commitment? There are two answers, closely related to one another, to account for the latency of Zeus. We must remember that the Zeus of this play bears little resemblance to the Zeus whom the Athenians knew from their epics and their civic rites. To bring him out into the orchestra would have meant evoking a conventional response which could only corrupt the meaning carried by the hidden tyrant. Again, the impact of his descent to earth would no doubt have blunted the effect of Prometheus' own tortured epiphany. The playwright wishes to exalt the hero; for the benefit of Prometheus' standing we must be satisfied with a lesser representative of necessity. Only thus can man's achievement in the face of an unfeeling, unpotential world blocking progress and creativeness be put in the proper focus. In *Faust* the hero is continually on the verge of losing his stage appeal because of the lurid attractiveness of his opponent. In the *Prometheus* the cold-blooded executioner, the abortive compromiser, the snarling opportunist cannot touch the greatness of Prometheus; by the scheme of the plot they are puppets rather than agents, and lack the credentials for a solid challenge.

But Prometheus is not entirely insensible to the provocations of an Ocean or a Hermes. Particularly the latter, with his shrill petulance and his brisk politicking, manages to rouse Prometheus to a pitch of resentment and bluster which threatens to cost him the chorus'—and that means the listener's—sympathies. Is the stridency of the messenger god, coming as it does near the end of the play, dramatically acceptable? That is to say, does it not tend to reduce the force opposing Prometheus to unduly minor proportions, and does it not promote in Prometheus himself a reliance on boasts and counterthreats unworthy of the hero? In any event, is vituperation climactic?

Again, the answers will have to be deferred. Meanwhile there is a further mystery connected with the status of Zeus. On several occasions Prometheus remarks on the fact that Zeus is a newcomer to the scene, a callow upstart, and compares the lateness of his ascendancy unfavorably with his own old age and experience. Does this mean only, as suggested above, that the scientist, in his struggle for the control of nature, experiences necessity and harshness as the price of a new dispensation? From the point of view of technological planning, it is the "new" which cannot be absorbed into the area of control; when the score of progress is cast and tallied, new difficulties, new pockets of necessity move into view and endanger the planning. Is that what is meant by the "youth" of Zeus? The answer is, Yes, *if* we read the *Prometheus Bound* as a neat allegory of philosophical issues. But the interpretation needs only to be mentioned to be rejected as patently forced and awkward and improbable. What, then, *is* the significance of the repeated stress on the youthful inexperience of Zeus? If it were merely a mythological vestige, a touch of Hesiodic color and nothing else, the emphasis would clearly be redundant and misleading.

Before going on with this problem, one final question. If the play, as has been agreed, is about the achievement and the suffering of thinking man, why are all the characters, with one apparent exception, gods? A glance at Aeschylus' trilogy, the *Oresteia,* is in order here. In the first two plays the action is carried out entirely by human characters; in the third, men are almost driven from the stage by the drama of the gods. The understanding is that in the *Eumenides* the fate of individual men has become less crucial, and the social crisis as such has moved into the limelight. The more a plot is conceived in terms of general human behavior, the more openly the gods become the dramatis personae. Where the action is presented as a struggle between individuals the gods fade into the background. In our play the issues stated or hinted at are so general that particular men, even men of myth, could not have satisfied the requirements of the plot. And yet, ironically, because the gods chosen are allegorical or used allegorically, there is a danger of greater preciseness than might have

been the case if the writer had elected men to carry the burden of the
message. Oedipus, though a particular man with a clearly defined
history of his own, is in many ways more Everyman than Prometheus.
In Oedipus, in his ambitious search and his crushing truth, we can
see ourselves more readily than in the undaunted intellectual ardor of
Prometheus. But then, this is not a play about Everyman, but about
a narrowly defined species of man, the fifth-century intellectual, pro-
claiming the cause of progress and the ameliorability of man's estate.
Still, the story is that of a class, of a movement, not of an individual;
and so the players are gods, not men.

It should be added that this sharpness of outline, the allegorical
perspicuity of the mask of Prometheus, contains an element of danger.
The clarity of a character or a situation might detract, in the imagination of the audience, from its reality. Life is not clear, it does not easily
resolve itself into philosophy. Hence, to maintain the illusion of
reality, the original allegory has to be softened and even obscured, in
various ways. As we shall see, Aeschylus, fully conscious of this demand, does indeed erase the fixed outlines of the intellectual image he
has created. He performs this erasure with such vehemence that he
manages to transform the divine characters, certainly Prometheus,
into full-blooded complex human organisms. At the same time, the
advantage of having gods, with their greater universality and their
acknowledged impressiveness, remains effective. Their presence indicates that the play is concerned with more than one incident in the
lives of heroic men, and that the action transcends the works and the
failures of any one individual.

Why, then, is Io mortal? Why does the writer disrupt the divine
homogeneity of his drama with the interpolation of a human being?
Actually Io is not mortal in the sense in which Antigone or Jocasta
or Helen or St. Joan are mortal. Her hybrid nature lifts her above
the concretely experienced, empirical run of women. She is the female
counterpart to a horned river god, and in fact daughter of a river
god, and bride of Zeus. By comparison with the great ladies of the
Homeric pantheon, with Hera and Athena and even Aphrodite, she
is of course a humble mortal. Still, considering the allegorical ob-

jective he had in mind the poet was wise to choose her, with her ephemeral trappings, rather than a canonical Homeric deity. What true goddess available to a Greek author could have suitably embodied the qualities of unreason and insecurity which needed to be formulated? Whatever might be said about the virtues and vices of the female inhabitants of Olympus, they are supremely intelligent. A mere girl, therefore, it had to be. But her connections and the miracle of her peregrinations make her into something that is more than a mere girl. Visually she resembles the daughters of Ocean, to whom she is tied through her youthful maidenly innocence and her want of stability. The only thing which sets her apart from them and from all divine creatures is her capacity for suffering, and in this she is linked with Prometheus. Thus Io is as much more than human as Prometheus is less than divine. They meet, and in their seemingly accidental meeting, a meeting neither well motivated nor organically developed, they embody the sufferings of humanity in its full extension from savagery to civilization, from pastoral nomadism to city refinement, from eidetic involvement to the rule of the intellect.

iv

I began this essay by trying to analyze the *Prometheus Bound* as a sort of manifesto, a philosophical tract, allegorically sketching the position of man in the modern universe, acclaiming his heroism and lamenting his weakness, through the broadening and concretizing mechanism of a masque. It is important for a treatise to carry a discoverable meaning, to present a pattern sufficiently transparent to allow reason to reflect on it and to find her special laws properly observed. This is, to a certain extent, true of the play. We can, and should, read it as a document recording certain trends in fifth-century Athenian thought, simultaneously corroborating the values of the enlightenment and combating its claims. The form is appropriate; heraldically set speeches alternate with shorter stretches of a dialogue without adornment, even prosy and garrulous. The dramatic machinery often creaks; the writing shows a romance-like unconcern for the motivation of dramatic climaxes. Generally speaking,

the tragic vehicle seems, at first glance, to be little more than an editori-
al cloak for material of an entirely different order. In a treatise the
units of meaning are plotted so carefully and so perspicuously that
the imagination requires no additional impetus to organize them for
itself in a balanced arrangement. The main purpose of a treatise is to
achieve a sense of order, and to bring about a situation in which few
major questions remain unanswered and no significant ends are left
undisposed. It is difficult to say how a genuine tragedy could be fash-
ioned from matter which affords so little scope for mystery and dis-
quietude. What, then, saves the *Prometheus Bound* from being just a
treatise, in spite of its frequent baldness and its lack of native momentum?

We have already noted several occasions on which the interpretation of the play as a tract failed to solve certain puzzles, or where it
made for new puzzles in its turn. The age of Zeus, the status of the
oracular art, and the closeness of Prometheus and Io are some of the
motifs which an allegorical explication failed to illumine. It is hints
like these which assure us, if we were not already convinced by the
emotional impact of the drama on generations of audiences and practicing poets, that the *Prometheus* is indeed much more than a discursive broadsheet dressed up in the garb of a chamber masque. The
difficulty arises when we ask ourselves precisely how the play transcends its function as a treatise. That is to say, by what means does
the poet succeed in creating a tragedy while at the same time preserving the allegory of scientific man? For the message evidently retains
its validity, whatever additional elements we may discover. I should
like to suggest that there are two main directions in which the play
goes beyond the semantic confines of the argument I have sketched
above. In the first place, there are several levels of meaning. The only
reason for not noting this earlier is that it seemed better to formulate
the allegory of science in isolation and thereby enhance its importance. And it does seem to me that this particular significance of the
drama is by far the most important, and one that the audience could
be expected to absorb more immediately than some of the collateral
meanings. But more than any other play in the Greek repertory the

Prometheus Bound dazzles with a multiplicity of significances, all of which interlock and reinforce each other in a way that does not permit paraphrase and that in the end defeats the allegorical intention. Each reference by itself is tolerably apparent. There is a political plane. Scene after scene we discover acute insights into the asymmetrical relations of power, wisdom, organized institutions, and liberating action. It has often been observed that many of the adjectives employed in the running controversy between Prometheus and the emissaries of Zeus are primarily political in color, and that Zeus is throughout pictured as a conventional tyrant, at least as the fifth century understood the nature of tyranny.

Then there is a cultural plane. In many ways the struggle between Prometheus and the complex of forces which opposes him reminds us of the historical struggle between Greeks and barbarians. Not only is Zeus the tyrant another Xerxes—one fifth-century thinker is said to have referred to Xerxes as "the Zeus of the Persians"—but the tribal and regional names which the poet chooses as symbols of uncivilized nature are generally taken from the contemporary Persian orbit. By the time of Aeschylus the Greek fiction that to be a non-Greek is to be not quite human, or human only in a superficial sense, had fully established itself. Equating uncivilized nature with barbarian mores had become a staple of public poetry, in spite of the occasional reminders by more historically oriented writers that Persia and Egypt could look down on Greece as a newcomer in the ranks of civilized nations. Prometheus is a Greek; Zeus, as the writer uses him, and Ocean and his daughters are not. The girls may perhaps sympathize with the hero's position; but they cannot really understand his mission. A cultural gulf separates them from him.

Finally it is possible to single out the sexual references at which I have only hinted. The juxtaposition of rational active man with nonrational passive woman carries our imagination beyond the scientific allegory and lends comfort to the masculine conservatism of the Athenian audience and, I dare say, of most modern audiences also. On this score the *Prometheus* has a remarkably old-fashioned ring, for one of the surprising things about Attic tragedy is the scope given in many of

the plays to female enterprise and female independence. Our play does
not feature an Antigone or a Clytemnestra; the male element stands
unchallenged in its place of power and strength. Themis is little more
than a shadow on the horizon, an abstraction without notable effect on
the dramatic action. The war is a war between males.

It is the critic's privilege to uncover these various nuclei of reference
and to study them in isolation from one another. In the play, of course,
they are not separate; cultural, political, and other symbolisms nudge
each other and overlap, to the advantage of one or the other of them.
But mostly the full response generated by the action is not narrowly
geared to this or that reference alone. The multiplicity of levels of
meaning and the mixed quality of the responses help to mitigate the
meticulousness of the logic, and to preserve the impression of a significant opacity which might endanger the success of a treatise, but
which a tragedy needs.

So much for planes of reference. The other factor helping to free
the play from the shackles of a too ostensible meaning is no less
obvious. Beyond the various analyzable themes there are nonprogrammatic factors; they do not share in a straightforward symbolic intention yet are powerfully operative in shaping the effect of the drama.
To cite one example: the interplay between stillness and motion, the
purely visual impact of the motionless hero standing as one crucified,
engulfed by the billowing blue gauze of the ancient Rhine Maidens,
generates an impulse of its own far in excess of any demonstrable
moral which it might be thought to enhance. Another instance of the
nonprogrammatic ingredient in the total texture is the residue of the
mythological tradition. We have already noticed that certain features
of the plot seem to be due to an acceptance of ancient tales even
where the terms of the tales threaten to conflict with the ends of the
allegory. We shall come back to this directly. Then there is the fact of
Prometheus' wrath. Like the wrath of Achilles or Lear or Kleist's
Michael Kohlhaas it is not the type of anger which interests social
scientists, a natural and predictable reflex stimulated by and commensurate to an injury received. In its monumental and shocking violence,
and in its incongruity rising as it does from the heart of the "thinker"

Prometheus, the anger belies any easy moral that might be drawn, and brings back into the play that more significant obscurity which assists us in getting past the barriers of a discursive meaning. "Brings back" is, of course, said from the point of view of the critic whose limitations have compelled him to approach the drama from only one side. In reality this enriching obscurity is part of the essence of the play from the beginning. Unfortunately it is more difficult to discuss the principles and the modes of this aspect of the tragedy than it is to reduce the action to the units of a debate.

The final scene of the *Prometheus Bound* may serve as a convenient sample of the interaction between meaning and nonmeaning, of the disturbing and exalting influence of alien factors on the terms of the allegory. In that last scene we learn, from the words of the hero which echo his introductory recitative, that untamed nature is in an uproar of indignation (1081):

> The ground is shaken;
> the low crash of thunder bellows
> close by, the fiery scrolls of lightning
> blaze aflame, whirlwinds wheel
> their dust . . .

Such are the turmoils of nature as it watches the hero disappear into the depth. That these are indeed tokens of compassion and fellow feeling is put beyond question by the declaration of solidarity issued by the Oceanids just before the elements are stirred up. At the same time the upheaval may also be understood as punishment, as the backlash of the crude elements against the man who wanted to tame and control them. That is the interpretation which Hermes puts on the scene when he prophesies it some time earlier (1014):

> Consider, if you do not trust my words,
> the irresistible attack of storms
> and waves upon waves of ills which will beset you.

Hermes' perspective cannot be dismissed. The unleashing of the natural forces symbolizes both sympathy for the hero *and* resistance to his purpose. Two planes of significance clash and merge in an irrational mixture. Furthermore the unrestricted fury of the physical powers is not only the setting within which the hero stands and against which he braces himself. It is also an external realization of the torment within his soul, of the anger and confusion which mark the limits of his allegorical personality. The sheer theatricality of the final burst and collapse—whether engineered on the stage or simulated in the rhetoric of the verse—goes, in its effect upon the imagination, far beyond any demonstrable programme. What starts out as a description of the suffering of knowing man in and with and against nature, ends up as an autonomous act of total strife and destruction. The world goes under; the triple statement, once by Hermes and twice by Prometheus himself, secures the feeling of inevitability.

Zeus also is a richer symbol, a less transparent personality than I have made out. To be sure, Zeus is the world as seen in a certain way, he stands for the senseless agencies which, in response to man's search for beauty and truth and loving comfort, concede an inch only to repossess a mile. But Zeus not only "stands for" one thing or another, he *is,* in a personal and immeasurable sense. However fully we explain the role of Zeus in this masque of thinking man, there is always something left over, and that remainder, difficult to analyze and tally, helps to lift the play above the level of a treatise or manifesto. Perhaps the most striking instance of the philosophical awkwardness of the figure of Zeus is his relation to the dark maternal powers of a bygone age (515):

> CHORUS: Who is the helmsman of necessity?
> PROMETHEUS: The Destinies' trio and the mindful Furies.
> CHORUS: Then would you say that Zeus is not as strong?
> PROMETHEUS: He is committed to his destiny.

Not even Zeus can escape the necessity embodied in these dark abstractions. Nothing is said elsewhere in the play to suggest that this is a private opinion or wishful thinking on the part of the hero rather than a truth which the author wants to convey to the audience. Now if we apply the standards appropriate to an allegory, this would have to mean that Zeus, besides *being* necessity, is controlled by necessity. Thus we pass beyond unambiguous conceptualization and enter into the world of literature and art where paradox is at home, and consistency, *pace* Aristotle, need not be a virtue.

The somber deities who are said to be stronger than Zeus are taken from the mythological tradition, specifically from the panoramic scheme of Hesiod, from that portion of his *Theogony* in which he reflects on the vast interlocking variety of social and historical forces rather than on the moral splendor of the rule of Zeus. They are part of his catalogue of generations; they are not involved in the cosmic trend toward Justice over which Zeus presides. The Furies are those released by the deposition of Cronus and the Titans; the Fates are a more general personification of dynastic transitoriness. Hesiod makes an effort to remove his Zeus from the entanglement denoted by these symbols; Aeschylus has no such concern, in spite of the ostensible universality of the god's might. Probably Aeschylus thereby reaffirms an older connection whose partial obliteration in Hesiod remained unsuccessful. In this reference to the authority of the Fates and the Furies, therefore, we witness an almost automatic carry-over of myth, a reassertion of the simple, naïve, and vital beliefs of popular divine lore, undigested and unreconstructed and, so long as we cling to the code of the treatise, contradictory. But without these bedeviling memories, without the disruption of meaning they introduce into the work of art, what would we have?

We know what we might have. In 1773 Goethe wrote a play entitled *Prometheus,* in two acts. First act: son rebels against father, refuses to be his servant; a domestic drama. Second act: men and their social problems; the first impact of death. Goethe dramatizes two major issues, the issue of freedom against servitude, and the issue of death versus immortality. In spite of its fragmentary nature and the early date of its composition there is considerable merit in the piece. The issues are clear, the language is unwaveringly true to the issues, and the revolutionary zeal which then inspired Goethe cannot but stir the heart of the most sluggish reader. But the clarity of the issues, the unambiguousness of the meaning, in the end prevents the sketch from being effective as drama, much less as tragedy. That the history of the writing of *Faust* might also be called a history of the progressive obscuration of the issues and conceptions with which Goethe started out, is fully recognized by all critics of that masterpiece.

Once we admit that denotative complexity and irrationality are of the very substance of a successful philosophical tragedy, two items which had earlier perplexed us gain fresh significance. It will be recalled that Aeschylus more than once insists on the point that Zeus is young and that his rule is new. At the time, we found that this newness could not be stretched into a symbolic scheme without lapsing into artificiality. Only the most ingenious interpreter could discover an allegorical significance in the comparative ages of the thinker and his enemy. But the fight of Prometheus will enlist our sympathies more readily if the enemy is not ancient and legitimate but young and of dubious authority. That is to say, the comparative ages of the two characters are not part of the *mathos,* of the veiled meaning of the action, but part of the *pathos,* the emotional persuasion produced by the quality of the personal relations in the drama *as* drama. It is important that the characters, however mythical or figurative, should deal with one another as men. They should have their foibles and encumberments as well as their specific and official purposes. We are not only to understand their significance, but to glory and suffer with them as ends within themselves. As human beings involved in a painful nexus they must not be referable beyond themselves. Even Zeus is not exempt from this demand; if he were not for the sake of the tragedy fitted into a system of subjective, nonallegorical relationships, the struggle of Prometheus would perhaps touch our intelligence but not our hearts. All this does not make our play a drama of character in the sense in which *Oedipus the King* or *Medea* is a drama of character. The tragedy does not flow organically from the interrelation of the various personalities. Such characters as there are do not originate the tragedy; they are designed to support a tragic mood in the face of an abstract allegory. The masks have taken on some of the features of the tangled skein of life; their hard outlines are here and there broken and distorted as if they were on the point of transforming themselves into living flesh and blood. The transformation does not proceed very far, except perhaps in the case of Prometheus himself; but the gain is sufficient to guarantee the desired success.

From this, further light is shed on the motif of the secret, the item of knowledge hidden from Zeus. To begin with, it appeared as if its fitful introduction into the argument was intended to infuse a semblance of progress and suspense into a static situation. Now it may be added that the secret is more than just a gadget to promote an artificial suspense. Like the youth of Zeus, the secret is taken from myth. We cannot be sure how well-known and important this motif was in the tradition familiar to Aeschylus' contemporaries. It is enough to note that Aeschylus recognized its usefulness and made it a cornerstone of his edifice of human relations. If the play were an allegory and nothing else, Zeus would have to be omnipotent. The myth of the secret limits his power, it reduces his authority to a level very near that of Prometheus, and by thus humanizing their relation opens the scope for a tragedy. No mere abstraction of overriding strength, the Zeus of the *Prometheus Bound* excites our interest and even a modicum of sympathy for this one crack in his armor of omniscience, without at the same time giving up one iota of the cosmic symbolism demanded by the allegory. Conversely, through his monopoly of the secret Prometheus ascends to the position of a minor Zeus, jealous, highhanded, unphilanthropic—if we may extend the term beyond the accident of mortality. And so his war against Zeus, that unlikely victim of a conspiracy of silence, becomes sufficiently ambiguous to accommodate itself to the needs of drama.

That the references to the Furies and the Fates are due to the same cause should now be evident. No more forcible reminder of the personal limitations of the god could have been devised. It is characteristic of the technique of the playwright that once again the humanizing touch is taken from popular myth. Why is it that mythology is made to supply those elements which help the author to counterbalance the theological or philosophical or moral burden of a drama? Perhaps, of all the pieces of common knowledge available to him, only the glittering escapades and the somber regulations of the divine tales were so familiar to the people that they could be digested whole and unreflectedly, without jarring or compromising the meaning of the material which they are drawn in to assist. That Zeus is subject to Fate is a thought to which people had become accustomed through countless pointed remarks in the Homeric epics and other classic tales. To have this truth once more enunciated in the present play is an effective instrument toward describing the "human" status of Prometheus' opponent. At the same time, the reminder does not arouse the curiosity or doubt to a degree which might imperil the impact of the heroic message of the masque.

It may be useful, in this connection, to discuss the portrait of Typhon (315–372) which most manuscripts put in the mouth of Ocean, though the majority of editors follow our oldest manuscript in assigning the speech to Prometheus. It is difficult to say which ascription is right. The answer depends on the answer to another question: whether Aeschylus means to emphasize the lonely pride of Prometheus or the conciliatory enterprise of Ocean, in this attempt of one of them to talk the other out of a proposed venture of "rashness." Fortunately the dramatic ascription of the speech is less important than the fact that it is where it is, particularly in this play in which statements are not as closely attached to characters as they would be in a more conventional drama. As it stands, the picture of Typhon battling and overthrown merges in our imagination with that of Prometheus. Typhon, the opponent of Zeus par excellence, the celebrated devil of Hesiod's poem, here becomes a fellow sufferer. He dared to stand up against the Olympians, he was defeated and hurled underground, and now spends an eternity plotting revenge against his torturers. The parallel with Prometheus is too close to be overlooked. Further, there is a vision of Typhon eventually breaking out from his underground chambers and once more hurling his weapons upward into the sky (367):

> . . . and then there will erupt
> rivers of fire tearing with fierce jaws
> the expansive plains of fruitful Sicily.
> Such seething bile will Typhon belch up high

with red-hot bolts of hideous turbulence,
though burnt to ashes once by the bolt of Zeus.

The language of this vision prefigures another rout, the mysterious
emergence of the "wrestler" (920) who will toward the end of time
outcrash and outfight Zeus and thus prepare the liberation of Prometheus. Within the imagery of the play as a whole, therefore, the
portrayal of the opening up of Aetna serves as a pictorial omen for the
humiliation of Zeus and the restoration of Prometheus.

But the choice of the sufferer also casts some light on the nature
of Prometheus himself. Despite the purity of his purpose and the nobility of his message Prometheus is in some ways another Typhon,
and Aeschylus manages, by his use of the myth, to enlarge the perceptions of the audience. The theomachy of Prometheus has about it
something brutal, even monstrous. The intellect also, the light of
pure reason directed against the stubbornly natural, may, when embodied in a human career, acquire feral dimensions. In the *Tempest*
the beastly is made comfortable, or at any rate endurable, through the
domestication of Caliban and the eventual self-mastery of Prospero.
In the *Prometheus Bound* there is no similar exorcism. The canons of
Aeschylean art stipulate progressive self-revelation rather than change
and evolution. The fierce streak which is part of Prometheus' being
remains with him to the very end, its terror tempered only by the
beauty of the rhetoric in which it is expressed. And because of this we
feel more closely attached to him than if he were a paragon of reasoned perfection. The brutality of Prometheus—we shall come back
to it—obeys the same purpose as do Zeus' blindness and subservience
to Fate. It ranges the enemies together in a concrete and familiar bond
which defies the allegory and authenticates their war.

We have already seen that the figure of Io is one of the richest
symbols in the play. Dimly we perceive that in spite of the obscurities
and the apparent irrelevancies of her part, her travels and her excess
of feeling signify a fulcrum for important aspects of the underlying
allegory. Nevertheless if she were nothing but a somnambulist of the
present, without memories and without beginnings, we would not
be satisfied. But she tells us that she was once a pretty girl, that she

has not always borne her present monstrous shape. Hence we are informed of more than a fact, a fixed pattern of behavior; we come to know a history, a singular shifting course of human events. This individual career, including the circumstances of her transformation into animal shape, is useless and a little awkward from the point of view of the meaning. In fact we note that Aeschylus decided to eliminate some features of the tale which might have obscured the meaning altogether. There is, for instance, no mention of Hermes' role in the killing of Argus, no doubt because it would have been embarrassing in this context to feature Hermes as a protector of the oppressed. But on the whole it is remarkable how much of the ancient story Aeschylus retains. Moreover he endows the events pertaining to Io's metamorphosis with an emphasis and a pathos which turn a tale of miracle into a tale of wonder. The account of her sufferings shapes our feelings; our pity proves that it is part of the tragedy, in spite of our inability always to clarify its bearing on the significance of her role. Thus pity and fear on the one hand, and insight and analysis on the other, come to be mixed in an unlikely synthesis to permit the full effect of meaningful drama.

Let me hasten to admit that the separability of the personal or biographical elements, their lack of necessary connection with the allegory, imposes a special obligation on the poet. Obviously not just any mixing of human relations and meaning will do. No technical rules can, however, be laid down to facilitate the successful combination of the two, to show what kind of persons must be put on the stage in order to create a drama with this or that message or moral. Success in this amalgam comes with the spark of genius; it can be tested only in the court of experience. Before the uniqueness of the achievement, approved by generations of theater-goers and readers, literary criticism can only demonstrate the fact. A theoretical distinction between an amalgam that is properly incongruous and a mixture that is merely confusing exceeds the limits of what is possible in criticism. All that criticism can do is show that a drama in which characters and meaning are completely harmonized must fail because it lacks the elements of friction without which drama cannot be fully alive.

V

The time has now come to look more closely
at the conduct of Prometheus, particularly at those facets of his behavior which are not closely linked with the symbolism of the play and
which may in fact be expected to have little to do with it. More especially I should like to comment on a number of qualities which this
particular hero exhibits but which, it appears, are found again and
again in the more famous examples of European high tragedy. It is
a remarkable fact that many of the tragic heroes of Western literature
bear a striking resemblance to Prometheus. The resemblance may perhaps be explained by the reminder that even today tragic heroes are
often conceived in the image of a theomachy, of man trying to assert
his individual and generic powers in the face of senseless and unpredictable agencies. At the same time, when we think of the Aeschylean Titan who braved Zeus, we are put in mind of a certain attitude,
a certain combination of gestures and feelings. More than any special
significance or intelligence, we recall the immediate impact of weight,
of truculence, and martyrdom. For most of us Prometheus is not a
symbol but a man, not an allegory but an experience visual, kinetic,
and emotional. It is this experience which, with countless variations,
has been duplicated time after time, until it has achieved an almost
archetypal status in the expectations of educated men and women.
It is, therefore, not amiss to attempt to define the ingredients which
have gone into the Aeschylean mixture of "Promethean" man.

The last three lines of the play are in the form of an incantation
(1091):

> O Mother, ever revered; O Heaven,
> revolving the light that is common to all:
> you see the wrong of my suffering!

With these words the play comes to an end, on a composite note of suffering, loneliness, a sense of outrage, and a feeling which under more
ordinary circumstances might be termed "arrogance." The critics
have preferred to call it "hubris," but the term raises too many questions to be useful here. These words of Prometheus echo his very

first utterance in the play (88–92), but with an important change in the grammatical structure. In the first episode Prometheus had called on the natural elements around him to look on his sufferings:

> O sacred heaven, and winged puffs of wind,
> streams and their sources . . .:
> see how I suffer, a god struck by gods!

Now, at the end of the action, he discards the imperative for the indicative mood. He takes it for granted that his sufferings are being witnessed; the stress is not on his desire for communication but on his concern with himself and his tortures. But though there is this change, though Prometheus is now apparently satisfied that he is not alone but surrounded by compassionate beings, the similarity in the wording of the two passages effectively neutralizes the advance. In spite of the repeated attestations of solidarity on the part of the Oceanids, both for their own persons and for the powers of nature which they represent, we feel that the hero remains isolated. Prometheus the fire-bringer, the founder of social organization, the champion of philanthropic intercourse, does not, in his own dramatic person, know the pleasures of friendship or sociability. His mode of existence is loneliness.

The stage setting of the *Prometheus* is the concrete realization of an image which is found several times in the *Iliad,* but which is perhaps most conveniently quoted from Sophocles' *Antigone* (586):

> Like a swelling of the sea when
> submarine darkness bestrides it with foul Thracian winds;
> it rolls black sands from the depth, and the cliffs
> struck by ill winds roar in response.

In Sophocles' play the promontory braving the winds and resounding to the breakers symbolizes the house of Laius buffeted by fate and *Ate.* In Homer the image usually underscores the unique heroic strength and stubbornness of the fighter hemmed in by his inconstant attackers. It may be assumed that this personal application in Homer was familiar enough to Sophocles' audience that it would refer the simile to Antigone as well as to her family. In the staging of the

Prometheus Bound the metaphor has become autonomous and entered the world of action. Or rather, reality and trope are set side by side in a novel arrangement. There is the cliff, the image of solitary strength and pride, lapped by the waves of Ocean and resounding to the hammer blows of an impersonal and unheroic hostility. But then there is also Prometheus, surrounded by the Oceanids and responding to the voices of his tempters with a roar of his own. The breakers are not all hostile; the daughters of Ocean certainly are not. But Prometheus treats them as if they were; his special nature does not acknowledge friends. Both visually and spiritually he merges with the rock. Visually he towers high above the rest of the characters, particularly above the chorus. They cannot reach him, nor can he reach them or reach out to them. Spiritually he is the rock. Brother of Atlas, he raises up the sky and is punished for his benevolence. In the older tradition both Atlas and Prometheus were associated with pillars rather than mountains; archaic vase paintings show Prometheus chained against a pillar. But pillars are ciphers of a settled world, of urban sociability. Aeschylus prefers to place him against a rock; the epic connotations of the embattled crag are exploited for a new conception of the fire-god, a conception in which loneliness, merited and self-imposed, is the dominant note.

This loneliness is not the ordinary sort, conditioned by time or circumstance. Shelley's Prometheus is a Platonizing Stoic, sufficient unto himself, hence not lonely. The hero of Aeschylus' play is the ideal man of the fifth-century enlightenment, of Socrates and Critias and the rest of the rationalists. Like Socrates he is unaware of the incompleteness of his nature; unlike Socrates he suffers the pangs of isolation. In the end the isolation forces him to surrender his brittle intellectuality. At first the loneliness of Prometheus presents itself as self-confidence; it springs from the intolerance of the thinker who works for the good of his brothers but does not love them. The thinker works alone and shuns assistance. But loneliness does not stand still; it feeds upon itself until it becomes that "modern" thing, the malaise of the intellectual cut off from the emotional springs of his being. The more keenly the malaise is felt, the more stubbornly the hero fortifies himself in his solitary stand, rejecting mediation and rebuffing old friends. And yet the anger into which he argues himself, the passion with which he defends his privilege, are hints of an essential compromise, of a range of experience first excluded and combated but now readmitted. For Prometheus is, after all, more than a rock. The edge of his resistance is not universally sharp; there is some crumbling in the hard granite of his purpose.

In the end Prometheus addresses himself to his mother, Themis. Social ties and family relations are important in Sophoclean drama where the hero stands and falls with his house, where the whole life of the character, including his acts and obligations as father or brother or son, is implicated in his tragedy. In Aeschylean drama, too, the hero is usually seen against the background of the house, and often the fate of the house carries the fate of the hero along with it. But intimate relationships between the various members of a family are not fully dramatized. This is particularly true, of course, if the hero is a god. That Prometheus should call upon his mother is not demanded by anything in the plot or by the character requirements of the allegory. Nor does the tradition offer a precedent, unless we are to regard the relationship between Achilles and Thetis in the *Iliad* as a source of the filial appeal. Furthermore, the identification of Prometheus' mother, Themis, with Gaia, the earth goddess (209), introduces an element of uncertainty into the scheme of the allegory. For do we not think of earth as one of the elements which alternately admit and repel the progress of man? The most that can be said, once more, is that Prometheus' call to his mother is not part of the treatise but a commentary on the special quality of the hero's sense of isolation. The family tie is etched in because it is felt to be one of the essentials in a cultured man to have such associations of kinship, friendship, and family. The conditions of Prometheus' achievement have brought him close to losing even the most fundamental of these ties. His appeal to his mother suggests that he has travelled a long distance from the sheltered life where she would be with him spontaneously. There is also an intimation that he has begun to feel his loneliness as a burden which, in spite of his pride, he would like to reduce.

His passion, his cry to his mother, are important clues revealing a Prometheus who is, notwithstanding his primary function, susceptible of warmth and understandable as a man. But, granted these humanizing touches, for the rest Aeschylus endeavors to formulate the loneliness of the hero as an overwhelming and all-informing condition of his role. At one point Prometheus says (197):

> It pains me greatly to have to say all this,
> but silence too is painful . . .

This is the dilemma of the lonely man who knows he will not be understood but must talk about his deed and his reward to make them live on and to assure himself of their worth. Technically there is no necessity for Prometheus' being his own messenger; psychologically there is. True, the type of the strong silent man, though not unknown in the epic, is foreign to the Greek stage where even Ajax, traditionally no mincer of words, practices the sustained rhetoric of the genre. But the oratory of Prometheus is more than a consequence of the dramatic form. Dramaturgic convention and psychological portraiture combine to produce a rhetoric which is not simply sustained but ostentatious and demonstrative. Deprived as the hero is of other forms of expression, he is all speech, all lecture and remonstrance. But speech is painful to him. His sentences and his descriptions are forced from an unwilling heart; the philanthropist despises men too much to consider them equal participants in discourse. His heroism, his superiority, carries with it the necessary adjunct of contempt. He is torn between silence and speech, with the result that the words which he utters seem to be addressed to himself rather than to anyone about him. Monologue and harangue rather than conversation: the pattern is pervasive in the career of Western high drama. More important, each utterance, conceived in a spirit of recoil and with the prospect of an unattainable silence before it, betrays its status as a surrogate by a special hint or inflection. Irony, bitterness, resignation, bombast; these are some of the moods supporting Prometheus' speech, and suggesting a fundamental disenchantment with speech as a natural social commodity.

The hero refuses to be an Aristotelian man, with the citizen's commitment to reasoned speech and to intercourse with other reasoned speakers. Nor is this the only item which he would wish to withhold from his fellows. He is jealous even of his sufferings. Whatever the meaning of his role, the hero divines that suffering is a necessary part of it, and that it is a suffering which transcends the treatise and enters into the core of his dramatic personality. Hence he must not share it with anyone else, and so Prometheus repulses Ocean when that worthy dignitary offers to suffer with him (345). He raises a wall between himself and others, always surprised at any initiative they show, always convinced that they live in comfort and sloth and flinch from exposing themselves. Here are his words to Ocean (299):

> How did you have the courage to leave
> the stream named after you and the rock-roofed
> self-established caverns, to come to the land
> where iron is born?

Unless the hero believes that the lives of other men are sheltered, automatic and soft, he cannot persist in the self-imposed isolation which gives him his strength to endure the "land where iron is born." He must despise in order to act and suffer. It is this heroic mode, not any calculable merit or status, which authorizes him to show himself impatient and brusque to his associates, at least toward the men. Toward the ladies he is more polite, to the extent of addressing them by name when they enter. They deserve consideration because nothing is expected of them. The chivalry of the tragic hero, like the brutal familiarity of the comic, takes for granted that in his scheme of things women are insignificant. Men are potential rivals, heroes-in-the-making, and need to be insulted and rebuked so that the uniqueness of the hero remains untarnished. It is not an argument against this rule that in many classical tragedies the women turn out not to fit the part which the men have naïvely assigned to them.

Thus the heroic tradition, inspired and embodied by Prometheus, makes for a self-conscious and recalcitrant principal, hard-pressed by what he conceives to be his unworthy friends as well as by his proper enemies. The artificiality of the self-dramatizing emerges most succinctly through an element in the writing which is particularly pronounced in the *Prometheus,* but which is not entirely lacking in any example of high tragedy. This is the self-righteous apostrophe, the charged epigram, not fully convincing in its succinctness but arresting and strangely satisfying, hurled in the face of disinterested or uninterested bystanders. Emil Staiger has demonstrated the similarity between the purposive drift of drama and the tension roused by the expectation of the final line of an epigram. The history of tragedy is full of such epigrams—"who loved not wisely but too well"—epigrams which are pregnant in sense, excessive in tone, and only rarely adequate to the meaning and the force of the play in which they occur. In them the peculiar blindness of the hero is interposed between drama and audience. His self-revelation is at best a partial thing, and usually misleading, for it focuses our eyes on the tortured pride of the man, on the dramatic dimensions of his soul, while distracting our attention from the total meaning of the play or even from the meaning of his role within the play. But that is as it should be, for if an epigram really had the power to tell us what the play was about or to inform us about the function of the hero in the plot, the play would fail to challenge our intelligence and our feelings.

The more revelatory such an epigram seems to be, the more we have to be on our guard. Usually we can learn from it what particular adjustment the hero has made to the tragic situation at the moment when he utters the phrase, but little else. Prometheus picks up the reproach of the chorus and replies in the terms of the criticism (266):

Transgression? Yes! But willed and unrecanted!

His mood of defiance prompts him to adopt the perspective of the enemy camp and to stamp his act a transgression. To have it so stamped supports him in his truculence. He would rather be wrong than not be an agent at all. Perhaps, in his dogged desire for independence, he would rather be wrong than right. His noble wish for notoriety has nothing whatever to do with the meaning of the action but is a special illustration of the heroic mood as such. The hero of high tragedy, in his loneliness and his thinly veiled contempt for others, becomes a law unto himself. The moral order loses its stringency when applied to him, and in his pronouncements he may toy with moral perspectives in a manner which appears to thwart the moral direction of the plot. The struggle of civilized man against brute nature is perhaps ambivalent, but it is no sin, especially within the framework of fifth-century thought. Yet within the play the hero may find it convenient, for the greater glory of his position, to don the garb of the sinner, in the knowledge that men are inclined to bestow greater admiration on a weighty transgression than on ordinary good conduct.

The moral orientation of the plot is not the only thing to be disturbed by the hero's self-dramatizing. Before the entry of Hermes, Prometheus predicts the dethronement of Zeus (939):

> What if he acts and rules for this brief time
> as he wishes? Soon his reign in heaven will stop.

Earlier (907) there is a more extended prediction of Zeus' downfall. Some of the lines of the prophecy are difficult to fit into the scheme of the plot. But it is important that they are all big and full-throated and exultant. Prometheus is preparing himself for the scene with Hermes in which he will need all his assurance to keep the lackey at bay. To gather the needed strength he pictures to himself the fall of Zeus, the humiliation and dishonor of the enemy with whom elsewhere in the play he appears willing to strike some sort of compromise (190):

> He will dissipate his rugged wrath
> and hasten to me in friendly union
> as I shall hasten to him.

The question of whether Zeus will fall or not is irrelevant and even a little ridiculous when one contemplates the meaning of the play. That this question could have been asked merely proves to what degree the utterances of Prometheus may, upon surface inspection, appear to conflict with the symbolism of the drama and to undermine the moral impact of the play. Only by imagining the fall of Zeus can Prometheus muster sufficient strength for his interview with the emissary of the god. We should not conclude either that the fall is imminent or even that it is effective as a hope. The epigram, which in this case happens to extend itself to the length of an oration, defines for us the momentary mood of the hero, and that is all. In any case we would be mistaken to read into it a reference to a projected salvation of the hero. Our play is complete within itself. If it was part of a trilogy, and another play followed, we have at present no means of discovering how the tragic complication was resolved. There are indications that the resolution may have been in terms of mythology; the figures of Hercules and Chiron are mentioned in the tradition as helping in the liberation of Prometheus. If so, the resolution may have been more apparent than real; given the deceitful stratagems of living drama there was no need for Aeschylus to go back on the message of the present play, which is that the struggle between Prometheus and Zeus is irreconcilable and eternal. Obviously Zeus cannot change, for though, in the interest of tragedy, he has some human characteristics, he is largely a symbol, and the reality which he symbolizes is immutable.

So much for the epigrammatic formulation of Prometheus' stand against Zeus. Similarly the mixture of ostentatiousness and agony in the final speech addressed to the elements is typical of high tragedy. The speech is proud because of, not in spite of, his defeat. He ends as he had begun, drawing attention to the treatment he, a god, has received from the gods. Prometheus would be lost if he did not have his audience, and if he does not have one naturally, he manufactures one, by hypostasizing the natural elements. There is nothing subtle or spiritual about his extrovert exclamatoriness. His suffering is important to him inasmuch as he can thrust his tortures before the eyes of others. Near the beginning of the action Prometheus cries (152):

> Why did he not cast me under the earth,
> into Tartarus, limitless house of Death,
> receiver of corpses . . .
> that neither god nor anyone else
> gloat over this sight?

Aeschylus is playing with us. He has Prometheus delude the audience

and perhaps himself also with a seemly show of modesty and fastidi-
ousness. But nothing could be further from the hero's wishes than
solitary confinement. Only by being seen can he be tragic. His repeated
request "Look at me" is answered by the chorus: "We see you, Prometheus." Sight is important throughout the play; it is the spectator's
wonder built into the drama, converting personal relations into a network of beholdings. This adds to the directness of what might easily
have been a rather abstract composition. The treatment of the story is
of the kind which has a special appeal to the senses. By fixing our eyes
on the towering figure of the hero we lull ourselves into forgetting that
the motives of his action may be less apparent. The hero insists on
being looked at rather than read about or talked with. Only by making
his role, his life and his sufferings, an object of sight for those whose
lives are less grandiose, can he be sure that he will gain the unreserved
and uncritical attention which the art of tragedy demands. No character in a novel, except in one which deliberately emphasizes the visual
in imitation of drama, exercises the massive and unrefracted impact
which distinguishes the tragic hero.

This peremptory claim on the senses verges on exhibitionism. The
simple bravado that we find in *Othello* or *Prometheus* is not the same
as the bravado mixed with contemplativeness which Shelley's Prometheus, for one, entertains. If such a generalization be permitted, a
Greek hero exhibits a minimum of doubt and self-analysis and a max-
imum of vitality, manifested through the vehicle of uninhibited rhetoric. Othello conforms to the Greek standard, Hamlet does not. But
the pagan simplicity carries its own safeguard, which prevents the
bravado from degenerating into bluster. By way of contrast, and to
indicate the dangers of a superficial classicism, one last reference to
Goethe will be in order. In a poem written in 1774 and entitled
"Prometheus," he sees the hero as an arrogant youthful protester
against Jehovah, hurling forth rhetorical questions and punctuating
his message with exclamation marks: We do not need a god! Any
gods that may exist are to be pitied! The speech is bouncy rather than
confident, filled with a sort of frantic hilarity. The mood is that of the
young Goethe; in his later years the poet would no longer acknowledge

the iconoclasm and the spirit of self-indulgence which light up these lines. There is nothing self-indulgent or destructive about the mood of Aeschylus' Prometheus. He does not rejoice in his pains; he merely advertises them. In spite of the anger and the truculence there is no reveling in torture, but an almost disinterested yea-saying, and a manly desire to hear himself echoed.

It is this special combination of Titanic incompleteness, of stubborn longing, of pride proud of its fall without malice or pettiness, which ensured the success of the *Prometheus Bound* in its own day and which delimited the course of high tragedy for centuries to come, particularly in Roman drama and the Renaissance drama directly indebted to it. These are for the most part nonallegorical elements, which have little enough to do with the meaning or message of the play. We expect the tragic hero to exhibit a sense of outrage; we can open our hearts to his protestations if the writer has done his job well. But if we ask ourselves precisely what prompts his expostulations, what it is that has hurt the hero, and whether he is fully justified in his complaints, there are no easy answers, perhaps because the questions are not meant to be asked in exactly that form. We begin to understand why Aristotle, who counted the *Prometheus Bound* among the plays worth citing, chose to discuss how the hero is likely to behave, and what sort of person he is likely to be, rather than telling us what a tragedy is about and what kind of issues are dealt with in it. We begin to understand why he is content to analyze the formal elements, the devices and manners and conventions of tragedy, rather than its nature. In a tragedy the characters and their behavior are bound to be bigger than the plot; and the conventions and machinery are likely to clash with a proposed significance. We must expect some incongruity between action and behavior, between meaning and manner. Without this disharmony we should have an open book, a treatise, not a tragedy. Precisely what this particular mixture of sense and nonsense, to use the positivist jargon, must be, is the real and probably insoluble task of criticism to discover. All that has been possible here is to point out that in the *Prometheus* sense and nonsense collide in an especially intriguing fashion. Tragedy does not communicate knowledge, as

Plato recognized; it stultifies knowledge and makes our knees tremble. At the end of the play, the audience along with Prometheus and the Oceanids are hurled into the abyss of darkness and despair. But it is a more substantial darkness, a richer despair, than we had known before; the special mixture of the play, whatever it is, is vindicated, by its effects.

Bacchae and *Ion:*
TRAGEDY AND RELIGION

Appear, in the shape of a bull or a many-headed
serpent, or lion breathing fire!
Come, Bacchus, and with laughing face
coil the deadly rope around the huntsman
of the Bacchae, to be trodden under by the
    women's stampede!

THUS THE CHORUS, immediately before the
messenger enters to describe the death of
Pentheus (1017). The invocation is signifi-
cant on many counts; for the moment we are concerned with the god's
laugh. "With laughing face" or "with laughing mask," the Greek
may mean either. The expectation is geared pictorially rather than au-

ditorily; the epiphany will be centered in the cast of the holy counte-
nance. But how are we to imagine it—that is to say, how did the Athenian craftsman shape the mask of Dionysus? Did he mold it into an
archaic smile, gentle, refined, charmingly supercilious, the smile of
the handsome marble youths who died in the Persian Wars? Or are
we to visualize a Gorgon grin, a grimace of malformed jaw and lolling
tongue? Is Dionysus' laugh bestial or Olympian, subhuman or superhuman? The latter, no doubt, at least so far as the maskmaker is concerned. The stranger is a handsome man, a pretty fellow, as Pentheus
readily admits (453), and an archaic smile would be just the thing to
create the visual effect of effeminacy. But if we can forget the maskmaker and the stage and the awkward requirements of a physical production, and listen to the poetry itself, the laugh turns out to be both
a smile and a grimace, a token of blessing and the sealing of a curse.
For such is the will of Dionysus.

In any case, the laughter is expressive of the gulf between god and
man. It is remarkable how few references there are in Greek literature, particularly in the epic and in tragedy, to men smiling or softly
laughing. We find much about derision and ridicule and triumphant
scoffing, the exultant shout which comes from the fear of defeat temporarily diverted. Ancient man, in most of the tragedies, is too busy
seeking the means of safety or of greatness to achieve by his own
strength the equilibrium and the wisdom without which happiness
and gentle laughter do not occur. The sea laughs; a meadow smiles;
so will the god, on occasion. But man cannot unbend and relax, for
he lacks the unselfconsciousness, the simple assurance of the natural
being. Except in the escapist genre of the romance—and that includes
the *Odyssey*—men are characterized by toil (620):

> Breathing hard he was, and sweat was trickling down his frame,
> his teeth were clamped on his lips, while I, close by,
> sat quietly and looked on.

This is how Dionysus describes the difference between the man of
action and himself, the breach separating human struggling from divine unconcern.

Divine laughter has nothing to do with sympathy or fellow feeling. The god does not love his children, though the Stoics in a later generation talked as if he did. In classical Greek thought the love of God is a matter of social distinction; God loves only those who are manifestly successful in the temporal affairs of this world. Divine love is not an axiom of theology but an explanatory concept ready to be cited whereever prosperity appears to be undeserved. Nor is the laughter of the god a chuckle of amusement. In the *Odyssey*, it is true, Odysseus manages to amuse Athena, but that is a sign of his uniqueness. Generally the gods of the epic amuse one another but they are not amused by the antics of men, and that is doubly true of the gods of tragedy. We may contrast the post-Romantic conception of Zorba, in Kazantsakis' recent *Zorba the Greek,* that Zeus smiles pityingly at the touching weakness of women, and that in fact he turns philanderer out of a mixture of sympathy and amusement. God is also a man, capable of suffering and sensing the sufferings of others. But this is not what we find on the Attic stage. Dionysus always stands apart from men; when he smiles—and he smiles throughout the play—it is the smile of the Sphinx, the icy mask of unconcern and abstraction.

Zorba tries to bridge the gulf between the divine tradition and social exigency. To find a fulcrum for his world of sentiment and temptation he remakes Zeus into a figure mixed in equal portions of Jesus and Don Juan. The Greeks of the classical period also were faced with the same difficulty, how to make sense of their accounts of the gods in the light of new social experiences, of the laws of the city, of marital ethics, of the values of a progressive civilization. But unlike Zorba, the Athenian of the fifth century B.C. is too enlightened to allow his god the benefit of human affections, particularly of human sympathy. Or, to put it differently, classical Greek tragedy does not permit sympathy or fellow feeling to provide solutions for the tragic dilemma. The gods do not willingly lower themselves to help men. But, if we are to believe the old stories told about them, the gods often behave as if they were the worst of men.

Apollo's fatherhood of Ion is a direct intrusion of the divine into human life. As for the *Bacchae,* the myth has it that Pentheus and

Dionysus are grandsons of Cadmus. The presence of Cadmus on the stage continually reminds us that the man and the god are blood cousins. This is not exceptional; both Greek myth and Greek religion range god and man in the closest proximity. Of Heracles and Niobe we are given to understand that they were both human and divine. Of Helen we know that she was a goddess before she came to be featured as a mortal heroine. Amphiaraus and Brasidas and Alexander were worshipped as gods though they had once, as everybody would admit, been men. Man is potentially a god; and yet the gods are infinitely apart. This is a paradox with which every Greek thinker worth his salt came to grips sooner or later. Plato and Aristotle wrestle with it in their discussions of the soul; the soul, they find, is both divine and human, both immortal and subject to change. Here we have the basic crux of the pagan creed, perhaps of all religion, but most pressing in a society that worships heroes and recognizes deification.

All Greek drama to some extent touches on this ambivalence. But usually the religious predicament is marginal, an element used for the dramatization of other, nonreligious issues. Only occasionally, as in the two plays under consideration, the question about the gods comes to inform the very heart of the drama. In one thing, however, all plays are agreed: the god must not be made to mingle with the mortals on the stage. The stage is reserved for sufferers and potential sufferers, and this disqualifies the gods, for, in spite of some thumping frolic in the *Iliad* and the extravaganzas of Orphic myth, the gods cannot suffer pain or grief, much less death. Hence when a deity appears in a tragedy he is set apart from the other actors and the chorus, often towering above them on a raised platform. If the god were to be one of the crowd, the effect would be comical, as is convincingly shown in Greek comedy. Generally, also, tragedy features him only in the Prologue and the Epilogue, outside of the dramatic action proper. Thus by virtue of the conventions of tragedy the god is kept free of the pollution of human involvement. The only extant play in which Euripides departs from the tradition and puts the god on the floor of the orchestra is the *Bacchae*. But even there he makes a distinction between the god who speaks the Prologue and the Epilogue—the true and undisguised divinity who has his epiphany on the roof of the palace—and the unearthly stranger who mixes and yet does not mix with the other characters. In spite of the disguise the audience knows that the stranger is Dionysus. Actually, can we speak of a disguise? It is unlikely that the Dionysus of the Prologue wears a costume and mask different from those of the Dionysus in the play. The pretty face and the delicate bearing were becoming recognized as important facets of the Bacchic personality; in art, too, the majesty of the black-figure Dionysus was being replaced by the languorous elegance of the fourth-century portraits of the god. If there is a disguise, then, it is one of conduct rather than clothes. The god in the play *seems* to be human. This is a daring attempt to picture the intrusion of the divine into the human scene in the form of living drama. Whether it is unique we cannot say; there were other plays about Dionysus, notably by Aeschylus, in which a similar technique may have been used. But those other plays are lost; for us the *Bacchae* remains an unparalleled experiment, an example of what can be done with the traditional material and the traditional forms by way of almost destroying tragedy as it is usually understood. For in writing this play Euripides seems to come close to creating the medieval mystery play. There is a critical widening of the tragic frame; human heroism and human suffering appear to be pushed into the background, and the miracle of divine being occupies the center of the stage. It is perhaps significant that the *Bacchae* was written at the end of the fifth century B.C., when classical tragedy had run its course. But this is not to say that the play is anomalous. As we have seen, Greek tragedy is a vehicle for many different ideas and many different intentions. The religious focus of the *Bacchae* is merely another realization of the rich potential of classical drama.

The stranger has no name. Even if he had one it would not be understood. "Does anyone understand the name of something when he does not know what the something is?" (Plato, *Theaetetus*, 147B). He is a walking mystery, an unintelligible mask. He refers to himself as a *follower* of Dionysus. But in the salient passages Euripides exercises a great virtuosity to avoid a clear-cut statement of duality. Those who know, the audience attuned to the ambiguities of the genre, will understand that when the stranger talks about Dionysus he is really talking about himself. Pentheus asks him (469) whether the god "forced" him—that is his term for "possessed" or "converted"; the verb he uses also means "to rape"—whether the god forced him at night or with his eyes open. The answer of the stranger, freely translated "face to face," is in fact untranslatable. Suffice it to say that he uses two participles of the verb "to see," one in the nominative and one in the accusative case, but without the assistance of a personal pronoun to apportion the activities distinctly and objectively. This is verbal conjuring. There are more tricks of the same sort (477):

> PENTHEUS: You say you saw the god; what is his shape?
> DIONYSUS: Whichever he chooses; it is not my decision.

Or again (495):

> PENTHEUS: Come, then, release the thyrsus; hand it to me!
> DIONYSUS: You'll have to force me; the staff belongs to Bacchus.

Compare also: "My locks are those of Dionysus" (494); "The god will free me whenever I wish" (498); "In injuring *me* you are imprisoning *him*" (518). The effect of all this is that in the minds of those who are alert to the divine charade, the stranger and Dionysus merge into one, as indeed they are one. In the unseeing eyes of Pentheus, the stranger produces the worst kind of mystification. But without some mystification a god cannot show himself on earth. Like an oracle, an embodied god must hedge his divinity with darkness and punning and formal proliferation. At any event, in spite of the tricks, the stranger does not become sufficiently part of the human scene to appear just cunning or deceitful. With his fixed smile he preserves his separateness and a kind of sublimity which even Pentheus can sense.

In the *Ion* Apollo does not show his face at all, neither within the drama nor in the Prologue or Epilogue. And no wonder, for a sovereign god in a tragedy ought to be shown as an august species of machine, colossal, imperious, automatic. But this will not do for Apollo the cosmic rake, the morganatic spouse of Creusa. So Euripides keeps him off the stage and has him represented by counsel, Hermes, a poor cousin, and Athena, a cheerful suffragette. Both of them are at best halfhearted advocates. Behind the expressions of solidarity and the diplomatic explanations one perceives a note of detachment, as if Hermes and Athena were not in their hearts convinced that Apollo has a case. Of course he doesn't; that is the burden of the play. And not having a case he forfeits bail and stays away from the courthouse on the day of the trial. In the *Bacchae* much of the power of the play derives from the presence of the god; in the *Ion* the important thing is the absence of the god. Here, then, are two plays, both working with a religious subject, with the intrusion into the lives of men of the world of the gods, both dealing with the gods' cruelty to man. And yet, how different in conception, in mood and form!

But *are* these religious plays, and if so, in what sense? We are inclined to think that the ancient repertory must include some religious drama, for we suspect that religious tragedy is possible only in a pagan world. Jewish monotheism has no room for it. True tragedy presupposes the unresolved coexistence of two opposed poles, of man and god, or of god and god, or god and devil. No such coexistence is possible in the terms of serious Jewish thought. In the realm of Christianity, too, tragedy can live only where pagan lingerings are strong, where being can be pitted against being and where the outcome is not foreordained by the omnipotence of the good. One may go further and say that tragedy cannot flourish except where paganism asserts itself over Christianity. Some of Shakespeare's tragedies are obvious cases in point. Goethe's *Faust* ceases to be a tragedy, if it ever is one, the moment the Queen of Heaven begins to exercise her grace. But if it is true that tragedy is uniquely a function of pagan thought, of the belief in many gods and in the godliness of some men, then it is only fair to expect that there is some ancient tragedy which is so closely tied to the religious experience as to merit the designation "religious drama." Both the *Ion* and the *Bacchae* are about the gods and their dealings with men. But are they religious tragedies in the proper sense of the word, that is, tragedies arising out of, and only out of, the problematic nature of religious faith or religious action, and grappling with the problems in a manner somehow parallel to that of the theologians or the philosophers?

The answer is that they are not, or at any rate that to call them religious tragedies pure and simple would do violence to the special intentions of each. In the *Ion* the divinity of Apollo is the *demonstrand* or *refutand* of a debate. With the telling of the myths Apollo's divine nature has become questionable, and with it the whole tradition of religious tales. A god is weighed in the scale of human standards and found seemingly wanting, a god with a *hamartia*, a flaw which causes a disturbance in the lives of men. Euripides has managed to write an inverted *Oedipus*, with the flaw located in Olympus rather than in a now unheroic humanity. Apollo is the real object of the play's search, he is not a symbol. But we should not forget that the Apollo whose sordid biography we are invited to contemplate is an Apollo of myths, a god of nursery tales and family trees, not the god whom Socrates saw fit to follow and whom Plato adopted as the inspirer of moral philosophy.

In the *Bacchae* Dionysus, in spite of his presence on stage, or perhaps because of it, is largely a symbol; the entity weighed in the scale is not a god, but men, as in all great tragedy. The precariousness of human greatness is here shown from a special angle: the god-likeness of man. For Pentheus, as a fighter against the god, places himself on the same level as his adversary. It turns out that this god-likeness is a trap and a deception, and that man is not so close to God as he may suppose. But this shows us that the concern of the poet is with man. As we shall see directly, even the religious experience described, the ecstasy and the hallucinations and the holy rolling, are not there as ends in themselves but mean to tell us something about the nature of man, man as a whole being rather than man as a worshipper. Thus, strange as it may seem, the *Bacchae* is less of a religious drama than the *Ion* is, and even the *Ion* is a very unusual specimen of the class.

ii

In the *Bacchae* the action of the god is direct and immediate; he touches the people and they respond. In the *Ion* it is not the god himself who affects the characters but what is told about him. As in the history of Herodotus we have here a distinction between what the Greeks call *ta onta* and *ta legomena,* between things which are and things which exist in reports, between reality experienced at first hand and reality mediated by word of mouth and pondered and analyzed. Both can be shattering in their effect. Some critics have said that the *Ion* deals with a rape, but that the plot is not sordid or squalid because the rape is committed by a god. One wonders what Xenophanes or Plato or Voltaire might have said to this. The truth is that the reality which sets the plot going is not a rape but the memory of a rape. The characters are affected, more or less directly, by a memory; their revulsion—and such it surely is—is not aesthetic, but intellectual and moral. It is of course true of all Greek tragedy, in contradistinction to that of Seneca, that it bypasses the bodily senses and makes its appeal to the imagination. Like death, a rape must not be communicated directly. To preserve the intended effect it must be stripped of its accidents and be entrusted to a messenger, who will unfold its essential magnitude. In the messenger's telling, or in the evocation of the memory, the rape attains an ideal status, and acquires the special purity which comes with isolation. At the same time this ideal concentration is brought about at the cost of material force. The rape does not shock, it merely worries and perplexes, and in the end generates questions as the viewing of the gross event could not have done.

Likewise the disappointment within the play is not so much for what Apollo has done or not done, but largely for what he has said or not said. He is a cad, but more important, he appears to be a liar. Again it is the intellectual phase of the problem which interests the poet. Apollo's failure to speak the truth is particularly disconcerting because he is supposed to be the exponent of oracular truth. Above all, this must be disturbing to Ion, the unspoiled youth, simple and good and credulous like Daphnis or Candide or any other adolescent hero of romance, with this distinction that he grows up to be a man. Ion thirsts for the truth, and in this he is more Apollinian than Apollo. He expects his god to behave like a god. As a matter of fact his expectation is unwarranted. If you have been raised on the kind of tales which Ion is bound to have heard from earliest youth, it is unrealistic to suppose that the gods do not lie and commit adultery. As it turns out, even this faithful servant of the god does not require much evidence to turn against his idol. The tales had conditioned him, and the present intelligence comes as a final confirmation. True, Euripides makes out that he is an unsuspecting youth and that Creusa's tale shocks him to the marrow of his bones. But Greek tragedy with its large-scale compression does not leave much room for a precise recording of the slow process of attrition which is involved in the overcoming of piety by doubt. Hence Ion begins to doubt as soon as the tale is out, and this makes psychological sense only because the speed with which his conservatism succumbs has its analogue in the hearts of the audience. Ion, like Creusa (1017), likes to think that the good and the bad do not mix. But he is an intelligent boy, and so he is quick to notice it when he finds Apollo offending against the canons of his strait-laced morality (436):

> What is happening to Phoebus?
> I must admonish him. To ravish young girls
> And then betray them? To beget sons in secret
> and callously let them die? No! As our lord,
> you ought to set an example . . .

Outwardly the *Ion* shows the same development as the *Oedipus Rex:* progressive self-recognition accompanied by an increasing insight into divine irresponsibility. But the analogy is trivial. For Oedipus the experience is deadly; it destroys his very being as a king and a man. In the *Ion* the knowledge gained is not ruinous but merely frustrating. Frustration is one of the keynotes of the play; at one time or another all the main characters are made to fret over the obstacles in their way. Even Hermes, ostensibly an uncommitted bystander, is subjected to

frustration, for the play does not come off as he had predicted in the
Prologue (69):

> When Xuthus enters this oracular shrine
> Apollo will hand him his own son, and say
> that Xuthus fathered him, so the boy will go
> to Athens and Creusa accept him, and
> Apollo's wenching will not come to light.

Everything said about the gods tends to associate them with meanness
but even more with ineffectualness. Apollo is a bounder, and with
him the gods in general are reduced to a low level of force and authority. With little respect for human feelings, they try to arrange
things as smoothly as they can, and fumble their operations. The accent is on the fumbling rather than on the intention. Eventually Ion
and Creusa and Xuthus turn out to be luckier than the gods, for their
mistakes are righted and their blindness is cured, while Apollo, in spite
of Athena's busy glossing, could not possibly forget all the botching
he has done. One may feel, though Ion does not, that a god has the
right to offend against human moral standards. But clearly a god
should be able to follow through with his actions and not have his
plans aborted. His rape of Creusa still leaves him a god; but this cannot be said of his various ill-fated attempts to cover up the affair.

Ion's discovery of his parentage is also a process of maturation.
Within the confines of the play the boy grows up to be a man. But
the mature Ion is no more understanding than the boy, only less at
ease with himself and less at ease with others. The simple, slightly
domineering familiarity which characterized his relations with the
chorus (221 ff.) is replaced by suspicion and resentment. In the
Oedipus the acquisition of knowledge touches the hero's relation with
himself; in the *Ion* it affects his relation to society. This is true also
of other plays by Euripides. The poet is interested in the group, in the
interaction between purposes and wills and destinies, rather than in
the fate or the feelings of an isolated individual. Often we are given
to understand that there is no reason why society should not function
happily, that the intentions of men if left to themselves are quite

compatible, and that friction sets in only when the gods decide to interfere and use men for their own amusement. That this is the case in the *Ion* requires no demonstration; the idea that human beings misbehave toward one another only at the instigation of the gods is basic to the dramatic plan.

The idea is powerfully supported by the use of specific elements of language and dramaturgy, such as the business of the Gorgon's blood (987 ff., 1054). When Creusa finds her position threatened by Ion, the availability of the Gorgon's blood suggests to her a way of eliminating him. That this is the heavy hand of the gods steering the human agent is made apparent by the form of the scene. Creusa does not simply say: "Here I have a vial with a deadly poison; let's use it." Nothing so straightforward as this, for it would saddle Creusa with the guilt. Instead she lectures the old man on a chapter of mythology. Pedantically, laboriously, she conducts him through the labyrinthine turns of the ancient story: the gods fought the giants at Phlegra, Earth bore the Gorgon to help the giants, Athena killed the Gorgon and used her dead form for manufacturing the aegis; later when Erichthonius, the founding father of Attica, was born, Athena gave him two drops of the blood of the Gorgon, stored in two golden capsules now attached to Creusa's wrist. One of the drops heals, the other kills, and this Creusa now proposes to use against Ion. Our brief summary does not convey the true feeling of the passage. Extending over thirty lines of text it proceeds with a slow, circumstantial monotony, as if every single step in the chain of causation leading back to the holy wars of the gods had to be fully cited to provide the plot with the proper authority. There is something of the rhythm and the mood of a ritual service about this rehearsal of the divine beginnings. Before she can kill her man, Creusa has to communicate with the gods through a sort of mock litany and assure herself of their participation.

Mythology furnishes many examples of the iniquities of the gods. The *Ion* bursts at the seams with mythological detail, especially as affecting the Athenian royal house. In the light of the stories about the gods' dealings with Creusa's ancestors, Apollo's failure to live up to his responsibilities becomes only the latest in a long series of divine

mischief. The chorus begins by describing scenes from the fights between gods and giants and monsters engraved on the metopes of the
temple (206 ff.). Then Ion asks Creusa to tell him about Athens, and
she obliges with detailed information about earth-born Erichthonius,
Cecrops and his daughters, and Erechtheus. The *Bacchae* has nothing
like this mythological fullness, not even in the speech of Cadmus,
where we might have expected to find it. In the *Ion* the mythological
décor is pervasive, it is a significant aspect of the style of the play.
That style is perhaps best described as baroque. The writing and the
structure are not pared down to bare essentials, as they are in some
other plays by Euripides. In contrast to the unpretentiousness of the
action and the obviousness of the emotions released by the action, the
language is lush and gilded. Take the description of the woven
tapestries in the tent where Ion almost meets his death (1146):

> And traced into the scheme there was a pattern,
> the Sky marshaling stars in his bright vault;
> the Sun driving his chariot near the glow
> of dusk, with glittering Hesperus in his wake.
> Black-mantled Night escorted by her stars
> careened along in a two-horse equipage.
> The Pleiades and Orion with his sword
> coursed through the midway of the sky; high up
> the Bear twisting his golden back around the pole.
> The orb of the Moon, divider of the month,
> pierced high into heaven; and the Hyades,
> the sailors' clearest sign, and, scattering
> the stars, light-wielding Dawn . . .

The description of the design on the tapestry continues. The translation tries to give a sense of the irregularities of syntax; the catalogue
seems to stumble along in a breathless and ill-organized fashion. The
significant thing about it is that all this is part of a messenger speech
which starts out as a call to the girls of the chorus to flee for their
lives. The terrible danger seems to be forgotten temporarily as the
girls absorb the colorful spectacle of the tent. There is no doubting the
lavishness of the decoration; expense is no object as Ion celebrates

his new-found importance. But what do the sun and the moon and the stars have to do with this phase of the action?

Again, take the design on the cloth in the cradle (1421 ff.); Athena's aegis and the Gorgon seem to grin down upon the action throughout. In this case the choice of the décor is meaningfully tied to the plot. But the particular choice is less significant than the emphasis on the pictorial as such. This insistence on externals and, on occasion, irrelevancies is a hallmark of the play. I suggest that the baroque quality and the concentration on the gods are strands of the same cord. For once, the life on Olympus forms the sum and substance of the drama. Homer is at his most colorful when he describes the comings and goings of the gods. When dealing with men a Greek writer must probe into their souls, into those intangibles of choice and action which call for compression and abstraction rather than for richness of color and expansiveness. The gods have no souls, particularly the species of gods with whom Euripides is here concerned. The life of the god is all on the surface; its meaning exhausts itself in splendid appearance and tangible façade. And when the god under consideration is a busybody or a rake, when the life placed under the lens is a night life, the tendency toward color and flourish is given full rein.

But the analogy with the *Iliad* is not complete. Homer shows us that the life of the gods among themselves has no real substance. They cannot die, they cannot suffer for long, and so their actions and interactions unfold themselves in an air of unreality, of weightlessness. It is impossible to take seriously the threats of an Ares or the boasts of a Zeus, for they are not supported by peril or doubt. As is well known, Homer often uses his gods for something very much like comic relief. When the human battle has reached its most critical stage, when mortal suffering has risen to its peak of intensity and pain, Homer changes the scene to the palaces of the gods and gives our sensibilities a chance to relax as we watch the escapades of those who can do all and risk nothing. In their affairs with men, on the other hand, the Homeric gods ask to be taken very seriously. When

Athena counsels Achilles or when Poseidon rallies the Greeks to resist, they become part of the human scene. Their personalities are affected by the weightiness of the situation which prompts their intervention. Not so in the *Ion;* here divine insubstantiality remains untouched even as Apollo descends to earth and performs his human business. A god who is concerned with preserving his reputation in the face of men, who tries to squirm his way out of the consequences of an ill-considered act, is a god who makes us laugh so long as he does not make us angry. The temple background suggests an aura of solemnity, but that is an illusion. The god of the drama is a funny god; and that means that the drama, in addition to being unusually colorful and extravagant in form, is unorthodox in spirit. In fact, it is not a tragedy in the modern sense at all.

The touches of humor are, some of them, broad; others are more subtle. Ion is perfectly satisfied with his lot as Apollo's spiritual son; in his piety he refers to him as "the father who begot me" (136); the sequel indicates that he is using a liturgical metaphor. But as soon as he finds out that the metaphor may not be a metaphor at all, his satisfaction changes into displeasure. Every blue-blooded Greek counted it an honor and a social necessity to be descended from a god, but it never occurred to them to understand this fiction literally. Ion's scruples coincide with the values of Plato's *Symposium,* in which we read that a spiritual progeny is more valuable than a physical child. But put in the mouth of this long-lost prince, such sentiments are bound to amuse rather than convince. The old servant also contributes to the fun. Creusa is not an Antigone, she needs an agent who will do the plotting for her. But the old man is not one of those wise and trusted counselors who direct the steps of heroes and heroines in other plays. He is drawn as a caricature of old age and of doting zeal. He is so ancient, so decrepit, that he can barely move his legs and has to be pulled along the Sacred Way as if it were a perpendicular ascent (738 ff.). And when he proposes to burn down the temple of Apollo (974) he is a comic and therefore pardonable Herostratus. Compare the *Clouds,* in which a somewhat different temple is actually burned, in response to a heartfelt desire on the part of the audience. The old man is a fool, but he is the sort of fool whom the people will suffer gladly, for his recklessness is a comic variety of their own.

One of the prominent features of Greek comedy is the parabasis, an address to the audience in which the members of the chorus disrupt the dramatic illusion by divesting themselves of their role in the play and talking about some topical issue which as a rule is unrelated to the subject of the drama. The *Ion,* too, has its "parabasis." This is the famous defense of women against the slander of unfaithfulness (1090 ff.), part of a choral ode sung immediately after Creusa and the old man have botched their plot. It is generally acknowledged that the thought of this passage has no discoverable connection with the theme and the plot, though Euripides takes some pains to pretend that it has. True, Euripides uses such choral thought pieces also in plays which contain no element of comedy. But here the lack of relevance is more than usually startling. The stanza reads as if Euripides needed to get this criticism of masculine prejudice off his chest and decided that this was as appropriate an occasion for it as any other. Similarly Ion's speech against the discomforts of being a prince in Athens (585 ff.) is a forensic argument which moves off on a tangent from the line of the play. Such ventures are possible only because the movement of the plot is not so compellingly aimed at an immediate target as to spurn embellishment and digression. The baroque brilliance of the drama leaves room for many things whose relevance is questionable but which in their turn contribute to the total effect of glitter and flourish and tumultuous fullness, of a kaleidoscopic world which teases the understanding.

This, then, is a play which is not high tragedy, which does not concern the inner man but god and society, which deals not with suffering but with adjustment. Its characters fight not for issues or causes but for survival and status. And the central character, who does not appear in his own person, is shown up as an irresponsible weakling, causing the human group dependent on him to forsake their decent ways for plotting and trickery and, almost, murder. Let us call the work a theological romance. As in the late Greek romances, decency is on trial, and men are herded through a baptism of pillage and rape and attempted slaughter before the hero and the heroine can once more settle down in domestic comfort. But in the novels the gods are not involved except to prophesy, to protect, or to punish. In the *Ion* the god is cast in the role usually reserved for the villain, the pirate, or the landlord who assails the virtue of the lady and sets off the chain reaction of pains and revenges. In some romances, as in the *Aethiopica* of Heliodorus, villains reform and turn into friends. In the pulp literature of antiquity this kind of conversion can be effected without much ado; characters count for less than the extraordinary events by which they are buffeted about, and the moral dividing-line between heroes and villains is remarkably thin. In fifth-century drama an analogous conversion must leave a residue of uncertainty and embarrassment. Apollo, through his representatives, attempts to see to the happiness of Creusa and Ion and Xuthus, but he comes up against the hard fact that human beings are not as easily manipulated as the romances would seem to suggest, and as the gods would like to believe. Men want their dignity and their rights; they think back and forward and connect the past with the future, and they worry if the accounts show a discrepancy. So the conversion from ravisher to protector runs into heavy opposition, and by the time the issues are settled the honor of the god is smudged beyond repair.

But in spite of the absence of smoothness and clichés, the story is a true romance. There is no tragic hero, and some measure of happiness comes to all. Men have something to which the gods are largely insensitive: kindness and sympathy. *Oiktos,* pity, is one of the key-words of the play (47, 312, 361, 618); even the temporary renunciation of pity, explicit as it is (970, 1276), testifies to the same emotion. In spite of the murder plot, and though Ion very nearly commits sacrilege and matricide, there is more downright humaneness in this play than in most other Euripidean dramas. The characters are civilized, generous people, easily injured, easily pleased, kind to slaves, ready to worship. Their warmth and their charity shame the gods. In the end Athena recognizes the strength of human benevolence. *Ex machina* she recommends a deception, from humane motives: to have

Xuthus go on believing that Ion is his son (1601 f.). The whole play may serve as a lesson that deception is often kinder than the truth. This is also the strength of the myths. Intelligent people know that the stories are lies or based on lies; at the same time they admit that the myths have a civilizing force of their own. The gods whose bungling and whose erratic ways are analyzed in this play are the gods of the myths. Euripides has his fun with them, by mixing the divine with the human, the mythical with the religious, the fictitious with the real. It is hardly likely that a romance such as this would seriously affect the faith of the worshipper. After all, the myths are myths, and worship is worship, and though there may be a tie between them, to relate them to each other as Euripides does is entertaining rather than disillusioning, much less heretical. A play about the deeds of the gods and their effects on men must, in the nature of things, border on the whimsical. It cannot be a tragedy.

iii

But does not the *Bacchae* show that this conclusion is wrong? Is it not about a god, and is it not a true tragedy? Above I made a passing reference to the great contrast between the two plays. The list of differences could be extended indefinitely. *Ion* deals with a dreamy youth foiled in his endeavor to lead a contemplative life: the *Bacchae* pictures a powerful man foiled in the conduct of an active public life. In the *Ion* the contemplative life is frustrated by scruple and doubt; in the *Bacchae* the active life is undone by raw experience. Both plays are full of irony. But that of the *Ion* is almost genial; it produces the pleasantries that we associate with a comedy of errors, signaling the fallibility of men and gods. When the incredulous Creusa replies to Ion's command that she leave the altar (1307):

Go, dictate to your mother wherever she is!

irony reaches and perhaps overreaches the limits of good taste, but it remains within the bounds of reason. In the *Bacchae* the irony is diabolical; it reflects not questions of personal identity but the identity of meaning and the problem of identity itself. The stage of the *Ion*—I am

speaking figuratively, for the real stages are of course indistinguish-
able—is filled with the clear bright light in which the metopes are
admired by the tourists from Athens (184 ff.). In this merciless light
the truth will out. It is the type of truth with which scholars and de-
tectives deal; as Ion says at one point (1547),

> I'll go indoors to scrutinize Apollo,

using the verb which a historian applies to his research. We are confident that the truth can be discovered, and we expect its formulation to
be simple and straightforward; for the vision of Apollo is plastic
and limited.

The illumination of the stage of the *Bacchae* is that of the womb; it
is the darkness of birth and passion and death. Within this darkness
the fire of Semele, the flame on the house, flare up with a foreboding
sheen. Only the remoter vistas opening up with the messenger speeches
are filled with the brightness of day: a contrast which marks the inner
contradictions of the Dionysiac. In the *Ion* we hear the boy-grown-man
say (1517):

> The incandescent ambience of the Sun
> opens our eyes to all that this day holds.

It is the same Sun whom Ion greets when he first enters the stage
(82 ff.), and whom Creusa invokes at the moment of her greatest
happiness (1445, 1467). But the Sun had shone also on the scene
of her first suffering (887):

> You came to me, Apollo, your hair
> shining with gold, as I was gathering
> into the fold of my dress yellow flowers,
> gleaming with a gold of their own bloom.

The golden radiance of the Sun is pervasive; only the catastrophe is
set in the chiaroscuro of the tent, with its artificial mirroring of Sun
and Moon and Stars on dark canvas. In the *Bacchae,* Pentheus asks the
stranger (485):

> When do you worship, at night or during the day?

The answer:

Mostly by night; there is prestige in darkness.

Finally, the plays are far apart in structure and movement. The *Ion* is a lively play, spirited and intricate, full of heated discussions, songs and arias, spoken exchanges of unparalleled length, extended messenger speeches. Now and then an oration is interrupted by song or chant, with chorus and actors performing responsively. Every formal means of creating a complex and varied structure has been utilized for the sake of the romance. There are surprises, reversals, true and false recognitions, plottings and resolutions: all the baroque elements which Aristotle desired in a tragedy and which to spite him are so much more frequent in plays which are not tragedies. Here is one example among many. Xuthus bids the chorus not to reveal what has happened (666); a little later the chorus does just that (760). Fewer than a hundred lines pass between the request and the exposé. Meanwhile the audience wonders whether the chorus will tell all, and when. This sort of suspense and this sort of technical brilliance are completely absent from the *Bacchae*. There the statement is terse, the pace regular, without the rallentandos and the accelerandos of the *Ion,* without elaborations or tricks, almost relaxed, if relaxation and compulsiveness can be said to go together. The fixed smile of the god suggests they do.

In the *Ion* the early scenes of temple worship, of rites performed happily and unaffectedly, are presented with great charm. As Ion addresses the broom on a note of homely camaraderie (112), the old-fashioned identification of simplicity and excellence, of beauty and virtue, seems securely established. We assume that the god is cherished and respectable and pure—for the Prologue, though disturbing, cannot by itself inaugurate a mood or a perspective—and repeated references to pure speech and pure thought (98 ff., 134 ff.) lull our senses into a false confidence. It is only with a violent effort, with a forcible reorganization of our feelings that we can face the scramble which follows. The *Bacchae* offers no similar misguiding; the disaster hangs over Pentheus from the moment he enters the stage. There is no rising curve, no choral acceleration, no emotional ups and downs, only an insistent heading toward the inevitable, formulated with economy and restraint. Here, in the case of a true tragedy, Euripides chooses to dispense with the frills, with dynamic and emotive refinement, and come straight to the point. It is like a return to the hieratic stiffness of the *Seven Against Thebes*. But Euripides goes even further than Aeschylus in removing the action from the undisciplined ferment of daily life. Both in the Prologue and in the entrances information is given out mechanically and abruptly. Whenever a character enters— Tiresias, Cadmus, Pentheus—he explains his status and his motivation, as circumstantially and undramatically as any clown in a Roman comedy. This makes for a full spectral illumination from the start; there is time enough later for dramatic confrontation. But it is not the random rhythm of the life of the streets, or of a work of art created in the image of that life.

iv

The *Bacchae*, like the *Ion*, is a tale about a god, but that is all they have in common. The *Ion* I called, perhaps for want of a better term, a theological romance. What, then, can we say about the *Bacchae*? Earlier I suggested that it is not intrinsically a religious drama. This flies in the face of certain critical assumptions which have recently gained currency. It has been suggested that Euripides' chief object in writing the drama was to give a clinical portrayal of what Dionysiac religion, hence Dionysus, does to men. According to this view, the *Bacchae* is a more or less realistic document, perhaps an anthropological account of an outburst of manic behavior, of a psychosis analogous to certain phenomena reported from the Middle Ages and not unknown in our own troubled times. The play has even been compared with a modern imaginative treatment of mass psychosis, Van Wyck Brooks' *Oxbow Incident*. I feel that this is mistaken, and for a very simple and obvious reason. Whatever one may say about the ancient tragedians, about the extravagant character of many of the plots, about the implausibility of much that is said and done, the fact remains that the writers are interested in what is typical, in the generic, or, as Aristotle has it, in the universal. To attribute to Euripides a study in abnormality is to indulge in an anachronism. Euripides is not the kind of dramatist, like Sartre, whose poetic urge is stimulated by small grievances rather than catholic insight. Nor is Euripides a scientific observer of sickness; he does not record, he creates. His material is ritual and mythical, and some of it clinical; but the product is something entirely different.

Pindar once uses the tale of Perseus cutting off the head of the Medusa as an image symbolizing the act of poetic creation: living ugliness is violently refashioned into sculptured beauty. The ferocity of the *Bacchae* is to be seen in the same light. By an act of literary exorcism the cruelty and the ugliness of a living experience are transmuted into the beauty of a large vision, a vision which is not without its own horror, but a horror entirely unlike that felt at the approach of the god. It is the kind of horror which Plato touches on in the *Symposium* and the *Theaetetus*, the sudden weakness and awe which get hold of the philosophic soul at the moment when she comes face to face with a like-minded soul and jointly ventures to explore the ultimate. Dionysus is only a means to an end; Euripides exploits the Dionysiac revels to produce a dramatic action which helps the spectators to consider the mystery and the precariousness of their own existence.

Aeschylus, notably in his *Agamemnon* but also in some of his other extant plays, appeals to the audience with an interplay of sounds and sights. With Aeschylus, language is not an instrument but an entity, a vibrant self-sufficient thing, working in close harmony with the brilliant objects filling the stage of the *Oresteia*. The word textures pronounced by the chorus, like the sentence patterns of the actors' speeches, stir the audience as violently as the sight of a crimson tapestry or the vision of evil Furies on the roof. Behind this sumptuous drapery of color and sound, personality takes second place. The characters are largely the carriers of images and speech. Sophocles introduces the personal life, the *bios,* into drama. Now a man is no longer largely the pronouncer of words, the proposer of ideas and emotions, but an independent structure involving a past and a future, a point of intersection for ominous antecedents and awful prospects. This emergence of the organic character, of the heroic life as the nucleus of drama, was a fateful step in the history of literature. Aeschylus also, in some of his later plays, adopted the new structuring for his own purposes.

Euripides goes further. He rejects the autonomy of speech as he rejects the autonomy of the personal life; instead he attempts to combine the two in an organic mixture of his own. In the *Ion* he gives us a parody of the pure *bios* form; mythology is squeezed into a biographical mold, with unexpectedly humiliating consequences for the great hero. In the *Bacchae,* on the other hand, it is in the end not the persons who count, nor the words or sound patterns though the play may well be the most lyrical of all Euripidean works, but the ideas. The *Bacchae,* in spite of its contrived brutality and its lyricism, is a forerunner of the Platonic dialogues. The smiling god is another Socrates, bullying his listeners into a painful reconsideration of their thinking and their values. That is not to say that we have here an intellectual argument, an academic inquiry into logical relations. That would fit the *Ion* better than the *Bacchae.* Rather, the *Bacchae* constitutes a poet's attempt to give shape to a question, to a complex of uncertainties and puzzles which do not lend themselves to discursive treatment. There is no clear separation of thesis and antithesis, of initial delusion and liberating doubt, nor is there anything like a final statement or a solution. Nevertheless the poem is cast in the philosophical mode. Sophocles, in the *Oedipus Rex* or the *Ajax,* takes a heroic life and fashions its tragic nexus to the world around it or to itself. Euripides, in the *Bacchae,* takes an abstract issue and constructs a system of personal relations and responses to activate the issue. He builds his lives into the issue, instead of letting the life speak for itself as Sophocles does.

The issue derives from a question which is simple and raw: What is man? As Dionysus remarks to Pentheus (506),

> Your life, your deeds, your Being are unknown
> to you.

For Plato, the human soul is a compound of the divine and the perishable, a meeting place of the eternal beyond and the passionate here. In the *Phaedrus* he puts the question more concretely. Socrates suggests that it is idle to criticize or allegorize mythology if one has not yet, as he himself has not, come to a satisfactory conclusion about his own nature and being (230A):

> I try to analyze myself, wondering whether I am some kind of beast more heterogeneous and protean and furious than Typhon, or whether I am a gentler and simpler sort of creature, blessed with a heavenly unfurious nature.

The word that I have translated as "creature" is the same that appears in Aristotle's famous definition of man as a "political creature," or rather, as "a creature that lives in a polis." "Political animal," the usual translation, is unfortunate, for in his definition Aristotle clearly throws the weight of his authority behind the second alternative of Plato's question. Man is not a ravaging beast, but a gentler being. But perhaps Aristotle is not as fully sensitive as Plato to the difficulty posed by the alternative. Is man closer to the gods or to the beasts?

Another question which is linked to the uncertainty about the status of the human soul is: What is knowledge? Or, to put it differently: How much in this world is subject to man's insight and control? Greek philosophical realism, beginning with the Eleatics and reaching its greatest height with Plato, taught that reality is unchanging, static, difficult of access, and that in general men come to experience it only through the veil of ever-changing patterns of sensory impulses. There is an inexorable friction between total Being and partial Appearance. Man is constrained to deal with the appearances, but at his best he comes to sense—or, according to Plato, to know— the reality behind the phenomena. The break-through to the reality is a painful process; it can be achieved only at the cost of injuring and mutilating the ordinary cognitive faculties. The perfectionists, including Plato in the *Phaedo,* submit that the break-through becomes complete only with the complete surrender of the senses whose activity stands in the way of the vision of reality. That is to say, the perceptual blindness and the phenomenal friction cannot be resolved except by disembodiment and death.

Now if this, or something like it, is the philosophical issue which Euripides is trying to dramatize, he is at once faced with a grave artistic difficulty. How is he, as a dramatist, to convey the universal scope of reality and the beguiling contradictoriness of Appearance, without rendering the formulation banal or bloodless or both? The statement "Dionysus is all" would be worse than meaningless. It should be emphasized again that Euripides is not trying to say poetically what could also, and better, be said discursively. What does a poet-metaphysician do to clothe the range of abstract issues in the living and self-authenticating flesh of poetry? Is it possible for a dramatist to convey ideas without having his characters preach them ex cathedra, which is by and large the situation we find in the *Prometheus Bound?* Can a philosophical idea which is refracted by a process of poetic mutation continue to score as a factor in a metaphysical argument?

To begin with, the Greek writer has an advantage over his modern colleagues. The ancient conventions of tragedy stipulate that the dramatic nucleus be essayed from a spectrum of approaches. From Prologue to chorus to characters to Epilogue, each constitutive part of the drama contributes its specific orientation. In the end the various perspectives coalesce into one and invite a unified though never simple audience response. This is the desired effect; sometimes the merging of the lines of coordination is not complete, and the spectators are left without a certain key to gauge their participation. Goethe's *Faust* is, perhaps, once again a fair example of such a case on the modern stage. The author is saying something profound about man and reality, but for various reasons the play leaves us with the impression of partial statements instead of a total imaging, because of the vast scope of the action, because Goethe has inserted certain curious elements of diffusion and fragmentation, and because he tries to play off one culture against another in an attempt to universalize the compass of the theme. Any Greek play is likely to be more successful on this score. The traditional spectrum of perspectives is offset by an extreme succinctness of speech and thought, by a narrow conformity to Greek ways, by an economy of character, and, last but not least, by the condensatory effect of hereditary myth. Myth is itself a condensation of many experiences of different degrees of concreteness. Greek drama simply carries forward the business begun by myth.

Dionysus, who is Euripides' embodiment of universal vitality, is described variously by chorus, herdsman, commoners, and princes. The descriptions do not tally, for the god cannot be defined. He can perhaps be totaled but the sum is never definitive; further inspection adds new features to the old. If a definition is at all possible it is a definition by negation or cancellation. For one thing, Dionysus appears to be neither woman nor man; or better, he presents himself as woman-in-man, or man-in-woman, the unlimited personality (235):

> With perfumes wafted from his flaxen locks
> and Aphrodite's wine-flushed graces in
> his eyes . . .

No wonder Pentheus calls him (353) "the woman-shaped stranger," and scoffs at the unmanly whiteness of his complexion (457). In the person of the god strength mingles with softness, majestic terror with coquettish glances. To follow him or to comprehend him we must ourselves give up our precariously controlled, socially desirable sexual limitations. The being of the god transcends the protective fixtures of decency and sexual pride.

Again, Dionysus is both a citizen, born of Semele, and a Greek from another state, for he was raised in Crete, like the Zeus of the mysteries—surely this is the implication of lines 120 ff.—*and* a barbarian from Phrygia or Lydia or Syria or India, at any rate from beyond the pale of Greek society. It is not as if the conflicting pieces of information had to be gathered laboriously from various widely separated passages in the play. All of them are to be found in the entrance song of the chorus. After the introductory epiphany of the god himself, the women of the chorus begin to assemble their picture of Dionysus, and it is indicative of what Euripides means him to be that even these first few pointers should cancel out one another. It happens to be true historically that Dionysus is both Greek and non-Greek; recently discovered Mycenean texts have shown that the god's name was known to the Greeks of the Mycenean period. It now appears that the foreign extraction of Dionysus may have been a pious fiction of Apollinian partisans. Dionysus the popular god, the god of mysteries, the emblem of surging life in its crudest form, of regeneration and animal passion and sex, was endangering the vested interests of Apollo, grown refined and squeamish in the hands of the gentry and the intellectual elite. One of the defense measures, and there were many, was to declare Dionysus a foreigner, a divinity whose ways, so the propaganda went, offended the true instincts of the Greek. There was some apparent justification for this. The genuinely foreign deities who were being imported into Greece often were kindred in spirit to Dionysus. At any rate the propaganda took hold. At the end of the fifth century all Greeks tended to believe that Dionysus came from abroad; and yet they considered him one of their own, a powerful member of the Olympian pantheon. Euripides exploits the discrepancy to the advantage of his purpose; he uses it to emphasize the unbounded, the unfragmented nature of the ultimate substance. But the arrival from foreign lands signifies a special truth; it highlights the violently intrusive character of the Dionysiac life, of the unlimited thrusting itself into the limited and exploding its stale equilibrium, which is a favorite theme of Pythagorean and Greek popular thought.

But all this would be bloodless metaphysics, dry-as-dust allegory, were it not for Euripides' grasp of the essential irony enunciated in the passage of the *Phaedrus* and skirted in Aristotle's aphorism. Man is both beast and god, both savage and civilized, and ultimate knowledge may come to him on either plane, depending on the manner in which the totality communicates itself. It is as an animal, as a beast close to the soil and free of the restrictions of culture and city life, that man must know Dionysus. But that means that in embracing Dionysus man surrenders that other half of himself, the spark of the gentle and celestial nature which, the philosophers hope, constitutes the salvageable part of man's equipment. The incongruity of the two planes, the political and the animal, becomes the engrossing puzzle and the energizing thesis of the play. The double nature of man is what the play is really about; the ambivalence of Dionysus is pressed into service largely in order to illumine the ambivalence of human cognition reaching out for its object, for the elusive pageant of truth.

V

How does Euripides use the animal in his art? In the *Ion* the relation between men and animals is simple and candid, though not devoid of some humor. At the beginning Ion wages a mock battle against the birds because they interfere with his daily cleaning operations. The kindly gruffness with which he rebukes them deceives no one. Once he threatens death to a swan that approaches too closely to the altar (161 ff.), but he does not take the threat seriously himself (179):

> To think I would murder you,
> messengers of the words of gods
> to men!

Ion is not so cynical as to remember that the swan is said to sing his truest song when he is about to die. Later Ion's life is saved when a dove consumes the poison meant for him (1202 ff.); he accepts the sacrifice gratefully but without comment. Near the beginning of the exodus Ion calls Creusa (1261) a "serpent . . . or a dragon"

> with murderous fire blazing from his eyes,

but this is a metaphor induced by rage, and in any case Ion is mistaken about her, as he acknowledges in the next scene. The history of Athens may have been crowded with serpents and half-serpents; the decoration of the tent features many beings half-man half-beast, including Cecrops himself with his serpent's coils. But the somber tent, as suggested earlier, is the exception. Through most of the action, and certainly at the end of the play when the causes of ignorance have been removed, men know their distance from the animals. Their humaneness entails this; the gentleness which characterizes the true inclinations of Io and Creusa and Xuthus takes us far away from the murky borderland where human nature and animal nature merge and where satyrs and centaurs ply their brutal trade.

In the *Bacchae* this borderland is always present. Men are identified with animals, not as in Aesop where the beasts aspire to be men and become moral agents, but as in a Gothic tale where intelligence and social grace and responsibility are renounced and the irrational, the instinct of blood and steaming compulsion, take their place. Characteristically this way of looking at life paralyzes value judgment. The gulf between men and animals is erased, but whether this is a good thing or not is by no means clear. When the women of the chorus, for example, call Pentheus a beast they do not mean to flatter him. He is the son of Echion, who was sprung from dragon's teeth, and there is dragon blood in his veins (1155). He is said to be a fierce monster (542) whose acts make one suspect that he was born of a lioness or a Libyan Gorgon. His mother also in her moment of visionary bliss sees him as a lion rather than as a man. For her, however, this is not a matter of disparagement; if anything, embracing a lion seems to her to offer a glimpse of perfection. Not so the chorus; in the passages cited they show an incongruous pride in human shape and human achievement. But in the fourth choral ode, as they reach their highest pitch of passion and frenzied insight, they issue the call which is quoted at the beginning of our chapter (1017):

> Appear, in the shape of a bull or a many-headed
> serpent, or a lion breathing fire!

In their first ode also they refer to Dionysus as the bull-horned god wreathed in snakes (100 f.). The god Dionysus, the stranger-citizen, the hermaphrodite, at once superman and subman, is a beast, for which the chorus praise him. This is the sacred dogma. Even Pentheus, once he has fallen under the spell of the god, acknowledges him as a bull (920):

> And now, leading me on, I see you as
> a bull, with horns impacted in your head.
> Were you a beast before? I should not wonder.

And Dionysus answers:

> Yes, now you see what is for you to see.

But what of Pentheus' own beast-likeness? Are the women suggesting that human beastliness is a mere parody of divine beastliness, and therefore to be condemned? Or have the ladies of the chorus not yet

travelled the full length of the Dionysiac conversion, and retain a
vestige of civilized values? Their abuse of Pentheus is couched in
terms which expose them as imperfect Maenads. Contrast that other
chorus, the band of Bacchantes hidden from our sight, whose mysterious acts of strength are reported to us in the messenger speeches.
From them rather than from their more civilized sisters on the stage
we expect the pure lesson of the new faith. And in fact they preserve no trace of a false pride in human separateness. They carry the
tokens of animal life on their backs and entertain the beasts as equal
partners (695):

> And first they shook their hair free to their shoulders
> and tucked up their fawnskins . . .
> . . . their spotted pelts
> they girt with serpents licking at their cheeks.
> And some clasped in their arms a doe or wild
> wolf cubs and gave them milk . . .

Under the aegis of Dionysus, men and animals are as one, with no
questions asked. The philosophical message is tolerably clear. But the
vestigial bias of the pseudo-Maenads on stage is more than a temporary
deviation from the orthodox Bacchic faith. In the interest of the message it would have been wiser to abuse Pentheus as a man, incapable
of going beyond the limitations of his anthropomorphism. The beast
imagery in the choral condemnation of Pentheus is cumulative and emphatic. The praise of Dionysus does not blot it from our memory. It
is, in fact, intended to serve as a counterpoint. The animal shape rules
supreme; but when all parties have been heard it is not at all clear
whether one ought to approve or not. The judgment is suspended, and
values are held in abeyance.

It is a mistake to consider the Dionysiac ecstasy a perversion of social life, an impasse, a negative situation. The *Bacchae* does not tell a
story of maladjustment or aberration. It is a portrayal of life exploding beyond its narrow everyday confines, of reality bursting into the
artificiality of social conventions and genteel restrictions. Waking and
sleeping are deprived of their ordinary cognitive connotations; who
is to say that sleeping, the drunken stupor which succeeds the rite, does

not expand one's vision beyond its commonplace scope? In the *Ion* the premium is on wakefulness; in the *Bacchae* we are invited to rest in a gray no man's land which is halfway between waking and sleep, where man shelves the tools of reason and social compact and abandons himself to instinct and natural law (862 ff., tr. Phillip Vellacott):

> O for long nights of worship, gay
> With the pale gleam of dancing feet,
> With head tossed high to the dewy air—
> Pleasure mysterious and sweet!
> O for the joy of a fawn at play
> In the fragrant meadow's green delight,
> Who has leapt out free from the woven snare,
> Away from the terror of chase and flight,
> And the huntsman's shout, and the straining pack,
> And skims the sand by the river's brim
> With the speed of wind in each aching limb,
> To the blessed lonely forest where
> The soil's unmarked by a human track,
> And leaves hang thick and the shades are dim.

This is the strophe of a choral ode; in the antistrophe the chorus invoke the divine order of things—*physis*, nature—which will assert itself eventually in spite of men (884)

> who honor ignorance and refuse
> to enthrone divinity . . .

The verses cited picture the pleasure and the awe of identification with nonhuman nature, with the life of the fawn bounding free of the snare but never quite eluding the hunter, a life of liberty which is yet not free. The animal senses the sway of natural law even more strongly than the man. Strophe and antistrophe, the vision of animal escape and the address to natural compulsion, are part of the same complex. But in the text they do not follow one upon the other; they are separated by that rare thing in Greek poetry, a refrain which is repeated once more identically, at the end of the antistrophe. Refrains in Greek tragedy always have a solemn ring; they are felt to be echoes of ritual hymns. The fixed severity of the repetition is something foreign within the headlong flow of the dramatic current. The mind accustomed to pressing on after the determined advance of ideas and plot is abruptly stopped in its tracks; time ceases for a while and the cold chill of monotony reveals a glimpse of Being beyond the Becoming of the human scene.

Here is an attempt to translate the refrain as literally as the sense allows (877, 897):

> What is wisdom? Or what is more beautiful,
> a finer gift from the gods among men,
> than to extend a hand victorious
> over the enemy's crown? But beauty
> is every man's personal claim.

Wisdom equals tyranny, beauty equals vengeance. The hunted and the hunter have their own jealous notions of wisdom and beauty, but their pretensions are drowned in the vast offering of the gods, the dispensation of natural law and the survival of the strongest. This is what the refrain seems to say; the message agrees well with the propositions of strophe and antistrophe. But note the didactic quality of the speech, the question and answer, and particularly the academic formulation of the last line which in the Greek consists of only four words: "Whatever beautiful, always personal." It is a line which might have come straight from the pages of Aristotle; better yet, it reminds us of a similarly scholastic passage in a poem by Sappho in which she contemplates various standards of beauty and preference and concludes: "I [think that the most beautiful thing is] that with which a person is in love." The poetess speaks of a "thing," using the neuter gender, and of "a person," any person, desiring the thing. Like a good teacher she starts her discussion with a universal premise. Then, as the poem draws to its conclusion, she discards the generality and focuses on the living girl and on the I, the specific poles of her love whose reality constitutes the authority for the writing of the poem. But the philosophic mode of the earlier formulation remains important; it reminds us that the specific poles of her present love are at the same time representatives of a universal rhythm. In Euripides' ode, also, it is this universal rhythm which comes into view through the hieratic stillness of the refrain and particularly through its last line. The words are almost the same as those of Sappho; the difference is that between a vision intent upon the small joys and sufferings of love, and a vision which comprehends man in the sum total of his powers and feebleness. The refrain may well be the closest approach to poetry shedding its disguise and showing itself as metaphysics pure and simple.

But the glimpse is short-lived, and the clarity immediately obscured. Again it is the chorus itself which is the chief agent of confounding the analysis. It does so by combining in the Dionysiac prospects of its songs the two sides, the real and the ideal, which are inevitably connected in the experience. Both ritual and hope, slaughter and bliss, dance and dream, the cruelty of the present and the calm of the release, are joined together as one. The paradise of milk and honey and the orgy of bloody dismemberment merge in a poetic synthesis which defies rational classification. Of this creative insight into the contradictoriness of things I have already spoken. To complicate the picture even further, Bacchic sentiments are superimposed on traditional choric maxims. In an earlier ode which begins with a condemnation of Pentheus' words and an appeal to the goddess Piety, the women sing (386, 397):

> Of unbridled mouths
> and of lawless extravagance
> the end is disaster . . .
>
> . . . .
>
> Life is brief; if a man,
> not heeding this, pursues vast things
> his gain slips from his hands.
> These are the ways, I believe,
> of madmen, or of
> injudicious fools.

We recognize the familiar adage of "nothing in excess," the motto of bourgeois timidity and sane moderation, at opposite poles from the Dionysiac moral of vengeance and expansiveness and the bestialization of man. The injunctions of moderation and knowing one's limits run counter to the hopes of those who worship Dionysus. The two people who live up to the injunctions, Tiresias and Cadmus, come very close to being comic characters, as we shall see directly. Why, then, does Euripides put the pious precept into the mouth of a chorus whose primary artistic function is to communicate precisely what it is condemning, the spirit of unbridled mouths and lawless extravagance? It may be noted that such injunctions in Greek tragedy are often illusory. Setting off as they do a heroic imbalance or a cosmic disturbance, they underscore the poignancy of the action. But in this particular instance the use of the Delphic motto is even more startling than usual. The direction of the metaphysical impact is rudely deflected and the opacity of the poem enhanced by this conventional reminder of irrelevant quietist values.

While the Theban women are away celebrating, the foreign votaries are in Thebes. This is a mechanical displacement necessitated by what Greek tragedy permits; for the Dionysiac revels must be reported rather than seen, and so the true Maenads are off stage. But that puts the chorus in an anomalous position. They are worshippers of Dionysus, but they must not behave like worshippers. Few Euripidean choruses are less intimately engaged in the action and in fact less necessary to the action. It is the chorus off stage that counts. Hence the curious mixture of halfhearted participation and distant moralizing, as if the poet were not entirely comfortable with the choral requirements. This may account for the perplexing admixture of Apollinian preaching which I have just mentioned. It may account also for the remarkable poetic color of many of the choral utterances. The poet, making a virtue of the necessity, calls attention to the detachment of the chorus from the heart of the plot—though not from the heart of the philosophical issue—by giving it some of the finest lyrics ever sounded in the Attic theater. This is not the place for a close appreciation of the poetry; that can be done only in the original. The analysis of ancient poetry is a difficult thing; there are few men who combine the necessary scholarly equipment with an understanding of what poetry is about. Further, some of the clues to such an understanding which in modern poetry are furnished by the experience of living speech are missing for the Greek. Nevertheless few readers can expose themselves to the choral odes of the *Bacchae* without realizing that this is poetry of the highest order. Imagery has little to do with it; in this as in most Euripidean plays the choral poetry is even less dependent on metaphor and simile than the dialogue. There is some pondering of myth, to be sure. But perhaps the most important thing about the odes is the wonderful mixture of simplicity and excitement. The women do not beat around the bush; their interest in life is single-minded, and they declare themselves with all the fervor of a unitary vision. This does not, of course, say anything about the poetry as poetry, but it may explain why the lyrics of the *Bacchae* touch us so powerfully.

There is one image, however, or rather a class of images, which ought to be mentioned: the container filled to the bursting point. In their first ode the chorus use the trope three times. They sing of Dionysus stuffed into the thigh of Zeus, golden clasps blocking the exit until such time as the young man may be born (94 ff.). They call on Thebes, nurse of Semele, to (107)

> teem, teem with verdant
> bryony, bright-berried;

the city is to be filled to the rooftops with vegetation, as a sign of the presence of the god. For illustration we should compare the famous vase painting of Exekias in which Dionysus reveals himself in his ship to the accompaniment of a burst of vegetation. Finally the women caution each other to be careful in their handling of the thyrsus, the staff of the god (113):

> Handle the staffs respectfully;
> there is *hubris* in them.

In all three instances it is the fullness of the container which is stressed, not the spilling over. But as the play advances, containment proves inadequate. At the precise moment when the stranger is apprehended by Pentheus' men, the Maenads who had been imprisoned earlier are set free (447):

> All by themselves the bonds dropped off their feet;
> keys unlocked doors, without a man's hand to turn them.

Their liberation is as real as the binding of the stranger is false.

The most striking *misé en scène* of the inadequacy of the container is the so-called palace miracle. Like that of the other passages, its function is symbolic rather than dramaturgical; after it has happened it is never mentioned again. It is not necessary to the progress of the plot, only to the effect and the meaning of the poem. We need not worry much whether the stage director engineered the collapse of a column or a pediment, or whether the spectators were challenged to use their own creative imagination, though I am inclined to assume the latter. At any rate, the vision of the palace shaking and tumbling is the most explicit and the most extended of a series of images pointing to the explosion of a force idly and wrongfully compressed. Eventually this concept converges on what I have called the friction between total Being and fragmentary Appearance, the friction which is worked out also through a series of antinomies: the brute wildness of the thyrsus versus the spindles abandoned in the hall, the fawnskins versus the royal armor, the civic proclamation versus the bleating shout, the beating of tambourines versus the steady clicking of the loom. Dionysus disrupts the settled life, he cracks the shell of civic contentment and isolation. Probably the most important word in the play, as a recent critic has well pointed out, is *"hubris."* It occurs throughout, and always in a key position. But it is not the *hubris* of which the tragic poets usually speak, the *hubris* which figures also in the legal documents, the thoughtless insolence which comes from too much social or political power. In the *Bacchae,* hubris is quite literally the "going beyond," the explosion of the unlimited across the barricades which a blind civilization has erected in the vain hope of keeping shut out what it does not wish to understand. That is not to say that the word is not used also in its more conventional sense, especially with reference to the campaign of Pentheus. As a result, the efforts of Pentheus take on the aspect of a parody of Dionysiac impulsiveness.

Similarly the hunt is a principal symbol because it catches the futility of organized, circumscribed life. From the vantage point of the larger reality, all worldly activity appears both hunt and escape. Hunting and being hunted are the physical and psychological manifestations of Appearance, the monotonous jolts of the process of generation and decay. Agave cries when approached by the herdsman (731):

> Run to it, my hounds!
> Behold the men who hunt us! Follow me,
> brandish your thyrsus and pursue them!

The Maenads are resting; they are communing with the god and sloughing off the sense of separateness when they are violently pulled back into the world of Appearance and resume their game of hunting and being hunted. In this case it is Appearance which causes the disruption; Being and Appearance are so related that one as well as the other may be the cause of disturbance and dislocation. There is a perpetual pull between them which never allows either to win a lasting victory. Without the constant friction there would be no tragedy; without the violent disruption of one by the other there would be no dismemberment. *Sparagmos,* the sacred dismemberment of the Dionysiac rites, is both a means to an end and an autonomous fact. As a means to an end it supplies the frenzied exercise which terminates in the drugged sleep. The explosion of energy, the tearing and mutilation of a once living body, leaves the worshipper exhausted and readies the soul, through a numb tranquility, for the mystic union with the god. But the dismemberment operates also as a self-validating event. Through it, symbolically, the world of Appearance with its contradictions and insufficiencies is made to show itself as it really is. The destruction of Pentheus, then, is not simply a sardonic twist of an unspeakable bloody rite, but a fitting summation of the lesson of the play. The limited vessel is made to burst asunder, refuting the pretensions of those who oppose Dionysus, of the partisans of unreality.

vi

Who is Pentheus, and why is it he who dies rather than one of the other Thebans? When the stranger raises the question whether the King knows who he really is, he answers (507):

> Pentheus, the son of Agave and of Echion.

Thus Pentheus identifies himself as a member of the ruling house, as an officer of the State. He bears a name which establishes his position within the hereditary political structure of his city. Even at the moment of death he throws off the leveling disguise of the ministrant and cries (1118):

> Mother, it is I, your son
> Pentheus, the child you bore in Echion's house.

In the judgment of Dionysus this pride in the house, the emphasis on the limited life, is ignorance. But is it commensurate with the punishment which Pentheus receives? Is there not something about him as a person which is more likely to justify the violence of his undoing? To ask the obvious question: Does Pentheus not exhibit an arrogance which cries out for retribution?

Here we must step gingerly. It is to be remembered that the action of the *Bacchae* is not primarily borne or promoted by the characters. Euripides does not in this play operate with idiosyncrasies but with lives. Suffering is constructed as the measurable content of a life, not as the unique unquantifiable experience of a specific irrational soul. And the lives, also, are largely catalysts for the release of social complications. These complications have nothing to do with the arbitrary contours of individual dispositions, but answer directly to the needs of the author's metaphysical purpose. The personal relations brought into play are devised chiefly as one of the means for the author to invoke his philosophical riddle. In the *Alcestis,* as we shall see in the essay on that play, character is all; in the *Bacchae* it counts for very little. It is sometimes said that the tragedy of Pentheus is not that he tried to do what was wrong but that he was the wrong man to do it —that he was, in fact, not a political strongman but precisely the unbalanced, excitable type of person who most easily falls a victim to the allurements of the Dionysiac indulgence. In other words, the character of Pentheus is too Dionysiac to allow him to oppose Dionysus successfully. But this argument will not stand up. Pentheus is no more and no less excitable or unstable than most of the heroes of Greek tragedy. An Odysseus, or a Socrates, is no more fit to stand at the center of a high tragedy than a Pecksniff or a Tanner. Odysseus is not a whole man, as Helen is not a whole woman; they are exponents of a partial aspect of the human range: intelligence in the case of Odysseus, love in the case of Helen. But Pentheus is a whole man, precisely as Oedipus is, or as Antigone is a whole woman. And because he is whole he is vulnerable, more vulnerable than the men and women who are weighted in one direction or another.

Of course he is not a moderate. His order to smash the workshop of Tiresias (346 ff.) is not well considered. He happens to be right; Tiresias appears to have turned disloyal to Apollo, and so will no longer need his oracle seat. Under the democratic spell of Dionysus, everybody will do his own prophesying. But even if Pentheus were unjustified in his harshness toward Tiresias, his lack of moderation, or, to put it more fairly, his capacity for anger, does not necessarily discredit him. Stability, self-control, discretion smack too much of asceticism and puritan artifice to provide a solid basis for tragic action. Pentheus is a whole man, with none of his vitality curtailed or held in check. But he is also a king, a perfect representative of the humanistic Greek ideal of the ordered life, a political being rather than a lawless beast. Being Aristotle's "creature living in a polis," he is destined to ask the wrong sort of question, a political question, when faced with the reality of religion. His query (473),

> What profit do the celebrants draw from it?

shows the political or educational frame of his thinking. The twentieth century, unlike the eighteenth, is once more inclined to the view that the question of usefulness when applied to religion misses the point, that religion cannot be adjusted to a system of utilitarian relations. But where did Euripides and his contemporaries stand on this issue? In all probability Pentheus' question did not strike the audience as irrelevant; it may, in fact, have impressed them as noble and responsible. At the end of the fifth century, as we can see in the *History* of Thucydides, the preservation of social and political institutions and traditions had become the overriding topic of discussion to which all other values tended to be subordinated. The *Bacchae* demonstrates that this sort of nobility, the exaltation of the political and educational thesis, is as nothing before the primary currents of life. But a nobility which goes under is not the less noble for its defeat. Pentheus dies, and the nature of his death, particularly of the preparations which lead to his death, is deplorable. But the fact remains that his stand, and only his, can be measured in positive moral terms. Clearly the force which kills him eludes ethical analysis.

Because Pentheus is a king he offers a larger area to be affected by the deity. His responses differ from those of other men less in their specific quality than in their intensity. As a king he suffers for the group; his name, as Dionysus reminds him (508), means "man of sorrow." But there is nothing Christ-like about him. He proposes to live as a rational man, to leave everything nonrational, everything that might remind us of man's original condition, behind him. Love and faith, the Christian antidotes of the dispassionate intellect, have not yet been formulated. In Plato, characteristically, it is love and reason together, or love-in-reason, which refines man and weakens the animal in him. Nonreason, in the fifth century B.C., is neither love nor hatred but religious ecstasy. This Pentheus means to fight, for he knows it is wrong. Pentheus is not a romantic hero, he does not search for a hidden truth. The same thing is true of the others; both the characters and the chorus are, each of them, convinced that they know best and that their way of life is best. For Pentheus the best is Form, the tested and stable limits of responsibility, law, and control. Against the chorus, which espouses the cause of excitement, of formlessness and instability, Pentheus is the champion of permanence and stability. Neither his anger nor his defeat are valid arguments against the merits of this championship. Like Ajax, as we shall see in the following essay, Pentheus is identified with armor (781, 809); like Ajax, the armed Pentheus, confined in the panoply of embattled civic life, turns against the forces which are wrecking his fragile cause. As a functionary he represents order and limit; as a man he is whole and robust and fully alive.

This cannot be said about Cadmus and Tiresias. For one thing, they are old men, their life force is diminished and stunted. This means that they cannot suffer as Pentheus can. It also means that they have come to terms with the world; there are no issues left for them to battle out, no difficulties over which to fret. Cadmus is a fine specimen of the *arriviste,* proud of the achievements of his grandson, but even prouder of the inclusion of a genuine god in the family. The god must at all costs be kept in the family, even if it becomes necessary to mince the truth a little. Here is Cadmus' humble plea to Pentheus (333):

> And if, as you say, the god does not exist,
> keep this to yourself, and share in the fine fiction
> that he does; so we may say that Semele bore
> a god, for the greater glory of our clan.

The distinction between truth and falsity, between order and disorder, is of no importance to him. At his time of life, a good reputation is a finer prize than a noble life, no matter whether the reputation is deserved or not. Tiresias likewise is not concerned with essentials. This Tiresias is not the Sophoclean man of truth, the terrible mouthpiece of mystery and damnation, but, of all things, a clever sophist, a pseudophilosopher who strips away the mystery and the strangeness of the superhuman world and is content to worship a denatured, an ungodded god. A squeamish deist, he does not hold with the miracles and the barbarisms of popular faith. In his lecture to Pentheus he pares down the stature of Dionysus to render him manageable and unoffending (272 ff.). Point one: he is the god of wine (280)

> which liberates suffering mortals from
> their pain.

That is to say, he *is* wine (284), precisely as Demeter *is* grain. By allegorizing the old stories and identifying the gods with palpable substances, we can dispense with whatever is not concrete and intelligible in the traditions about Dionysus. Point two: he is a perfectly natural god. The distasteful tale about Zeus sewing him up in his thigh produces a quite satisfactory meaning once it is understood that the grating feature is due to a pun. Like Max Mueller in a subsequent era of facile enlightenment, Tiresias believes that the mystery of myth is caused by a linguistic aberration; with the discovery of the cause, the mystery disappears.

Finally, in the third part of his lecture, Tiresias does pay some attention to the irrational virtues of the god, to his mantic powers and his ability to inspire panic in strong men. But this part of the assessment is underplayed; it is briefer than the other two, and one feels that Tiresias adds it only in order to have a weapon with which to frighten Pentheus. The reference to soldiers strangely routed and to Dionysiac torches at home in the sanctuary of Delphi is not a confession but a threat, calculated to appeal to Pentheus in the only language he understands: the language of military and political authority. Tiresias' heart is not in the threat; what interests him is the theological and philological sterilization of the god. Neither he nor Cadmus really understands or even wants to understand what the god has to offer. But they know that his triumph is inevitable, and so they try to accept him within their lights. They are fellow travellers, with a good nose for changes of fashion and faith. To take them seriously would be absurd; a Tartuffe has no claim on our sympathy.

They do not understand; hence nothing happens to them.[1] Pentheus, on the other hand, is fully engaged, and he is a big enough man to perceive the truth beyond his own self-interest. He is capable of appreciating the real meaning of Dionysus; though he does not approve, he understands. But understanding, in a man of his power of commitment, is tantamount to weakening, and in the end, to destruction. This is what Euripides dramatizes with the sudden break-up of Pentheus' royal substance. Abruptly the officer of the State turns into a Peeping Tom. One shout of the god (810) and the manly general becomes a slavish, prurient, reptilian thing, intent on watching from a safe distance what he hopes will be a spectacle to titillate his voyeur's

---

[1] The metamorphosis which Dionysus inflicts upon Cadmus in the Epilogue is a datum from mythology. Because of the bad state of preservation of the final portion of the play we do not know how Euripides motivated the metamorphosis, and what the punishment—for such it is said to be (1340 ff.)—is for.

itch. The civilized man of reason is gone, and in his place we find an animal, living only for the satisfaction of his instinctual drives.

Is the rapid change psychologically plausible? Once more, the question is not pertinent. There is no character in the first place, only a comprehensive life-image to symbolize one side of a conflict which transcends the terms of a uniquely experienced situation. Whether it is possible for such a man as Pentheus is shown to be in the first half of the play, to turn into the creature he becomes after his conversion by Dionysus, is a question on which psychoanalysts may have an opinion but which does not arise in considering Euripides' purpose. The truth is that the change is not a transition from one phase of life to another, much less a lapse into sickness or perversion, but quite simply death. When a tragic hero in the great tradition is made to reverse his former confident choice, especially if this happens at the instigation of the archenemy, the role of the hero has come to an end. We remember Agamemnon stepping on the crimson carpet, after Clytemnestra has broken down his reluctance. The blood-colored tapestry is a visual anticipation of the murder. Instead of the corporeal death which will be set off stage, the audience watch the death of the soul. With Agamemnon slowly moving through the sea of red the contours are blurred and the king of all the Greeks is annihilated before our eyes. Aeschylus uses a splash; Euripides, less concretely but no less effectively, uses a change of personality.

That the hero has died in his scene with Dionysus becomes even clearer when the god, with a Thucydidean terseness, announces the physical death (857):

> Now I shall go and dress him in the robes
> he'll wear to Hades once his mother's hands
> have slaughtered him . . .

His death, then, is an agreed fact both while the chorus sing their ode to Natural Necessity and also during the terrible scene which follows in which Pentheus arranges his woman's clothes about him. The King joins the Maenads, but he goes further than they, for he adopts the bisexuality of the god. All this is meaningful as a picture of the complete and devastating victory of reality over unreality, of the natural over the institutional life. But it is not without its psychological aspect, and here, curiously, we may see an ironic parallel to one of Plato's most troublesome concerns. In his discussions of dramatic poetry, Plato takes it for granted that the spectacle affects the soul of the spectator, even to the extent of transforming it in its own likeness. This is what drama demands; the audience must allow what they see to shape their souls, without struggling against the impact. Plato recognizes the legitimacy of the demand, and decides that therefore drama is too dangerous to have around in a healthy body politic, except the kind of drama whose effect is beneficial. Pentheus also is about to see a spectacle, a Dionysiac drama of the type which as a responsible man of the city he had condemned. Euripides knows that Plato's act of censorship is in a hopeless cause. A life which does not reach out to embrace the sight of a greater reality which tragedy affords is incomplete. Watching a play may mean a partial sacrifice of the soul, a surrender to the unlimited and the irrational, but we cannot do without it. Pentheus holds out against it for some time, but in the end he throws down his arms, with such finality that his soul comes to be transformed and enriched even before he goes off to spy on the mysteries.

Pentheus is drunk, without the physical satisfaction of strong drink (918):

> Ho, what is this? I think I see two suns,
> two cities of Thebes each with its seven gates!

This is one way of formulating his conquest at the hand of Dionysus. Drunk he sees more keenly, or at any rate more completely:

> And now, leading me on, I see you as
> a bull . . .

And Dionysus replies:

> Yes, now you see what is for you to see.

For the first time Pentheus' eyes are sufficiently opened to see the god in his animal shape. His vision is broadened; but his role as Pentheus is finished. The disintegration of the king is made particularly painful by the emphasis on the feminine clothing. With Dionysus assisting as his valet (928) the one-time upholder of the *vita activa* becomes fussy and vain about the details of his toilette. Does the cloak hang properly? Is he to carry the thyrsus in his right or in his left hand? The energies which had once been directed toward the mustering of armies and the implementation of public decisions are now bestowed on the arrangement of his Bacchic vestments. Along with this attention to the correct fashion—behold, another Tiresias—to the external signs of his new-found anonymity, there goes an internal change which is equally preposterous. The blocked doer turns into an uninhibited dreamer (945):

> I wonder if my shoulders would support
> Cithaeron and its glens, complete with Maenads?

His speech, formerly royal and violent and ringing, has become pretty and lyrical; he pictures the women (957)

> like birds in the thickets,
> contained in the fond coils of love's embrace.

Compare this with his earlier comment (222) that the women

> slink off by devious ways into
> the wild and cater to the lusts of males.

His imagination has been fired, his surly prejudices are gone. The vision which neither Cadmus nor Tiresias was able to entertain has come to Pentheus and is inspiring him. The Bacchianized Pentheus is a visionary and poet. But it is a poetry which lacks the saving grace of choice. He contemplates the prospect of his mother carrying him home from the mountains, and the prospect pleases him. The political man has become woman *and* child. Having rid himself of the social restrictions and classifications, he savors infancy, a sentient creature for whom the mother's cradled arms offer escape and bliss. He is woman and child and beast, an amorphous organism susceptible to all influences and realizing itself in a life of instinct and unthinking sense. The victory of Dionysus is complete; the king is dead, and the man has been found out, in the god's image.

vii

This, roughly, is what the *Bacchae* is about. The vast recesses of mystery and abomination which it explores make it difficult to talk about the play without some measure of doubt and uneasiness. Not so with the *Ion*. The *Ion* deals with a portion of Greek mythology. Selecting an ordinary incident from the traditions about the gods, the poet turns it this way and that to highlight its absurdity in the light of modern culture, and incidentally also to re-emphasize the worth of the human achievement. The spirit in which this is done is, on the whole, playful. But the plot which Euripides sets up features enough scheming and resentment and disillusionment to make us wonder whether the author's purpose is not quite serious. It is indeed, but the seriousness is that of a dramatist who takes no human suffering lightly, who regards the feelings of men as more precious and essential than the events which befall them. He finds that even the silly nonsense about gods fathering human sons can, if taken at face value, produce momentary effects which threaten to cripple generosity and fellowship. Eventually kindness triumphs; human culture is too tough and too secure an institution to be disrupted for long even when one of its chief supports, the veneration of the gods, is jarred.

The *Bacchae* questions what the *Ion* extols, by asking: Precisely what is human culture, and what is man? Plato chose to believe that, at his best, man can divest himself of his animal trappings and rise to a station in which the divine in him remains in sole control. Euripides shows that the divine equals the bestial, and that man's special achievement, the social graces and comforts fondly sketched in the *Ion*, are at the furthest remove from the reign of the god. Pentheus is a "political animal" whose veneer is stripped off, who is forced to return to his origins as a creature of instinct and sense, without the protective coloring of social conventions, without the benefit of activist illusions. In this original state before the fall into grace he will be a simple beast, with the pleasures and the dangers of an animal existence. To save his dignity, the king must die; the death images the ephemeral nature of

the civilized veneer. A few seconds of consciousness are given to him
to double the pathos and to ratify the horror (1118):

> Mother, it is I, your son
> Pentheus, the child you bore in Echion's house.
> Have pity, Mother, do not kill your son,
> though my transgressions furnish cause enough!

This brief abortive glimpse of what has held him up in the past and
what is now becoming the instrument of his defeat, the social compact,
is like a trope of all cultured life. Between the realm of the beasts
from which man is born, and the realm of the gods presided over by
the great beast of heaven, civilized existence and human fellowship
are a minute enclave, hard-pressed and short-lived and utterly without
hope. Social conventions are fictitious, they offend against nature and
the natural law. However noble and glorious the human achievement
may appear to the enlightened, it makes barely a dent upon the true
structure, the real being of the animate world which defies reason and
order and progress and engulfs man in its eternal rhythm of animal
necessity.

Everyone will agree that this is a most depressing moral. But it is the
moral pronounced by the play, and we cannot doubt that it is a view
held by the author. Fortunately we know that it was not Euripides'
only view, for we have the *Ion,* in which men are very substantial indeed, far removed from the realm of the wild beasts, and where the
god is so civilized himself—and, we should add, so ineffectual—that
the vista of a greater reality which is neither rational nor cultured does
not even suggest itself. I said earlier that the *Ion* is about the gods and
the *Bacchae* about man. But that is only a matter of emphasis. In truth
both plays are about God, both are about man. But they have to be
read together so that we may understand the full range of Euripides'
thoughts on the subject of religion. As dramas they are autonomous;
each exercises its own special effect and wants to be taken on its own
grounds. But once we begin to think about the issues developed in
them, we must in all fairness admit that what for want of a better term

may be called Euripides' philosophy is not fully presented in either play. Even together they do not give us a complete picture. But they help us to realize that a good drama, especially a good Greek drama, must bear down significantly on a narrow front. If it tries to say too much and to cover too many stations it dissipates its strength. A Greek drama is, ideologically or philosophically, an unbalanced thing, especially if, as in the *Bacchae,* its objective is to dramatize a philosophical truth. But the imbalance is our gain; the force generated by the concentration is unmatched in the history of dramatic literature.

Ajax: TRAGEDY
AND TIME

I<small>T IS SOMETIMES SAID</small> that the *Ajax* is not a
well-constructed play. Now structure, in a
Greek drama, is an elusive commodity. In
its heyday Greek tragedy was seen and heard, not studied. To what extent is the aesthetic appeal of a religious service, or of a political rally,
determined by structural factors, and what are the structural criteria of
such a communication? I do not intend to enter into this inquiry, which
is one to which classical scholars have only recently become alive. But
at the least, structure is more than a symmetrical arrangement of sung
and spoken lines; it has something to do with the distribution of stim-

uli of emotional response. In the light of this it should be noted that at the exact center of the play, thrown into relief by the horror which precedes and the mortification which follows, the chorus has an ode of joy (693):

> I throb with passion, joy lifts me up high!

All pain and fear and resentment are forgotten, and in a paroxysm of relief the sailors shout to Pan and Apollo to lead them in their dance of happiness. Alas, their happiness is out of place, the result of a characteristically Sophoclean device which is often found near the middle of a play: false hope. On this occasion it is the hero himself who misguides their affections, with a speech which begins as follows (646, tr. E. F. Watling):

> The long unmeasured pulse of time moves everything.
> There is nothing hidden that it cannot bring to light,
> Nothing once known that may not become unknown.
> Nothing is impossible. The most sacred oath
> Is fallible; a will of iron may bend.

And later (670):

> The snowy feet of Winter walk away
> Before riper Summer; and patrolling Night
> Breaks off her rounds to let the Dawn ride in
> On silver horses lighting up the sky.
> The winds abate and leave the groaning sea
> To sleep awhile. Even omnipotent Sleep
> Locks and unlocks his doors and cannot hold
> His prisoners bound for ever.

This stately homage to Time is by no means unique in Greek literature, though it may well be the most successful of its kind. "The moving likeness of eternity," as Plato calls it in the *Timaeus,* held a great fascination for all thinking Greeks. Reflecting upon its various operations they made the discussion of time a Greek specialty, with a rich vocabulary to mirror the variety they discerned. Every reader of Greek finds in his earliest lessons a number of words for "time" to tax his ingenuity as a translator: time as motion *(chronos),* time as status *(aion)*, time as juncture *(kairos)*, and so forth. Time, in all its manifestations, was felt to be a particular mark of the human life. It was sensed to be part of the complex of a meaningful existence on earth, of human weakness and achievement and self-consciousness. God knows no time; beasts live *in* time but cannot be said to recognize its laws or to suffer from its restrictions. Only man, who, as the tragedies remind us again and again, hovers precariously between divinity and beastliness, becomes aware of the power of time.

The lyric writers were the first to develop the theme of man as a time-bound being. But the poetic possibilities of the insight are not fully exploited until the dramatists adopt it for their own. The *Oresteia*, the *Oedipus* plays, the *Prometheus Bound,* the *Ion,* all build their dramatization of the contingency of men's works around the focus of time. Usually it is time as motion, or flux, which serves the poets as their guide. For, as the lyric poets had recognized, the defenselessness of man emerges most clearly when time is visualized in its most cruel guise, as an enemy of stability and solid anchorage, as a stream.

But time as flux may itself be considered under various perspectives. Let me mention four. First, time may register itself as moving past the subject into the future. This is the historian's line of vision, or the scientist's. Of all the perspectives it is the least disturbing, for on this view the beholder is scarcely involved in the flux. Such time is calculable; the beholder knows the past, and on the basis of his knowledge he may freely predict the future. But calculability does not fill it with meaning. Because I myself am not engaged in the processes of time, the direction and the character of the advance toward the future remain irrelevant to me as a moral being.

Contrariwise, time may be experienced as a function of one's own development. As Lucretius[1] puts it:

> Time by itself does not exist; but from things themselves
> there results a sense of what has already taken place, what
> is now going on and what is to ensue. It must not be claimed

---

[1] R. E. Latham (trans.), *Lucretius: The Nature of the Universe* (Harmondsworth, England, Penguin Books, 1951), pp. 40–41.

that anyone can sense time by itself apart from the movement
of things or their restful immobility.

This is the philosopher's time; it stems from introspection, from the
discovery that man himself is a part of the moving world around him.
On this view, also, time is calculable. But unlike the historian's time,
the philosopher's time has meaning; it is nothing if not read from the
significant phases of my own growth and successes and failures. Yet
in a sense, as Lucretius suggests, to speak of time in this way is a tautol-
ogy. The flux contemplated has meaning and is relevant, but there is
no allowance for a meaningful relation, much less tension, between
the flux and the self. A time which does not exist outside the moving
self rouses neither hopes nor fears, it does not oppress nor does it inspire. Hence poets have no interest in this perspective.

Third, time presents itself as a stream which sweeps men along as
mountain torrents carry along stones, or as rivers carry flotsam and
wreckage. On this view time is both meaningless and incalculable; the
stones and the wreckage have little control over the direction and the
rate of speed of the current which pulls them along. If there is an element of calculability, it is merely this: that the operation of the stream
upon the man enveloped is not likely to be beneficent.

And finally, time may be thought of as moving, not past the agent,
or with him or around him, but straight through him. In such a case
time reveals itself not only as incalculable but as a shatterer of the
substance of man.

Like the philosopher's time, the historian's also fails to fit into the
scheme of dramatic poetry. Negatively, of course, it may be put to some
use. When Hamlet says, "The time is out of joint," he thinks of himself as an onlooker, an outsider, a scientist who judges and manipu-
lates at will. He assumes that a man may penetrate the vagaries of
time without being touched in his own person. As he finds out eventually, his own life becomes affected when for him, temporarily,
time stands still; he discovers himself in a "dead vast and middle of the
night" which paralyzes and ultimately transforms him. His feeling
that he was born to set time right is a delusion, as we are made to
recognize in the course of the play. In the world of the poet, time is

an active power. Hence only the last two perspectives of the four I have mentioned are to be found in the plays. Time affects man, either as a container or as an aggressor. If as a container, time functions as the life of the cosmos, the structure of fate or chance, the superhuman rhythm which molds the human existence to its will, numbing or healing or perfecting but always determining the character of its charge, while never granting a glimpse of its intentions. If as an aggressor, on the other hand, the intention is obvious, and the outcome clear: such time kills.

In the drama to which we shall now return, Ajax is the undisputed hero. Even though Sophocles has him die halfway through the play, the whole action is centered on his person. And he stands alone. The other characters have their disagreements between themselves, but their quarrels are as nothing if compared with the great gulf which separates Ajax both from his enemies and from his retainers. This stark cleavage between the hero and the rest of the characters is of course quite usual in Sophocles. But in the *Ajax* the incompatibility between hero and nonheroes is rendered with extraordinary pathos. And one of the means whereby the writer manages to make the contrast so impressive is his handling of the concepts of time. Menelaus and Odysseus, but also Tecmessa and Teucer, might say with Shelley's Urania:

But I am chained to Time, and cannot thence depart.

Time is the movement of the cosmic stream, and the cosmos is prior to its parts. Hence living men are hollow specters or empty shadows, as Odysseus puts it early in the play (125). The insubstantiality of man is the greater because the rationale of time is not apparent. The philosopher who said "Everything is in motion," also said "Time is a child playing a game of draughts; the kingship is in the hands of a child." In the eyes of the nonheroic characters of tragedy, then, man is not the master of his fate, nor even of his personality, because he is molded and refashioned continually as a stone is polished in the stream which carries it.

But the container need not be inimical, or at least so men's optimism prompts them to suppose. In a friendly guise time pretends the role of a companion or a protector. The delusion can go further, as in this quotation from Plato's *Laws* (4.721C3):

> Mankind are coeval with the whole of time, and are ever following, and will ever follow, the course of time; and so they are immortal, because they leave children's children behind them, and partake of immortality in the unity of generation.

The delusory concept of time as a fellow traveller and sanctifier of man is an index of the recuperatory power of the human soul, but also of its need to be supported and comforted. Man welcomes the bearing which he himself, hopefully, reads into time; he clings to time because it appears to incorporate a sequence, a structure, which may give meaning and direction to his own existence.

So long as there is felt to be a direction, it is not really important whether the direction perceived is forward or backward. When Ajax has died the chorus sings (925):

> You were destined, alas, hard-hearted one,
> you were destined to drain an evil share
> of numberless infinite toils.

Here the movement is toward a predestined goal. The suffering, and in the end the death, are interpreted as the final causes of Ajax's adventures from the start. But then, less than ten lines later (933):

> A great inceptor of sufferings was
> that time when the contest for the arms
> engaged the hands of the best.

For the chorus, time is either a movement coming to a head or a movement from a source. Hindsight creates the illusion that we know which of the two it is that rules our affairs. But in actual fact, as the two conflicting formulations show, there is no way of ascertaining the flow of the stream. It implicates the witness in its suprapersonal sweep, but that is all we can know about it until whatever additional knowledge we may gain no longer matters.

Time the companion is a popular misconception. And so is time the softener of pain. After Tecmessa has given her rousing report of the killing of the cattle, she remarks on the beginning of Ajax's recovery (306):

> . . . and at long odds, with the help of time, regains his senses.

Tecmessa believes that time, even injurious time, provides its own healing. Once the disease has run its full course, the very length of the aberration will function as a palliative. Compare the chorus, in their ode of joy (714):

> Great time assuages all!

The phrase is an echo of Ajax's famous lines cited at the beginning of this essay, but there is a difference. Ajax, in his apostrophe to cosmic and social instability, had said that time reveals and hides beyond reckoning, as if it were an immense receptacle consuming and regurgitating by turns. The chorus cannot for themselves entertain so philosophic a picture. Its purely dynamic quality does not furnish them with the solace they need. So they see time as quenching or softening all. The greatest fury or passion or suffering, and that means: whatever is hard and brittle, is mellowed and abated with time. This is the worship of time as the great inurer, the dispenser of balm, which— or at least so they think—always operates predictably. The sentiment is common and indeed plebeian. What saves it from triteness is the particular verb used by the chorus which I have translated: "assuages." Its original meaning is "to put out a fire," and we may well regard as a burning flame the madness whose subsidence the chorus is anticipating. But by the time of Sophocles the verb had generally come to mean "destroy," "make wither." So even the built-in healing power of great time is not respectful of substance. It cancels out the evil; but it cannot be expected to put anything in its place. Softening is not transformation, but deprivation.

ii

The notion of time as a stream or a container, or, more mercurially, as a companion or a healer, is the notion held by the men and women ranged opposite Ajax. It is the popular, the non-heroic perspective, for lesser men, or rather for all men, except the hero. Men must either cower before time, or nestle in its lap, or measure their achievements against an imagined direction and speed of time, to preserve their sense of purpose and substance. The perspective may be mistaken, or even immoral, as the hero might suggest. But without the feeling that man is dependent upon time and subservient to it an important prop would be missing from the basis of social life and social cooperation.

Now in spite of the vulgar optimism which claims to be able to read a sense of progress or alleviation from our involvement in the current of time, there are moments when even the most optimistic see neither direction nor speed. It is then that men speak of *tyche,* fortune. The Latin *fortuna,* based on the verbal stem *fer-,* which means "to carry," plainly points to the image of the stream which I have been developing. The Greek *tyche* has a slightly different orientation. Literally it means "structure" or "tissue." When Tecmessa or the chorus refer to their situation or their prospect as *tyche*—and they do this repeatedly—they acknowledge their awareness of a structure, of some larger fabric of which they declare themselves to be captive members. Along with the presence of the structure they also acknowledge their own blindness vis-à-vis any meaning or purpose the structure may embody. By the time Sophocles wrote his plays the emphasis in *tyche* had come to rest on the unintelligibility of the tissue, or on the oppressive tightness of it. When a person speaks of *tyche,* the current of time is felt to be so densely poured about the victim that all sense of motion is lost. The only thing left is hope, the hope that the chance is after all flowing properly and toward an auspicious end.

Tecmessa has learned of the announcement by Calchas that Ajax will come to grief unless he is kept within the camp on this one day of his life. Terrified, she implores the chorus to protect her against what she calls (803) "coercive fortune." Exactly the same words had been used by her earlier when speaking to Ajax about the unkindness of her fate which reduced her from princess to concubine (485). The appeal to fortune, or rather the mixture of protest and surrender to it, is once more representative of ordinary unheroic humanity. "Coercive fortune" may be experienced as a single incident or accident, as when, in Euripides' *Electra,* Orestes is said to have died of it: he fell from his chariot in a race. But more properly, and more profoundly, it designates the whole tight web of untracked circumstance. Plato's principle of Necessity, for instance, is of this order. Tragedy prepared this concept of a structure without meaning, of a fabric whose function it is to oppress without revealing its nature or identity. *Tyche* may be broken up into many points, each of them blind, unrelated, gratuitous. But most significantly *tyche* is not event but circumstance, the whole web rather than its strands.

When Ajax is at the height of his madness, Athena asks him what he has done with Odysseus. Literally the question runs (102): "At what point of fortune do you have him stand?" Odysseus, like all other ordinary mortals who mind their manners and worship the gods, has his fortune which determines his successes and failures. The significant thing here is that Athena tricks the raging Ajax into believing that he, Ajax, can plot Odysseus' fortune for him. That is indeed madness, for fortune cannot be plotted or engineered. But it is a madness which is characteristic of the heroic intelligence. For, as we shall see later, Ajax's handling of time bears a close resemblance to such tampering with fortune.

Fortune as an object of popular reflection and hope and despair is one of the pervasive themes of Greek tragedy. In the plays of Aeschylus references to fortune are especially prominent in the choral passages, particularly in the *Persians,* and in the speeches of heralds and servants, and in the warnings issued by the heroes. For their own persons, the heroes do not rely on fortune. The only one who seems to do so, King Pelasgus in the *Suppliants* (380), does so at a juncture when he has declared himself subject to popular vote, and that means: when he has ceased to be a hero. Thus from the very beginning of the writing of tragedy, heroes are treated differently from other men; they do not feel themselves embraced and controlled by a *tyche.* Much later, in Euripides, the rule comes to be relaxed. As is to be expected in a playwright whose heroes are "people like ourselves," enmeshed in atrocious circumstance, Euripides does feature the concept of fortune in the self-appraisals of his heroes. In Sophocles, however, the older tradition was fully kept up, in all plays, that is, except the *Oedipus Coloneus* and the *Philoctetes,* where the chief characters, bowed down by old age or sickness, do not enjoy the sense of freedom and animal vigor which characterizes the more typical Sophoclean hero. In the *Oedipus Rex* the rule of fortune is emphasized by the chorus, by Jocasta, and especially by Tiresias, the riddling prophet, mouthpiece of the people, chastiser of kings and heroes. Oedipus steadfastly refuses to acknowledge so irrational a structure as fortune. Only toward the end, just before his eyes are fully opened to the terror of his situation, does he, in a frenzied speech, ostentatiously call himself the son of Fortune. And by doing so, by accepting the vision of Jocasta and Tiresias and the messenger and all the others who lack in heroism, he temporarily betrays his mission as a hero (1080).

In the *Oedipus* it is Tiresias who spearheads the attack of those who flock to the standards of fortune. In the *Ajax* the same function is performed by Calchas, his colleague in the skill of prophecy. There is, however, a difference in formulation, and this introduces us to yet another conception of time, allied to that of fortune. When the web of fortune becomes, as it often will, too oppressive to be endured, the hard-pressed victim attempts, not to tear and break the fabric, but to find a natural opening, a chink in the structure, to crawl through into what he hopes will be freedom. Then men are like mice trying to escape from a maze, busily seeking the one hole which leads into the open. This chink, or as we may call it, this nick in the strands of time, rarely discovered but always hoped for, is the object of many sighs and prayers in Sophoclean tragedy, and especially in the *Ajax.* Its discovery would furnish the answer to the feeling "So long already . . .," which expresses not a sense of progress, or even duration, but merely weariness and exhaustion. The Greek word for the nick in time is *kairos.* Before the classical age it denoted the vacuum between two strands of the warp. By the time of Sophocles, and actually long before, the meaning of *kairos* had been narrowed down to refer to one fabric only, the fabric of time.

When Teucer and Agamemnon almost came to blows over the

question of the burial, Odysseus, as the chorus acknowledge (1316), comes in the nick of time to prevent bloodshed. When Teucer recapitulates the past deeds of Ajax, reminding the Greeks to be grateful to a man who has done so much for them, he stresses that Ajax once saved all of them in the nick of time (1274):

> When you were penned within your own defenses,
> your very lives poised on the turn of a spear,
> he came and rescued all of you, unaided,
> as flames were licking round the edges of
> the towering ship-decks, and while Hector pressed
> across the ditch to leap into the hull.

Circumstance is here pictured as a dense envelope of barriers and fire and smoke and attacking foes, until Ajax shows a way out of the impasse. The actual word *kairos* is not used on this occasion, but the language points to the same basic conception.

The nick of time, with its overtones of last-minute salvation and miracle and happy ending, is an eminently popular concept. This is obvious not only from the tragedies but more significantly from another genre to which I have already made reference to verify popular attitudes, namely, the late romances, the pulp literature of the ancient world. The heroes and heroines of the romances are constitutionally incapable of seeing anything but coercive fortune. They are thoroughly immobilized by this vision, for, by the conventions of the genre, their superior status renders them more sensitive to the tyrannic rule of fortune than other men. In the end they require the assistance of friends or trusted slaves, less intelligent and less sensitive but cleverer and more inventive, to find the hole in the net which imprisons them. Similarly, though less obviously, *kairos* plays an important role in the ancient arts of medicine and rhetoric. The instinct for the best moment, for the singular occasion when the practitioner could cut through the limiting conditions and achieve the results which ultimately lead to conversion or salvation: this attention to *kairos* looms as large in the writings of the Hippocratics as in the handbooks of the rhetoricians. Neither the orator nor the medical man is foolish enough to think that he can subvert the massive processes of organic or spiritual life. But his skill tells him that the processes are not completely closed, that there are gaps and openings in the structure which he may ascertain and through which he may hope to effect his ends.

In the tragedies the nick of time, or the main chance, is of course the central concern in the plays of intrigue, such as the *Philoctetes* or the *Electra*. For the rest *kairos* is in the popular domain. Aeschylus indeed does not make much use of the notion; in Euripides the nick of time, like fortune, has come to be associated with the hopes of the heroes as well as with those of the commoners. But in Sophocles, *kairos* is an object of popular expectations and of popular despair. In our play, *kairos* is, toward the middle of the plot, used as a pivot of the action. From Calchas, via the messenger, we learn that Athena's wrath is destined to strike Ajax only during this one day, and only under certain conditions. If he can be kept in his tent, safely out of reach of the divine punishment, in careful and sorry seclusion, he will be saved (753, 756, 801 f.). To cite the colloquial comment of the chorus (786):

> It's a close shave; somebody won't be happy!

This is the people's perspective, romantic, bustling, subservient to chance. Ajax will have nothing to do with it. It is beyond good and evil; the fact that on this particular day Ajax could be saved is not related in due proportion to anything he has done or not done. For any crimes he may have committed he has been punished already, through the madness and through his loss of prestige. If the possibility of salvation is to be understood as a reward for his earlier conduct it is surely unworthy of his great merits. The salvation which would accrue to him in the nick of time is self-generating, meaningless and sordid, an application of plebeian hopes, enacting the survival of the unfittest. And so Ajax deceives his retainers and escapes to die.

Finally, perhaps the most useful fiction as regards time is the dogma that time is not an unstructured mass but that it is articulated, and that clock time is a realistic apprehension of time as such. This is a view which comes close to the philosopher's interpretation of time as a function of our own development. As a matter of fact the most suc-

cinct formulation of the view is found in Aristotle: time is the counting off of motion; its nature is numerical. Characteristically, throughout Aristotle's discussion of the subject in the fourth book of his
Physics, we are conscious of a certain mercantile flavor, as if Aristotle
meant to say that time made us into shopkeepers who handle weights
and measures and reduce the business of life into distinct quantities.
In spite of the stirring picture of the high-minded man in Aristotle's
Ethics, the general tenor of his moral philosophy is practical and businesslike. Even the best man, the philosopher, is a reckoner, a de-
cipherer of mysteries and a calculator of astronomical relations.

In tragedy, business, or engineering, the meticulous tracking and
analyzing of numerical relations is usually a mark of the nonheroic.
At the very beginning of the *Ajax,* Odysseus comes forward as a
tracker following the footprints of Ajax. Significantly the language is
not so much from hunting as from business (5):

> . . . measuring
> his freshly minted tracks . . .

The use of the countinghouse image stamps Odysseus as an ordinary
man. Others are similarly characterized. Tecmessa, for one, though
an honorable lady, counts like a fishmonger. On one occasion (265)
she establishes, by a bastard syllogism, that because two pains are
worse than one, the present condition, after Ajax has awakened to
his crime, is worse than that before.

But not until it is applied to time does the counting theme find its
most natural validation. Again and again the chorus literally count
the days, as though the counting could convince them that time was
advancing toward fulfillment rather than merely grinding them down.
In their last ode, not a particularly distinguished song but typical for
the use of the counting theme, they ask: (1185, tr. Jebb):

> When, ah when will the number of the restless years be
> full, at what term will they cease, that bring on me the
> unending woe of a warrior's toils?[2]

---

[2] R. C. Jebb (ed. and trans.), *Sophocles: The Plays and Fragments,* Pt. vii: *The
Ajax* (Cambridge, England, Cambridge University Press, 1896), p. 179.

On that occasion their counting does not give them joy; on others it
is their only sustenance. And of course the hope that on this one day . . .
in this nick of time . . . matters will be righted, is itself a convergence
of the counting urge upon one critical date in the calendar. Without
the fiction of the calendar and of red-letter days most men would be
lost. Not so Ajax; he disdains such reckoning and despises the reckon-
ers. When he places his sword in position to receive the thrust of his
body, he says (815):

> The slayer stands where he should do his work
> of cutting best, supposing anyone has
> leisure and interest for such calculations.

His contempt for numbering is shown most acutely at the point when
he first decides to commit suicide and ponders the business approach
to life (473):

> Only a coward hankers after the
> full tally of his life . . .
> What joy is there in the totaling of days,
> each crediting or debiting death by turns?
> I would not buy a man of no account
> who heats his heart with empty expectations.

The hero does not count, he lives, and when life becomes a sordid
business of ticking off days, he sacrifices life.

Once, it is true, Ajax himself turns enumerator. He has come out
of the tent to show himself to the chorus and Tecmessa. As he begins
to recover his calm and change from singing to spoken verse he ex-
claims (432) "Aiai!"; and then, after suggesting a punning connection of this cry of pain with his own name, he continues:

> Once, twice, three times I must cry out "Aiai!"
> to match the torment of my present pains.

Is Ajax here indulging in a harsh parody of the common pose, or has
his torment temporarily reduced him to the sensations of an ordinary
man? The four words which make up the last line of our translation

might be thought to reinforce this interpretation; more literally Ajax says: "Such are the troubles in which I am fortuned." But an uncertainty remains. The passage clearly forms an exception to the ideological pattern I have traced. It seems to me rather unlikely that Sophocles would use such key-notions as "fortune" and the counting theme for the purpose of psychological realism, to mark the ups and downs of an unstable personality. Unless, with some classical scholars, we are willing to believe that in Sophocles fixed characters count for nothing and that each scene or action creates its own imagery and precipitates its own mood, the language of Ajax as he begins to address the chorus remains puzzling. It will, perhaps, be best to remind ourselves that symbolism in Greek tragedy is not a hard-and-fast technique, distributing terms in accordance with a rigorous plan. It is too often assumed that the images in a Greek drama respond to a sort of mathematical analysis. There are occasions when the imagery defies a complete reduction. This is one of those occasions, and it is probably the wisest course to leave the puzzle as it is, a suitable reminder that the critic's machinery is never perfect.

iii

Ajax's general position, at any rate, is unmistakable, and we must now try to assess it. Aristotle tells a tale about certain men in Sardinia who slept with the gods, and upon awakening did not feel that time had passed. Similarly in the first book of the *Iliad*, while Achilles converses with Athena time stands still; nobody else notices that Achilles is taking time out, and when the conversation is over he and Agamemnon continue their quarrel where they had left it, as if no interruption had occurred. By virtue of sleeping with the gods or conferring with them, a man may hope not merely to crawl through a chink in the texture of time but to leave time behind grandly and without effort. Dionysus and his mysteries hold out the same hope, offering the comatose sleep of the wine-soaked as a special instrument for the conquest of time and the achievement of timelessness. But this is the plebeian way; sleeping with the gods is incomparably easier than talking or, as the Bible has it, walking with a god. The achievement of timelessness is difficult enough; the conscious enjoyment of it is an exceptional privilege.

Yet the hope persists, above all in the breast of the man who feels himself to be different from the common run, and who wishes to preserve his being as a definable identity. Any change, according to the Greek view, is in its nature a disturbance, the dislocation of an identity. A man who is somebody, who has achieved a standing of his own and wants to retain it, must begin to regard time as aimless and destructive, as an effacer of achievement and status. As a result he conceives the wish to place himself beyond the effects of time, and to oppose its functioning. But this can be done only at the peril of his life; by insisting on his identity and braving the advances of time, the hero cuts himself off from his surroundings. In the end he may find that he has preserved a shell rather than a living soul. Archilochus drew the picture of a man rolling himself up like a hedgehog and presenting nothing but bristles to the hostile influences from abroad. But does a hedgehog permanently rolled up continue to live as a hedgehog? Does he not rather become a generic specter of the race?

The Sophoclean hero, and in fact many tragic heroes, are in precisely this position. He is not as other men are, he has a distinct being, more real than that of others, which cries to be preserved from contamination and change. Exactly what this being is, he may not know himself in every instance; we ourselves are hard put to it to define the heroic nature. But whatever it is, we do know how it behaves. It seeks to perpetuate itself against mutation, and to stabilize the world which it dominates. And to do this, it must oppose the agent of change, time.

Lucretius, it will be recalled, claims that time does not exist apart from things. That is the philosophical view, the view from the study, across the top of the desk. For the hero times exists because in his insistence on his rights he challenges it to a duel and thereby provokes its operation. He summons time, and time, rising to the challenge, attacks and destroys. There are only two things time can do when its current is blocked and it is bidden to turn against a man. It can either strip off the presumptuous veneer and lay open the common weakling under the heroic mask. We then speak of Time the Revealer, time which brings out into the open the hidden truth, the heart of the man. Or, if the challenger is a true hero, time must cut straight through him and kill. Time breasted either reveals or annihilates.

It is part of the subtlety of Sophoclean drama that we are tempted halfway through the play to think that we have witnessed the work of Time the Revealer. When Oedipus calls himself a son of Fortune, or when Ajax makes his gentle speech about the irresistible mastery of time, the disguise seems to have dropped off, and the hero seems to have joined the ranks of the commoners after all. Antigone's "break-down," when she is about to be led off to burial (806 ff.), is of a similar nature, and equally illusory. For these are heroes through and through, and time cannot cease until it has entirely demolished their mortal status.

In the present play the lever of time's attack, or better, the cause of hostilities between Ajax and time, is a part of the antecedents of the plot: the award of the arms of Achilles. From Teucer we learn (1135) that Menelaus and some of the other leaders had exercised an improper influence on the voting. In the eyes of Ajax and his party the contest for the arms was decided by a rigged election. The con-sciousness of this maneuver helps to feed the glow of their resentment, for the corruption of the others is thought to be sufficient proof that Ajax is in the right. But even if the election had been perfectly fair and proper, nothing would have been different. The use of the ballot expresses the views of the people, and the hero must not be subject to their whims.

The manner in which the decision was reached pales to insignifi-cance beside the outcome of the decision itself. The result of the con-test shows that, given the old-fashioned warrior, Ajax, and the mod-ern man of reason, Odysseus, the leadership now goes to the latter. Historically speaking, Ajax is getting to be out of date. He finds him-self at odds with the advance of time, in the sense of social and po-litical progress. In the simple, unselfconscious terms of Greek political thought: time changes the good man into the bad. The man who has been looked up to and imitated in one era will be laughed at or dis-

regarded in the next. The Homeric soldier has become worse than useless in the age of democracy and committee work and elegant compromise. Reason and reasonableness are the new ideals; fixity of character,
the proud unbudging manliness of the old order, is felt to be coarse
and dangerous. Calchas, the representative of the people, gives voice
to the new creed of flexibility and circumspection. As reported by the
messenger he says (758):

> Excessive and unthinking bodies are
> struck down by massive hardships from the gods,
> . . . when a mortal man
> thinks thoughts outranking his mortality.

Athena also at the end of her epiphany, before the entrance of the
chorus, announces the creed of humility, though in terms at once more
traditional and also less relevant to the situation at hand (127): Do
not talk back to the gods, do not pride yourself on strength or wealth;

> a single day may elevate or abase
> all mortal things; the gods love and protect
> all men of reason, and the bad they hate.

Where it stands, Athena's little speech has an air of unreality, if not
cynicism, about it. Ajax has not prided himself on his wealth, nor has
he, yet, spoken unbecomingly to the gods. But beyond all doubt he is
not a reasonable man. Thus it would seem that in the opinion of
Athena his lack of sophistication puts him in the same class as the
nouveaux riches and the blasphemers. This is disconcerting; but Sophocles complicates the puzzle even further. To emphasize the monumental stubbornness of the hero on the stage he has Athena pretend to
the audience that in the past, in the pages of the *Iliad,* Ajax had
been an excellent man at thinking ahead and meeting emergencies
with forethought and intelligence (119):

> Could you have found a man more provident,
> more gifted to effect what chance required?

Athena wants us to believe that before Ajax was overwhelmed by the
storm he had worked in harmony with time. This epitaph on his al-

leged former self, proffered at a moment when Ajax is suffering the worst pangs of his hallucinations, is a bare-faced mockery of the truth. Even in the old epic Ajax was in no sense a pliable or thoughtful man. His present truculence and rigidity are simply the continuation of a personal pattern set from the earliest beginnings of the tradition. Athena pretends the opposite only because, from the vantage point of the gods, Ajax's resistance to time is a betrayal of the human portion, hence Ajax must have changed. Or, conversely, Athena cannot admit to herself what happens to be the truth, namely, that the gods have changed along with the society which they symbolize. The gods are eternally true to themselves, hence Ajax is not the same as before. This is what Athena says; but the drama refutes her judgment.

Ajax offers himself to be crushed by insisting on a role that is no longer viable, and by opposing time with the same unerring vigor that had laid low so many opponents in the past. Time attacks, and in a mighty explosion the magnificent unrepenting self is disintegrated and the remains handed over to *Ate,* the ruinous demon that infests all fallen angels. This *ate,* this damnation, has a grandeur of its own, the grandeur which attends a catastrophe of major proportions. Odysseus, too lightly moved to fellow feeling, pities Ajax for his new companion (123), but the chorus, in one of their passages of poetic insight, thrill at the vision of their lord (195)

> burning with a heavenly *ate.*

They sing this when calling on Ajax to come out of his seclusion in the tent and fight for his soiled name. Literally the line may be translated in two ways: either "fanning the flame of an *ate* that reaches the sky," or "burning with an *ate* sent from the sky." I suspect that the chorus mean the former; they think of Ajax deliberately kindling the flame of his madness. The implication that he could, if he wished, quench the fire is flattering, and indicative of the esteem in which they hold him. But alas, the second interpretation is the correct one; the curse is heaven-sent because it is the tragic concomitant of the victory of time.

When eventually Ajax recovers his senses, there are many symptoms to show that he is a broken man. Witness the terrible cries (308, 317) such as he had never uttered before; the man of the terrifying battle shout becomes a person of shrill wailing and piercing lament. In a rapid succession of unheroic moods he begs the bystanders to kill him, he rails at them for not leaving him alone in his misery, and he complains that the villains whom he meant to slaughter got away. This mixture of moods makes it apparent even to the chorus, blind and forgiving as they are in their regard for their master, that the old authority is gone. In a bitter, undignified outbreak against Odysseus, the modern man, Ajax stoops to using slang, the sort of mobsters' cant known to us from Aristophanic comedy, as if the destruction of his old manhood had made him over into a glib member of the hated crowd (381, 389). In the end, exhausted by this exhibition of meanness and vulgarity, Ajax has an apostrophe to

> Darkness, my light,
> most brilliant gloom!

and prays to be admitted to the nether world. It is at this point (401), when the full measure of his undoing begins to dawn on him, that Ajax recognizes the role of Athena in his destruction.

We may well ask about the function of Athena in this tale of the hero unstrung. Generally the tragedians use the gods for any one of the following purposes. One: the presence of a god may herald an immutable truth or symbolize some reality or trend which is greater than individual men. Of this there is very little in the play. The Athena who gloats over the sickness of Ajax is not comparable to the Zeus who stands for Justice, or the Aphrodite who stands for the cosmic power of Love. Two: the gods may be employed as stage hands, to assemble an enormous and superhuman event, which must be shown to flow from a higher source if it is to be properly impressive. This we do find in the play, for Athena is the ostensible creator of the sickness which overpowers Ajax at the moment of his defeat. Homer had taught his followers that even the most revolting disease will appear petty in the scheme of things unless it can be shown to have been sent by a god. We cannot like or admire the Athena of the Prologue, but her divinity is unquestionable, and through the fiction of her responsibility the madness of the hero takes on an aspect of majesty and awesomeness which it would otherwise lack.

Three: the gods are given the task of humbling men, either to humanize or to barbarize them. If tragedy is, as is widely held, a dramatic treatment of the fall of the proud, this function of the gods as levelers and agents of punishment is a necessary component in all tragedy, not only ancient drama. The proud cannot fall unless they are pushed, and somebody has to do the pushing. This is not just a matter of texture or technique, for the moral situation demands that the punisher be more powerful than the proud. That humiliation at the hands of the gods is an important element in our play is obvious. But if that were all we should have to ask why Sophocles chose to present Athena only at the beginning, and why he drew her character as he did. For the Athena of the Prologue is less a punisher or discipliner from the heavens than a churlish and rebellious friend, a former associate turned disloyal and resentful. Indeed, the personality of the goddess as pictured by Sophocles goes far to rule out the probability that her appearance in the tragedy was designed *primarily* for the purposes mentioned under Two and Three. She does not have the necessary majesty to be entirely successful in turning the sickness into a splendid horror, and she is too vindictive to satisfy the requirements of divine justice and retribution.

Athena's principal role in the *Ajax* is to dramatize the collapse of the hero. This explains why her appearance is restricted to the Prologue. We come to be acquainted with Ajax through her, and when we feel we know him she leaves the stage, never to return. Her departure and her absence are felt keenly not only by Ajax but through him by the audience. For, as Athena herself recalls to our memory (90), she is his ally and chief assistant. Historically that is correct; she had been his champion in the past, both in his own past and in the past of the audience, in the tales learned at school. But—and this is where the difficulty began—she had also been the champion of Odysseus. In Homer both Ajax and Odysseus are the chosen warriors; the dual character of the goddess, mingled of fierce militancy and cool calculation, had found something in each of them to respond to. Now a new day has arisen and Athena must declare herself for the one or the other. The decision is never in doubt; as the protecting divinity of democratic Athens, as the people's guardian, she must espouse Odysseus. This means, as Tecmessa perceives (953), that she must hurt Ajax.

But this is mythological superstructure. It is not that Athena turns against Ajax, but he destroys himself in his heroic stand against time, and Sophocles uses the violent swagger and then the abrupt departure of the goddess to highlight the self-destruction in a way which is not accessible to a more direct portraiture. With Athena gone from his side Ajax is a doubly broken man. He is obsessed with his loss; again and again he ponders the disappearance of his ancient ally. Significantly he never mentions her by name; his sense of injury and the memory of his former greatness permit nothing more than hints and circumlocutions. The catastrophe is, after all, of his own making. The brief materialization of the goddess at the beginning, when he is mad, helps to underscore his desolation when he recovers and finds her gone. But he is too honest to deflect outward upon her what he knows in his heart to be the fruit of his own commitment.

iv

> Now our fierce, magnificent leader,
> Ajax, is brought low,
> sickened with a turbulent winter.

Thus Tecmessa (205), at her first appearance. That Ajax's behavior when the play opens is due to a sickness, a malignant demon attacking the soul of man and perverting his actions, cannot be doubted by anyone. There are many clues which underline the strangeness of his conduct. We learn, for instance, that in moving out against the Greek chieftains he proceeded stealthily, under cover of night (47). This method of warfare may have been effective enough in the bloody guerrilla actions of Sophocles' own time, but it is contrary to what we would have expected of the historical Ajax, or of the Ajax of the tragedy as he sees himself. Unlike Odysseus and Diomedes he is not likely to go on night patrols, pouncing on men in their sleep and massacring them without the sanction of challenge and counterchallenge. The truth of the matter is that the sickness has begun long before he starts cutting down the cattle. It must be thought as originating with his loss in the contest for the arms. The sickness, then, is not so much a consequence of his defeat by time as a symbol of it. The killing of the cattle is only the final spasm of the ordeal, coincident with the final demolition of the heroic soul. Further than this the sickness cannot go; Ajax must wake up, to find himself destroyed.

The butchering of the cattle is one of those conceptions which make the spectator wince both at the enormity of the thing and at its appropriateness. All the characters in the play refer to it, and several describe it in detail, as if each wanted to outbid the others with the picturesqueness of his report. Tecmessa even describes the scene twice. But only the second version is a report in the proper sense of the word. The first is part of an excited exchange with the chorus, chanted rather than spoken, and conveying the awful truth through the mediation of an image, the image of the wintry storm. The chorus of sailors conjure up the spectacle of a tempest, with the raging Ajax at its center and the swell of ridicule tossing the waves. "Pull for safety!" the chorus shout to one another, and try to make their escape. Thus this account of the madness is garbed in a vision more immediately relevant to the professional interests of the choristers, and appealing strongly to our love of metaphor. For the time being, the imagery cushions our perceptions. But then Tecmessa declares the storm ended (257):

> But wait! The lightning is gone; like the wind
> from the south, though at first violent and sharp,
> he is calming down.

She invites the chorus to join Ajax in waking up to the truth and surveying the terrible results. And now, finally, we are in a position to listen to her detailed communication, without taking refuge in metaphorical extensions and extenuations.

As she tells the story, the savagery of Ajax's treatment of the animals is thrown into cruel relief, and so is the senseless confusion of the deed. The cutting, the dismembering, the severing of tongues, the torturing, and the grim jubilation, all are sharply etched in our memories. But there is some uncertainty concerning the identity of the animals killed. Tecmessa speaks of bulls, and the image is almost flattering to the sons of Atreus intended by it. But elsewhere the talk is of rams, or even he-goats (cf. 237, 297, 309, 374, 1061). It does not matter; it is enough that Ajax sees his enemies as less than human, and that the reporters capture the violence of his mood. A too nice distinction between the several species might have done an injustice to the quality of his delusion. It is the treatment of the victims which counts, not the specific nature of their animal disguise. Two of them are killed outright; they stand for the sons of Atreus. One is flogged and flayed before he is put to death; that is Odysseus, suffering the fate which in the eyes of Ajax he deserves, the fate of an impious runaway slave.

What kind of a madness is it that makes a man mistake innocent cattle and sheep for his enemies? Or rather, is "madness" the right word for it? For the similes in Homer suggest that Ajax is acting out a fantasy which, in its way, is as truthful as the reality he wakes up to, and, who knows, perhaps even truer. Later in the play Sophocles gives us a number of hints that, seen in a certain perspective, men and cattle are ranged more closely together than our waking experience would allow. Tecmessa in describing the shrill wailing of the broken Ajax comments (319):

> He used to think that to indulge in such
> laments was good enough for dreary cowards.
> Himself, instead of high-pitched strident wails,
> would give a husky groan, like a bull lowing.

His enemies employ the same comparison. Witness Agamemnon, who contrasts the old-fashioned warrior with the new (1253):

> A little whip causes the big-flanked ox
> to trot obediently along the path.

Agamemnon is wrong, of course; more than a little whip is needed even in the case of Teucer, to whom this statement ostensibly applies. But the comparison is in order; like Ajax himself all the characters tend to put the traditional hero in the same class as the lead-animal of the herd. A Homeric warrior is like a bull, or a ram. But for reasonable people that is all; a comparison is only a manner of speaking and no more.

Ajax goes further. He reverts to a mentality which preceded the advent of reason and culture and kindliness. In a throwback to primitiveness he chooses to live in a world where man and animal are not distinct, where the leader is not *like*, but *is*, a bull or a ram, and mutual preying and killing are the norm. What more suitable condition for a man who has set himself against time? If this interpretation seems fanciful a piece of etymological evidence may help to remove our scruples. *Presbys*, the Greek word for "elder," literally means "chief bull." I am not suggesting that the Greeks had once known a totemistic social organization, or that the contemporaries of Sophocles were completely aware of the etymological components of the word. But the existence of the word and its derivation suggest that dignity and leadership among the group were at one time seen as analogous to the standing of the lead-animal in the herd. Mythology with its hybrid shapes, the simile, and the theriomorphic objects of popular religion kept alive in the Greeks an understanding of the aboriginal identity of man and beast. By a punishment worthy of an Orphic hell Ajax is forced to live the life which in his resistance to time he has put himself on record as wanting to live. The killing of the beasts becomes not so much a madness as the full realization of his appetites.

The man-beast identity is not the only synthesis, to use the Freudian term relevant to the experience through which Ajax goes. Another unity of the same order is that which exists between Ajax and his armor. The self-induced hardening of the man is symbolized by the constant reference to the weapons he wields or to his military dress. Unlike the beast synthesis, which is largely compressed into one frenzied experience, the focus on the arms is used more subtly to give direction to a variety of scenes. Whether Ajax is on the stage or is being talked about while absent, whether he is mad or sane, he cannot be conceived apart from his arms. The nearest parallel is the biblical picture of Saul leaning on his spear or brandishing his spear or hurling it. Like Saul vis-à-vis David, Ajax persists in his attachment to his weapons at a time when diplomacy and flexibility have put the arms of the strong man out of the running. In the case of Ajax there is the added irony that the arms with which he is identified are not the arms of Achilles, hence are second best in addition to being out of date. But as he clings to the trappings of his glorious past he does not seem to realize that he is cherishing what at one time he was ready to reject.

In his so-called madness, his instrument is his sword. The first time Odysseus refers to him he calls him (19) "shield-bearing Ajax." This remains true throughout; references to the man always draw particular attention to his arms, as if they alone constituted his authority and accounted for much of his personality. By contrast the stress on Teucer's bow is minimal, and the others are associated with no weapons whatever. Ajax cannot act without at the same time activating his armament. Tecmessa is (211) "captured by the sword"; we are not allowed to forget that his past achievements, and that includes his marriage, are owed to the sword. As Ajax prepares himself for death he prays that Teucer will be one of the first to find him (828)

> fallen upon this sword still freshly moist.

The sword is placed in position, and Ajax becomes truly one with it, and Tecmessa finds him "folded around the sword," as the business-like Greek has it (899).

By the repeated emphasis on the tools of war, the suggestion of unwieldy size and hardness and isolation, Sophocles reduces the hero to a shell of his former flesh-and-blood self. His resistance to time has left him a hedgehog permanently rolled up and showing only his barbed armor. Ajax continues to treat Tecmessa as if he were the old Ajax of the proud days gone by. He demands obedience, refuses to think of her as an equal partner—never calls her by name—and barely regards her as a human being. He has none of the social graces, none of the fellow feeling toward social inferiors which the new age has made the fashion. When his son does not answer his summons immediately he breaks out in a fury; when the boy comes he forces him to look on the carnage of the cattle as if the scene of slaughter were a source of pride. In literary imitation of Hector's speech to Astyanax in the *Iliad,* he too addresses his son who is characteristically called "He of the Broad Shield." But the venture is only a surly replica of the old model. He praises the father of the boy, and expresses the hope that the boy will some day become like himself. He continues in his refusal to face the fact of time and development, even for his son. Instead there is much talk of his own father (434, 462, 471); he prefers to measure himself against the familiar dead past.

All this means that the attractive Ajax of the Homeric wars has been stopped in his tracks and has turned into a mockery of his former self. Instead of manhood he shows cruelty; instead of self-reliance, self-centeredness; instead of bravery, desperation; instead of pride, vanity and arrogance; instead of fighting strength, slaughter and mutilation. In an hour when he comes as close to kindness as he can he says to Tecmessa (594):

> You are, I think, a fool
> to suppose that you can educate my nature.

Time has killed off the man and then passed him by. On a stage as lively and hectic as that of any play in the Greek repertory, including even a shift of scenery and an exit and fresh entrance of the chorus—which is the sort of liveliness on which Aristotle frowned—Ajax rests at the center, outwardly joining in the busy play but inwardly hostile to involvement and setting his face against the commotion. It is instructive to contrast him with that other great figure of heroism, Prometheus, outwardly fixed in his chains but in his heart seething with social instincts, with programs of action, with a will toward progress. Prometheus, the crucified, is eternally young; Ajax has cut off his ties with life long before he goes into his death.

v

Both the plot and Ajax's belated insight into his situation demand that he die. But when the time for his death arrives, Sophocles has made things difficult for himself once more. By introducing the mechanism of the nick of time, with the suggestion that the hero might be saved on this one day, Sophocles has opened up the possibility that death will not be necessary after all. Yet the prospect of continued life for Ajax is intolerable and, worse than that, dramatically useless. A heroic death appears tragic only to the degree that it seems to be enacted by necessity. And so the playwright devises a means of neutralizing the intimations of *kairos:* the two blasphemies. In the Prologue, when Athena points self-righteously to the ravings of the hero and states that it is a deserved sickness, she says nothing about specific misdemeanors which might have brought on the punishment. There is nothing in the whole first half of the play which might temper our impression that Ajax suffers because of what he is, not because of what he may have done or failed to do.

But when Ajax has removed himself from the stage to die, though none of his followers suspects that this is the object of his excursion, the messenger who comes with news from Calchas upsets our assumptions. For the first time, and utterly without warning, we are told about two earlier occasions when Ajax showed himself less than discreet toward the gods (764):

> "Son," said his father, "bend your mind to win
> by the sword, and let the gods help you to win."
> But he, his pride blotting his sense, replied:
> "Even a nobody, father, could gain power
> if gods assist him; I propose to attract
> my glory by myself, without assistance."
> Such was his boasting. And later, again,
> when great Athena spurred him on and called
> on him to bathe his hands in enemy blood,
> he answered with a word of blasphemy:
> "Mistress, go and assist the other Greeks!
> Here where I stand the battle will be easy."

To speak thus about the gods, or to address them as Ajax is said to have done, is indeed blasphemous. If these tales are true we must revise our views concerning the background of his punishment. But there is something disconcerting about the reports, and particularly about their timing. If the audience was not familiar with these incidents—and I suspect that it was not, notwithstanding the ancient scribe's notice that there was a story in which Ajax threw Athena bodily from her chariot—then it would appear that Sophocles cites them remarkably late in the proceedings, and with a minimum of emphasis. Perhaps the moralizers needed an aetiology for Ajax's suffering, at a point just before the suffering culminates in death. The unthinking are happily reconciled to the death once they feel that it is a deserved penalty for specific crimes. But the two acts of blasphemy are mentioned only, as it were, in passing, and forgotten immediately thereafter. We must, I should think, conclude that Sophocles did not want to have the incidents understood as touching on the heart of the tragedy. The timing, the scope, and, not the least, the source of the information conspire to play down the importance of the crimes, for Calchas is not, in this play at any rate, an entirely reputable informant. The drama is saved from being just another morality tale about a proud mortal being punished for not sufficiently honoring the gods. The simple-minded in the audience, with whom an Athenian playwright always had to reckon, may have found satisfaction in such an interpretation, but those to whom structure and imagery and thematic development meant something would want to shrug it off.

And yet, the reports cannot be shrugged off entirely. Though the intelligence is late and inconspicuous, Ajax had dishonored the gods. His punishment, if it is a punishment, may not be related precisely to the blasphemies; but they are symptoms of a tendency inherent in all heroism, the tendency toward isolation and self-sufficiency and the cutting off of social ties. The new man, with his reason and his smallish sympathies, does not present an impressive front when compared with the true hero, but he is sure to adapt himself more easily to the whims of the gods. Let us say that Calchas' revelations illumine the character of Ajax from an angle which is more readily appreciated by the people than some other manifestations of his personality. The blasphemies are not the cause of his punishment; but they do give tangible evidence of the sort of man he is, on a level of action and behavior which can be judged more concretely than some of the subtler strokes of the artist's brush. The blasphemies help to round out the portrait of the man who is out of touch, and who attempts to regain his lost prestige by a factitious outbreak against authority.

Ajax first begins to think of suicide when the sickness is wearing off, immediately after the great storm has ended. He knows he is broken, and when he sings (412)

> Foaming courses of the sea,
> caves by the ocean, headland groves,
> too long, too long you have kept me here
> a prisoner in the Trojan land!

he temporarily adopts the outlook of the commoners. From an attacker, time has turned into an oppressor breaking his back. A little later he delivers his great speech on time, nonheroic time, that is. A speech not so much of dissembling, though there is some of that also, as of euphemism and apparent surrender. He now admits, or supposes, that he pities the woman—still no names—and the child, and that he regrets having to leave them among his enemies (652). He declares that he was wrong to rebel against the sons of Atreus; for without a hierarchy, without a chain of command, the world would collapse. And now the application: I must give in, for even the greatest powers give in in their time. The seasons give way to each other, night gives in to day, sleep to waking. Nor do values achieve stability; friendship lapses into enmity, enmity into friendship.

All this is of course foreign to the old Ajax. But it is no lie, for the old Ajax no longer exists, except fitfully and uncertain of himself. The attack of time first made him into a parody of the ancient warrior. Now it has made him over, for a short spell, into the new man; it has refashioned him so that now he travels with it instead of against it. But tragic heroes are not changed; they are undone. In this scene, with his magnificent baroque showpiece of a speech, Ajax has his hero's death. The corporeal suicide must follow. No explicit announcement is required, though there are enough double meanings embedded in his oration to give warning to those who know what a hero can do and what he cannot do. Later, in his monologue at the scene of death, when he is by himself on the beach, he conjures up his old personality once more, calling down curses upon the sons of Atreus and Odysseus, and unburdening himself of the vulgar perspective which gained him a free exit from the tent. But then it is too late.

How could Ajax be expected to live in a world in which mutation rules supreme? It is the tragedy of Ajax that the stable moorings of the heroic age as envisaged by Hesiod have been replaced by the relativism of the iron age, in which parents will quarrel with the children, host with guest, friend with friend. What Ajax does not realize is this, that the iron age is not entirely devoid of the better sentiments, of reverence and justice and the other social goods which Hesiod portrays as leaving men to their own foul and indeterminate devices. In truth, the new fluidity has its own attractions and its own positive values which Ajax cannot see, for his temporary admission of the universality of flux is a weakening, or a ruse, but not a conversion. Even in his unstrung, moribund state, he cannot see that change has either value or charm.

As he gets ready to die, Ajax prays, not to Athena, for obvious reasons, but to Zeus, the ancestor of his house; to Hermes, the guide from life to death; to the Furies, spirits of vengeance who can brake the flow of time and punish the sons of Atreus long after Ajax is gone; and to Helios, the bridger of space who is to inform Ajax's father of his death. The invocation of the Furies (835) is particularly interesting. It shows us an unreconstructed Ajax, one whose lapse into mildness and subservience now appears to have been only a brief episode—this will be important directly; interesting also because under the aegis of the Furies time relations are canceled out, the son suffers for the deeds of the father, so does the grandson, to revalidate the primitive pretemporal concept that the house is one and unanalyzable, and that the son and grandson live again, or better: live, the life of the father and grandfather. Similarly, in his prayer to the Sun (845) Ajax calls upon Helios to halt his course and stop his chariot, to interrupt the rotation of the day, when he comes to the place in the sky which looks down upon Salamis, in order to give the message to his father. On the threshold of his death, then, Ajax once more strains his whole being to interfere with the stream of time, and to re-establish the sacred fixity without which he cannot live. And this brings us to the turning point in the drama.

vi

The oracle had suggested that Ajax could be saved if he stayed safely home instead of venturing out into the open country. This is taken quite seriously by Tecmessa and the chorus. They are interested in saving life (812), no matter what sort of life. Now if Ajax had stayed home, physically and figuratively, he could have gone on living perhaps, but his life would have been a shadow existence, not unlike the kind of life which the Homeric heroes are compelled to live in Hades, a spectral existence without feeling or body or purpose. Even the beautiful poetry of the speech on time cannot deceive us into believing that the new Ajax is alive or real. For the hero, salvation must have a nobler meaning, not the commonplace romantic excitement associated with the nick of time, but a salvation which puts its stamp on the eternity of values, which preserves the true being of the man rather than the embers of his soul. This is what the second part of the play gives us. It shows us an Ajax who is saved more than if he had stayed alive, in disgrace, mocked and shunned. We know from Plato's portrait of Socrates in the *Apology* and the *Phaedo* that death can be regarded as a more effective means of preserving a man's special function and his individuality than a timid avoidance of death. Ajax dies and is saved, as a hero and a saint, a demon henceforth insolubly and perennially linked to the soil and fate of Athens and her citizens.

Here we have come to a point in the drama which was more meaningful to a Greek audience than to us. But we, too, by an act of the historical imagination, can learn to appreciate the propriety of what

Sophocles does with the material at hand. As suggested toward the end of the essay on the *Seven Against Thebes,* the demon, the life-giving and protective spirit whose dead body, resting in the soil of the land, ensures its fertility and its happiness, is a common Greek institution. If we look around among the various heroes chosen to be demons by the Greeks we find that all of them had in their lifetime committed some terrible crime. We need think only of Oedipus, of Heracles, and of the sons of Oedipus, all of them men whose acts fell far beyond the pale of civilized behavior, but who had nevertheless, or perhaps because of the immensity of their crimes, been transformed into protecting demons. The assumption seems to have been that the excess of vitality which made these men so dangerous in their mortal phase could now be counted on to benefit those whose powers are more circumscribed. Ajax, in Athens, was such a demon. One of the ten Athenian tribes was named after him, and the citizens relied on his beneficent presence to help Athens through many of her political and economic difficulties.

Hence, when *ate* makes Ajax commit slaughter and treason and sacrilege, he is already well on his way toward canonization. His sickness, ironically, becomes the instrument of his salvation. And when, on the verge of death, he invokes the Furies against the sons of Atreus, he is already practicing the arts of the competent demon cursing the enemies of his land. The suicide itself, though not perhaps regarded as sacrilegious as it is in modern religious thought, contributes its share to the making of the saint, by arousing the horror which always attends any forcible snuffing out of life. It appears, therefore, that in this special case time is not only destructive of the proud heroic self, but also creative of something new. The act of creation and its result are as unpredictable as the force destroying the man is mysterious. In Ajax it leads to demonship, and so the creation of time must also be recognized, in a sense, as a victory of Ajax. He is shattered as a hero, but reborn as a demon—in Greek, the word for "hero" and "demon" is the same—achieving the permanence for which he had longed, and justifying the harsh grandeur of his former self.

Now because Ajax is destined to be a demon, because, in fact, he is a demon the moment he has thrown himself on his sword, the question of burial comes to be of the greatest importance. Sophocles was fascinated with the theme of interment; in two of his extant plays he dramatizes the difficulties which block the burial of a demon in the making. In the *Antigone* the tragedy enacted is in part that of the burier. In the present play it is exclusively that of the buried. In both plays the author forces us to look upon the body of the dead, if not in the flesh, then through the reporting of messengers and mourners. In both plays the action revolves about a body and its disposition.

At first the body is shrouded from sight by trees (892). The act of death itself, I assume, was not witnessed by the audience. For the purpose Ajax steppped behind some stage obstruction where Tecmessa ultimately finds him. When the choristers ask to see the corpse (913) it is pulled into the open, but not before Tecmessa has thrown a coverlet over it. Only after Teucer has entered the stage, and on his orders, is the body fully revealed. This intercalation of a period when the body is not visible cushions the break between Ajax the crashed hero and Ajax the hero reborn. There should be no slow transition, no organic development between the two phases. For, as I have tried to suggest, they are really one, though human eyes may see them as irreconcilables. By withdrawing the body from open view for a short while, the author evades the ticklish question whether to dramatize the demonic status of Ajax as a corroboration of the old or as a radical departure from the old. Like the exit and re-entry of the chorus, the temporary concealment of the body serves as an interruption to make the audience forget everything that was pitiable or repugnant in the hero's behavior. At the least, it serves to obviate the wrong kind of question.

For a while, supposedly, Ajax's new status is no more assured than his old heroism had been toward the eve of his age. By a clever twist of dramatic irony Teucer comes only in the nick of time, as prayed for by Tecmessa (921), to preserve the body against the machinations of the detractors. But even if Teucer had not come in good time to forestall the enemies, the damage would have affected only the Athenians

themselves, not Ajax, who is now beyond the reach of temporal af-
flictions. In spite of the abuse heaped upon him, he is secure in his
demonship. When Teucer, Tecmessa, and Eurysaces in a touchingly
intimate ceremony cut their hair in sacrifice over the corpse, we are
assured that, whatever further wrangling may be in store, Ajax is now
at rest, even before he is put in the grave. His survival underground
has been authenticated by those nearest to him.

The acrimonious exchanges which follow are not likely to make us
miss the fact that with the death of Ajax the progress of the play has
come to a dead stop. While Ajax was alive, though only the broken
tally of a man, things moved swiftly and with deadly purpose. All
action, including Ajax's speech of resignation and dissembling, had
been directed toward a cogent end. Now that he has died there is no
further development. What follows is merely a protracted illustration of the congenital inability of most men to recognize a saint when
he is in their midst. While Menelaus and Agamemnon on one side, and
Teucer on the other, hurl their insults, nothing happens, time is
empty, and though this is not at all the kind of standstill which the
living Ajax had desired, the simple fact that time does interrupt its
course while the fate of the body is being decided carries its own
sardonic justice.

vii

As intimated at the beginning of the essay,
it has been asked why Sophocles chose to write a play in which the
hero dies before the plot is half done, and whose second half is
curiously flat and unheroic in mood and style by comparison with the
first. That a play with a hero who dies halfway through need not be
inartistic, Shakespeare has shown. But more than that, given Sophocles'
purpose of dramatizing the hero's struggle against time, or better,
the assault of time upon the hero, the structure of the *Ajax* is well
suited to the purpose. If I may apply a biblical motto in a sense not
originally intended: By their fruits ye shall know them. With
the hero dead, the world is the loser. What follows is the pettiness of
the unheroic, flexing their wizened muscles and wagging their tongues

in a total void, unsustained by the vital currents and the solid am-
bience which made every act of Ajax a Titanic effort rather than an
empty gesture. The flatness, the lack of tension and weight in the
second half of the play are symptomatic of the advent of the common
man. Even a broken hero is a more substantial thing than the Agamem-
nons and the Menelauses, who do not know what it is to fight against
a foe greater than other men and who, though beneficiaries of time,
have no insight even into their own ephemeral estate.

The contrast between the two halves of the play is not only one of
mood and substance. In form also Sophocles marks a decided change.
Before the death of Ajax the quality of the drama is largely musical.
The chorus chants or sings lengthy passages of sustained grief or joy,
and both Ajax and Tecmessa join with the chorus to produce those
musical exchanges which on the Greek stage achieve the most brilliant
emotional effect. After he is dead and the exaltation of tragedy proper
is exhausted, music is restricted to one ode by the chorus, and to one
exchange between Tecmessa and the chorus accompanying the search
for the body and its discovery. The dominant characteristic of the
second half is speech—we might almost say prose, the prose of thrust
and parry, the pro and con argumentation of the law court—rather
than the music of madness, or the music of reflection, or of mourning, or of hate. There are speeches in the first half also. But because
they give voice to the character of Ajax, and his isolation, the speeches are monologues, not orations designed to convince or convict. After
the death the orators take over and attack and counterattack. The rhetoric of the soul gives way to the rhetoric of the forum. But the body in
the center of the stage cannot possibly be touched by the brittle logic
chopped at its feet.

The men against whom the loyal Teucer tries to defend the corpse
are a singularly undistinguished lot. Menelaus' presence in the war
councils seems to be due to an oversight in the nepotism regulations.
He stresses the respect which is due to temporal authority, in a tone
rather like that used by the luckless Creon in the *Antigone*. He feels
that if only respect—or, as the outspoken Greek has it, fear—were
fully implemented, social organization would be successful and per-

fect. But the comparison with Creon is too flattering. In the mind of
Creon the appeal to fear is backed up by an avowed faith in law, and
law is a matter to which Menelaus pays only the most cursory attention. It will be useful to quote from his speech at some length, to underscore the contrast between Ajax and this specimen of the new man
(1077):

> Even a mountain of a man must know
> that one small blemish will produce his fall.
> But one attached to fear and reverence,
> you may be sure, salvation is his gain.
> Where wilfulness and *hubris* rule supreme,
> behold the city after running well
> before the wind, shipwrecked and plunged below.
> Let there be fear, I say, in its right season;
> let us not think that we can act at will
> without paying the price in grief and pain.

Salvation, running before the wind, the proper season, reckoning the
price: we have come to know the mentality well enough. But perhaps
the most revealing touch in this creed of the new age is the sudden
mention of the city. Menelaus starts out by talking about an individual agent, a doer, a potential hero. Now he substitutes the city, the
safe, comfortable group, as if he were afraid even in thought to venture out alone into the uncertain sea of life. The change from the
singular to the plural is unannounced, probably unnoticed by most. It
is the herd perspective asserting its proper categories.

Agamemnon, who appears next, is more subtle. At first sight it
appears to be a poor example of dramatic economy to have both
Menelaus and Agamemnon oppose Teucer's aims. They are brothers,
their objectives are the same, and the plot does not seem to be ad-
vanced further by this twofold version of intervention. But "dramatic
economy" is always a dangerous phrase. The notion that the short-
est route between two points is the most effective is not easily applicable to drama. In the present case it would not have done to
bring on stage only one specimen of postheroic manhood. One of the
significant things about Ajax was that he was alone, one man at odds

with the rest of men. His opponents, then, must be presented as many, acting with a fair unity of purpose but seeking safety in numbers. Greek tragedy does not favor crowds. Not that it would have been technically impossible to arrange for a milling mob in the vast orchestra of the theater in Athens. In fact some choral dances, as those of the Aeschylean *Suppliants,* must have come rather close to producing the effect of a mob stirred into action. But for its speaking roles tragedy relied on selective samples, on representative individuals to carry the burden of popular interests. In Attic drama, with its severely restricted number of actors and characters, two is a crowd. To enhance the pathos of the uniqueness of Ajax, Agamemnon must succeed Menelaus and share the limelight with him. Their near-identity betrays their lack of quality; because they are made from the same mold, neither has the distinctive powers which heroism demands.

But once the dramatic need for a representation of plurality has been satisfied, the author may wish to make the second actor a variation rather than an exact replica of the first. Agamemnon is more subtle than Menelaus, and his greater subtlety in the end prepares us for the appearance of Odysseus, whose refinement is destined to give an entirely new complexion to the conflict. Agamemnon's appeal is less to fear than to the law which sanctions fear, and less to political law than to social regulation (1246). Also he sets out, in the best traditions of the intellectual revolution, to discredit brute strength and to elevate the power of intelligence (1250). With this evocation of the teachings of Xenophanes and Heraclitus, Agamemnon declares his membership in the vanguard of the enlightenment. But underneath the gospel of liberating reason there is a political motivation. In a revealing line, close to the end of the play, he says (1350):

> To reverence tyrants is no easy matter.

Agamemnon too is a delegate of the people, of the little men who curse the hero because he is not like them. His utterances are not downright vulgar, but his sentiments are little different from those of his brother.

And what of the chorus? Ostensibly, of course, they are on the side of Ajax. They followed him to Troy, and their fate continued to be linked to his. But their loyalty aside, they think and feel like the sons of Atreus. They are simple men who have learned the lesson of fear and prize nothing above safety and anonymity. Their sailors' talk, on the Attic stage, immediately stamps them as democratic and unpretentious folk. Timidity, constraint, cowardice are their avowed companions. The thing they abhor most is ridicule. This, at first sight, somewhat resembles Ajax's own insistence on being admired, and his anticipation of jeering when the prestige is lost. In truth, however, Ajax did not fear laughter. He fully expected it, and loathed the prospect, but when it came he took it as his due from the blind rabble. His retainers, on the other hand, cringe at the thought of the slightest taunt. For them mockery is more than an insult, it is the collapse of the precarious role which they have constructed for themselves out of the leavings of their master's pride.

For a full understanding of the tragedy, this is perhaps the most painful note, that at first blush the people's response to the death of the hero should resemble the hero's own disposition. In this play, as in most Greek tragedy, and for that matter in comedy, each person considers his own welfare and his own advantage before he gives himself an opportunity to consider others. Altruism and self-effacement are not the stuff of dramatic poetry. But there is an obvious difference between the proud isolation of Ajax harshly rejecting all encroachment on his terrain; and the chorus anxiously pondering the question of what will become of them now that their protector is gone; or Tecmessa pressing the claims of wife and family; or Teucer ever oppressed with the consciousness of his bastard birth (1006), clinging to Ajax because he knows that the hero alone is big enough to disregard social convention and accept him at his own worth. Compared with Ajax, even the best of them, like Teucer, are men whose horizon is bounded by their needs and their resentments. They do not know the glory of the kind of struggle which Ajax undertakes, for they have tried to adapt themselves to the position which the advance of time has found for them. They travel along with the stream, their association with Ajax notwithstanding.

viii

Finally a word or two about the most explicit champion of accommodation and stream-time, Odysseus. He too is self-centered and desires his own advantage, but he knows that he does, and he builds a philosophy of enlightened utilitarianism on his appetites. Menelaus and Agamemnon refuse to acknowledge that they cannot match Ajax on his level. The members of the chorus are too ready to admit their inferiority. Odysseus is the only man who recognizes that he is different from Ajax and yet puts a positive interpretation on the difference. Of the adversaries of the hero he is the one most likely to elicit our understanding and sympathy. It is significant that Odysseus is the only character in the play who seems to undergo a development. At the beginning, when compelled by Athena to witness the madness of Ajax, he tries to block out the sight (80):

It would content me if he stayed within.

Not that he is afraid of Ajax, as some commentators have suggested. Rather he is afraid of the contaminating air of the madness which is bigger than either himself or Ajax. He is not sufficiently humane to endure the sight, much less the touch. For a dramatic character who no longer fears the contagion of madness or divine sickness we shall have to wait till we come to the Theseus of the *Oedipus Coloneus* or the Theseus of Euripides' *Hercules,* both written after the Athenian plague had revolutionized the attitude toward disease. The Odysseus of the *Ajax* may think of himself as emancipated, but he is old-fashioned enough to avoid contact with an obvious victim of the gods' displeasure.

But more than that, his desire not to be contaminated is chiefly a desire not to be involved. His brand of isolationism, though far different from that of Ajax, is a legitimate brand nonetheless. But at the end of the play he is changed, he is willing to be involved, and he risks misunderstanding and opprobrium to bring about the measure of peace and reconciliation on which the drama ends. Part of the explanation is that his isolationism never extended to his feelings, but only to his actions. Indeed, his initial revulsion may be said to spring from an excess of sensibility and fellow feeling stabbed into inaction. The key-word of his opening scene is *oiktos,* pity, and remarkably enough he includes himself among the members of the pitiable breed (124). In the end his pity rouses him to overcome his reluctance to act. Hence the statement made above has to be emended: Odysseus does not undergo a development, he simply recovers his ability to act. This happens once the initial shock of seeing Ajax in his fury has worn off, as soon, that is, as the new Ajax has taken the place of the victim of *ate.* Nevertheless it remains true that in Odysseus the author presents us with a character whose actions do not flow substantially and predictably from a public pose. He is a varied man, capable of fine gradations in thought and conduct, a worthy antithesis to the monolithic stiffness of the hero.

In his conversation with Agamemnon (1359 ff.) Odysseus revoices the Heraclitean sentiments of Ajax's speech of surrender, the paean to the instability of things and values. Odysseus even uses some of the same examples: friends are potential foes, foes are possible friends. But this revoicing of the relativist position is no duplication. When Ajax makes his speech, the weight of his remembered personality shows the perspective to be pusillanimous. So long as the living example of the hero's greatness was, despite sickness and despair, concretely before our eyes, the apostrophe to time could charm and impress but not convince. But now that Odysseus confesses to the same perspective, his pleading on behalf of his former enemy makes us question our ready condemnation of the philosophy of flux. From the premise: "A friend today may be a foe tomorrow" and its converse Odysseus concludes (1361):

A rigid spirit has not my support.

"Live and let live and bury the dead" falls short of expressing a heroic sentiment, but as a rule of action it is neither immoral nor trivial. At the very least it is an insight which accepts the inevitability of change and man's bondage to it, and still allows for some freedom of choice and conduct. Through the agency of Odysseus the merits of the popular morality, of liberalism in the modern sense if one so wishes, are restored to their rightful station from which the dulling force of Ajax's contempt had briefly removed them.

Teucer concedes the respectability of Odysseus' persuasion. When he thanks him for his mediation (1393) he refers to him as the son of Laertes, a far cry from the earlier scolding by the chorus, who had talked of Odysseus as the son of Sisyphus (189). The change of filiation is an index of Odysseus' changed moral standing in the eyes of his former adversaries. As in the *Odyssey,* Sisyphus, the archknave, is replaced by Laertes, the pious grower of fruit; and as in the *Odyssey* the shifting of the focus to Laertes inaugurates the final settlement. It is difficult to say to whom the settlement applies, and what its terms are, except that the burial is now made possible because for the supporters of Ajax the Heraclitean maxim has become a reality: a former foe has turned into a friend. In point of fact the burial signifies a truce rather than a settlement. Agamemnon and Menelaus will continue to carry their grudge, though they will abstain from acting upon it. What matters is not the terms of the truce itself but the moral authority with which Odysseus invests it. His plea for forgiveness (1322) is formulated as a recommendation to grant even to your enemies the right to preserve their own particular values and their own special prerogatives. Each man has his natural excellence, his own claims against prestige, and these we must, Odysseus feels, respect in our neighbors even when they conflict with ours (1339, 1356).

Like Pericles in Thucydides' funeral oration, Odysseus attempts to bring together two disparate worlds, the world of Agamemnon with his affirmation of respect and law, and the world of Ajax, the world of excellence and status and rugged individualism. The moral enunciated by Odysseus on the whole favors the camp of the people, the social group that looks for progress through compromise. The words he chooses are taken from the sphere of heroic action and aristocratic pride. The terms *arete,* excellence, and *time,* prestige, had long been catchwords of a philosophy which derived its inspiration from the past and spurned the egalitarian tendencies of the present. But now the prestige to be acknowledged is not the exclusive, jealously guarded status of the great lord but a prestige which is only one of many, and which allows the privileges of others to coexist. In spite of the overtures to heroic terminology, the great truce turns into an instrument for leveling. When men "conceive in harmony," their conceptions possess little grandeur. Peace is restored at the expense of greatness and of artlessness. The mutual attunement, the humaneness of the new creed as formulated by Odysseus, is built on two interlocking premises. One demands that "whatsoever ye would that men should do to you, do ye even so to them"; according to the other (1365),

> I too shall one day be in need of burial.

The ethics of the businessman is combined with the ethics of the graveyard. We do not aspire to be gods, the river of time is good enough for us; let us try to swim rather than float so that our bodies will not hit one another. But above all, no building of dams to stem the tide.

Lest it be thought that this is a moral which Sophocles means to support, that he throws the weight of the drama's lesson on the side of Heraclitus and the Sophists, let us recall that Odysseus is, dramatically speaking, not entirely successful. Though he is now willing to touch the body of Ajax and help carry it to the sepulcher, Teucer politely vetoes this (1393):

> I hesitate, son of ancient Laertes,
> to let you minister in this burial,
> lest my permission irritate the dead.

The people have relented, but Ajax preserves his exclusiveness to the end. He is carried to his tomb in full panoply (1407), as if this renewed emphasis on the armor made it plain that he is not included in the general truce. The tragedy had come to an end with the death of the man. What we have witnessed in the second part of the play is the plebeian backwash of the heroic act, the humble societal arrangements prompted by the act. The treatment is necessary to indicate the gulf which separates the hero from ordinary men. But the detail and, in the case of Odysseus, the loving care with which the common man is studied should not trick us into believing that the age of the hero is dead, that reconciliation is resolution, or that kindliness or utilitarianism is more substantial than heroism with its cruelty and its ponderous unbalanced strength. Ajax stood with the gods, and fought against time. He perished as a man, but his heroism survives, beyond good or evil, beyond the reach of time, in the pure air of everlasting life which even in tragedy is the reward and proof of an earthly existence purposefully spent.

Alcestis: CHARACTER AND DEATH

IN HOMER'S *Iliad* the uneasy truce which ac-
companies the duel between Menelaus and
Paris is, after the disgraceful withdrawal of
Paris, broken by Athena, who persuades a lesser Trojan, Pandarus,
to shoot Menelaus (4.104, tr. Richmond Lattimore):

> Straightway he unwrapped his bow, of the polished horn from
> a running wild goat he himself had shot in the chest once,
> lying in wait for the goat in a covert as it stepped down
> from the rock, and hit it in the chest so it sprawled on the boulders.
> The horns that grew from the goat's head were sixteen palms'
>   length.

201

A bowyer working on the horn then bound them together,
smoothing them to a fair surface, and put on a golden string hook.
Pandaros strung his bow and put it in position, bracing it
against the ground . . .
                                      . . . and took out an arrow
feathered, and never shot before, transmitter of dark pain.
Swiftly he arranged the bitter arrow along the bowstring . . .
He drew, holding at once the grooves and the ox-hide bowstring
and brought the string against his nipple, iron to the bowstave.
But when he had pulled the great weapon till it made a circle,
the bow groaned, and the string sang high, and the arrow, sharp-
     pointed,
leapt away, furious, to fly through the throng before it.

Everything conspires to make the shot firm and true. That Athena,
the instigator of the disturbance, then turns around and deflects the
arrow from Menelaus is another matter. It merely proves that divine
power transcends divine partisanship. If the goddess had not interfered
with the direction of the missile, it would surely have found its intended mark. That is the impression created by the build-up of the shoot-
ing, and particularly by the prehistory of the bow itself. By tracing
the various steps which went into the making of the bow, by dwelling
on the size and strength of the animal and on the effort whereby it
was made to render up its horns, Homer manages to convey to us
that this is a superbow, an unerring instrument in the hands of any
warrior, but particularly so in the hands of the man who had killed
the goat and thus made the bow his own. A bought weapon, or a
stolen one, is not likely to give the same kind of service. The quality
of a thing, then, particularly of a thing used by a man, is regarded as a
function of its history. How it came to be, what happened to it in its
inception and afterward, is decisive in fixing its nature and its ef-
fectiveness.

The principle that in the area of physical things, status or efficacy is
determined by origins, is well known to Greek writers. The many
aetiological tales in Greek mythology, providing imaginary origins
and histories for numerous segments of our experience, argue the same

understanding. These stories show that the principle is not restricted
to inanimate things, but operates also in the area of organic life. Indeed most of the tales are about animals or plants, answering such
questions as: Why does the swallow not sing like other birds? or
Why is the weasel more ingenious than other creatures? or Why does
the heliotrope always turn its face to the sun? The character of an
organism is, according to this method, explained by pointing to a past
event. Men also are subject to aetiology. In Homer, as in most of the
writers of his tradition, the prowess or cowardice of a fighter is pre-
sumed to be conditioned by his family background. If a man comes
from good parentage he can be expected to prove himself a stalwart
warrior; if his parents are undistinguished, the chances that the son
will make a mark for himself are slim. This is, of course, a wide-
spread assumption; in Greece it prevailed until the rebels of the
classical period began to question it, but even then the natural prefer-
ences of the writers continued to favor the belief in inherited characteristics. Deviations from the rule were regarded with some uneasiness or, occasionally, with the excitement of a strange discovery, as
in Pindar's *Sixth Nemean,* written for a family in which athletic skill
was found to be handed from grandfather to grandson rather than
from father to son. The poet is intrigued by the enormity of what
the facts seem to indicate. But it is noteworthy that even here the
athlete's talent is not thought of as a personal matter, but as a gift
granted long ago in the family's past.

Now if it is true that the aetiological question—how did the thing
come to be?—was a powerful guide in the Greek approach to the puzzles of individual life, to the riddles of physique, status, and achievement, one might plausibly expect to find the same outlook also in
Greek analyses of human character and social behavior. If Helen is
under the compulsion of Aphrodite, if Homer's Agamemnon betrays signs of what today might be diagnosed as a feeling of insecurity,
or if Theophrastus' Grumbler is never satisfied with anything that
happens to him, we wonder whether the reasons for their behavior
might not be traced to their historical antecedents. Did something
happen, either to them or to their parents or their parents' parents,

which laid the foundation for the development of an excessive tendency to love, or doubt, or grumble?

Here and there in the Greek writings it may seem as if this approach was indeed taken, as if, that is, the principle of aetiology was
explicitly applied to the analysis of conduct or character. In Aeschylus'
Agamemnon, for instance, Clytemnestra furnishes her own interpretation of why she is different from other wives. It all started, she
tells us, when her husband sacrificed their daughter Iphigenia. But
it is significant that the argument is that of Clytemnestra herself, and
not of the chorus, who alone qualify as a conveyer of the poet's critical
comment. The chorus, in fact, make no allowance for characters.
Their understanding of the world is lyrical; for them everything is a
texture of events, of colorful units of life attracting and repelling one
another and in the process creating complex patterns of meaningful
association. The lyrical perspective is essentially descriptive; because
of its extreme vulnerability to sensory stimuli it is incapable of analysis
or explanation. But even Clytemnestra's argument is not so much
an explanation as a rationalization. She recognizes the monstrousness
of her deed, and looks for an excuse in the past. The wrath released
by the killing of Iphigenia may explain an act, but it cannot be designed to explain the whole complex tissue of traits and tendencies
which Aeschylus has embodied in Clytemnestra. In any case her retrospective explanation is the exception rather than the rule. In general those Greek authors who are interested in matters of the soul, in
psyche and *ethos,* do not give us history. Instead of uncovering antecedents they draw a picture; instead of analyzing motivation they nar-
rate; instead of providing an aetiology they list the symptoms.

The Greek writers were not familiar with psychoanalysis. More particularly, they had to do without the tidy terminology and the clinical
orderliness of the Freudian school. But as we have seen, the aetiological
principle was not foreign to them. It would be a mistake to suppose
that they were *not yet* capable of analyzing men's actions in terms of
events and influences in their earlier lives. The poet who tried to explain the deadly aim of Pandarus' bow by investigating the history
of the bow could, if he wished, have explained the tormented career

of Helen by pointing to an incident or a series of incidents dating back
to her childhood in Sparta. That he did not do so has nothing to do
with intellectual progress or the lack of it. It is simply that he was not
interested in this kind of explanation, or in any other kind, when
dealing with exceptional human characters. Great writers have an insight into the complexity of the psyche which allows them to create
convincing characters and to set forth human relations of great in-
tricacy. But they need not regard it as their concern to supply reasons for their creatures being the way they are.

Homer's characters are remarkably subtle, as everybody would agree.
He is a connoisseur of individual modes of behavior, a shrewd practitioner of the art of psychology. So is Euripides, especially in the
plays which do not end unhappily. Aristotle, in spite of his essay on
the soul and his treatment of the emotions in the *Rhetoric,* does not
have the sharp insight of the poets, perhaps because his science and
his system get in the way of his very considerable sensitivity. Nor do
all great poets necessarily have this insight. A writer like Faulkner
often does not have it, or does not wish to communicate it, because
his tragic figures are conceived as either automata or monsters. Restoration comedy does not have it because it deliberately puts on the stage
men and women who are monomaniacs, hence false to the legacy of
the complete man. Proust does not have it because his preoccupation with the past and with the sources of the present mortifies the
instinct for the vitality of the present.

It is a commonplace of literary criticism that the meticulous regis-
tering of channels of motivation may run counter to the interests of
psychological realism, if not of art. The great and most enduring portraits are often the least overtly analytic. Their creators leave it to the
readers to take their cues from faint hints, or from the actions themselves, to establish the possible causes and motives to their own satisfaction, if they so wish. What made Hamlet the man he is in the
drama may be an interesting speculation, but the question does not
enter into the aesthetic response except peripherally. Especially on
the stage an explicit plotting of motivation is likely to be disastrous in
its effect. If a playwright were to give us the exact causes of an action

in terms of the soul's evolution, he would risk reducing that action to the level of a standard mechanism. On the stage a character should be both singular and interesting; hence motivation must be either obscured or left entirely to our imagination. By concentrating on the evident patterns of behavior and response the playwright makes his characters more immediately and more generally appealing.

Modern interpreters usually frown on any attempt to emphasize psychological variety and finesse in a Greek play. In a recent admirable edition of the *Alcestis* we read: "So far from considering the *Alcestis* a full-length study of *naïveté*, weakness, hysteria, egotism, character-development, and so forth, I do not believe that apart from the *hosiotes* [piety] Euripides had any particular interest in the sort of person Admetus was."[2] It is true that there are Greek dramas in which issues or lyric perceptions are more important than character delineation, and in which the personalities of the agents are so shaped and distorted as to answer to themes and objectives beyond themselves. I have already discussed some of them. But the existence of such dramas should not blind us to the fact that there are in the Greek repertory other plays which are nothing if not portrayals of interesting characters in action and interaction. If critics have lately been unwilling to concede this, their reluctance is perhaps due to a commendable reaction against the fashion of reading the plays as studies of case histories. Freudian interpretations of Shakespeare or of Aeschylus may have their use, but they start from so irrelevant a premise that they defy the basic intentions of the writers. Greek drama is not concerned with motivation; the question of why a particular character may be acting as he is carries us far away from the nucleus of the tragic business. But some Greek drama is very much concerned with character elaboration. It would be wrong to impair the tough fiber of Euripides' plan by translating his terms into professional jargon, or by filling in what he has chosen to leave uncharted. But to explore the richness of the vision, and the subtlety of the psychological

[2] A. M. Dale (ed. and comm.), *Euripides: Alcestis* (Oxford, England, The Clarendon Press, 1954), p. xxvii.

perceptions, is very much to the advantage of an understanding of the play. It is no longer feasible to assume that a classical work of art is necessarily a monolithic sort of thing, unselfconscious, natural, in a state of paradise. We must acknowledge complexity and refraction where we find them, even in so simple a tale as that about Admetus and Alcestis.

ii

The catalyst which Euripides employs for the isolation of character is death. In our play death is the principal theme. This immediately raises two questions which are, in some indirect way, connected with each other. First, should a play about death be a tragedy? Second, should the treatment of death in a drama involve the use of symbolic devices or not? As for the latter, it is to be noted that the Greeks did not have a word for "symbol," and though Greek literary criticism does discuss such things as metaphor and simile, it generally regards them as stylistic techniques or mannerisms, as substitutions for the real thing, and not as self-validating formulations of a poetic reality. At the same time it is obvious that the poets knew the value of symbols. Medea's chariot, Pentheus' pine tree, the "Chalybian stranger" in the hands of Oedipus' sons are the kind of meaningful substances which the ancient critics do not take under advisement, but which nevertheless contribute, and must always have contributed, significantly to the aesthetic effect of the drama. The crimson tapestry in the *Agamemnon* is not merely an embellishment of royal proportions, but helps to shape the mood and the meaning of the action as only a visual symbol can. It is, therefore, legitimate to say that the poets did use symbols to put across their literary intentions.

In modern discussions of symbols, ritual is usually not very far behind. The obvious parallelism of myth and ritual has led some writers to regard all symbols as mental correlates of ritual patterns of behavior. In the play before us, Hercules goes off to fight Death at roughly the same time Alcestis is being put in the grave. The simultaneity of contest and sacrifice is too tempting to resist; it smacks of the rites of spring, of mortification and invigoration and in the end, jubilation. In the words of T. S. Eliot's *Family Reunion:*

> Spring is an issue of blood
> A season of sacrifice
> And the wail of the new full tide
> Returning the ghosts of the dead,
> Those whom the winter drowned
> Do not the ghosts of the drowned
> Return to land in the spring?

To read the *Alcestis* as a symbolic representation of the death and re-birth of Nature is especially tempting because this type of interpre-tation has been proposed for much of Greek drama by an influential school of critics.

Yet, in the case of this play at any rate, the ritual interpretation is to be completely rejected. The characters of the *Alcestis* are not the dependent parts of a larger organism, they do not feel themselves to be members of a cosmos with which they must keep in tune and which in turn determines their fears and hopes. On the contrary, in spite of the myth of fate and death which informs the play, the chief characters are autonomous, undetermined, self-reliant men and wom-en, in no way tied to the vegetative life around them. They are human, they are bourgeois; and the bourgeois life is insensitive to the work-ings of ritual patterns. It does not function as a knowing or unknow-ing participant in the periodic cosmic processes of expansion and con-traction, of seasonal life and death. If Admetus and Alcestis and Pheres were participants in a drama of cosmic crisis, they could perhaps take some dubious comfort from their role. Even if they were not, as agents in the play, themselves aware of their ritual standing, the reader would remedy the lack and regard their actions as positive min-isterings in a natural cause. But as Euripides conceives the King and his Queen, no such facile comfort is appropriate. They stand alone, without hope and without purpose, stripped of a sense of belong-

ing, having surrendered their chance of ritual reconciliation. They
are, in fact, modern men.

To come back to the second of our two questions, what means are
available to literature of talking about death, Sappho says in one of her
poems:

> A great desire grips me to die and see
> the dewy banks of lotus-covered Acheron.

Her formulation is twofold, first, colloquial speech, and then metaphor, specifically a metaphor taken from two different mythological
sources, the story of the lotus-eaters, and the concept of the river separating the world of the living from the world of the dead. Sappho uses
the two formulations side by side, but they are of course alternatives;
either would have been adequate, and both are equally natural, at
least in the terms of Sappho's poetics. Why Sappho in this case chooses
to reinforce the colloquial with the mythological or vice versa we
cannot tell; the rest of the poem has not come down to us. The possibilities of the colloquial are severely limited, even in the supple
Greek, whereas the range of mythology is, notably in this matter of
death, almost unlimited. Death may be visualized as a person, as a
winged messenger who along with his brother Sleep returns the
Homeric hero Sarpedon to his grave in Lycia. Vase paintings have
taught us that in this role Death is a handsome young man, a gentle
guarantor of elegance and peace. Or again, Death may appear in
the person of the fearsome Charon, him of the burning eye and the
matted beard, whose unlovely visage stares at us from a number of
Etruscan paintings. Or he may be experienced as Hades, the majestic
inmovable ruler of the dead. Ancient writers greatly benefited from the
variety of mythological formulations. Depending on the special objectives of the work at hand, they could pick this or that formula, or they
could combine several for a particular effect. And they were always in a
position to choose between the colloquial and the symbolic in the
first place. In this respect the Greek authors may be said to have had
an advantage over their modern colleagues. Homer even manages to

present the maturing of Achilles by his use and nonuse of mythology; in the first book of the *Iliad*, when Achilles needs to control his passion, he is assisted by Athena, while in the last book of the work he is able to master a similar outbreak of anger without outside help.

But personification has its disadvantages. The concentration of an experience into the contours of a person, however august and brilliant, will usually be false to the abstractness or the mystery or the power of the experience. Personification works by subtraction, and a great deal that is important in the intangible that is personified, comes to be sacrificed on the altar of clarity and visual charm. Hence mythology offers complementary symbols of death, nonanthropomorphic symbols which may be adopted by themselves or used in combination with others. There are the images of the *Odyssey*, such as the vicious beasts Cerberus, Scylla, and Charybdis; or the lotus-eaters, or the clashing rocks. Death can be represented as a flock of vultures or Furies on the roof, door posts sweating blood, a palace tumbling to the ground, a curtain rent. Aeschylus' plays, as is well known, are full of such nonpersonal symbols of death.

One rule of writing which was well understood by the ancient authors is this: when symbols of death predominate in a work of literature, the physical happening of death must be kept in the background. That means that in drama, generally, heroes do not die on the stage. And this is true in the great majority of the plays that have come down to us. But it is not true of the *Alcestis;* the heroine's death takes place right on the stage. What is more, the physical death is so conspicuous that it becomes the pivot of the dramatic action. Consequently the scope for symbolic utterance is greatly minimized. To be sure, Euripides does make some use of the metaphorical material which I have mentioned, and the personification of Death becomes one of the subsidiary agents of the plot. Nevertheless, as I hope to show, the stress in the play is on realism, on the everyday formulation, on Sappho's "I wish to die" rather than on symbolic transformation. And there is a good reason for that. Death as an object of fear, as an ominous prospect, registers its most telling impression via symbols. So will death as a hoped-for release from suffering. But the question of the meaning of death, and especially the group of questions taken up in the *Alcestis*—how, and why, and with what results does a man face or not face death, and what does death mean to the living?—these questions must be asked in a setting that is immediate and colloquial. To dramatize the meaning of death, symbols are useless; it is behavior that counts.

The overcoming of death is a universal theme of folk literature. Of the Greek heroes, Hercules, Theseus, Pirithous, and Orpheus, among others, attempted to descend into the nether world and outwit Death. Each of them, with the exception of Hercules, either failed in his purpose or proved himself a rascal rather than a hero. The most rascally of them was Sisyphus, who tried to evade death by bidding his wife not to bury him after he had departed for the underworld. The result was that the powers of death could not claim him fully as their own. So he struck an agreement with the king of the dead to let him go back to the living for a day, in order to see to his proper burial. He reascended, tried to go back on the agreement by staying on among the living, and was finally fetched down again and punished.

The folk tale about Admetus and Alcestis on which Euripides modeled his play was very similar to this story about Sisyphus. Our play, like the folk tale, is concerned with death not as a dire prospect, but as a fact already experienced and known. As a prospect, death creates confusion and uncertainty, and induces us to turn our eyes away from human concerns to the mysteries of the universe. As a fact, it allows us to concentrate our attention on what it does to men. For both the protagonists, death is a fact. They are committed, even dedicated, to the fact. One has decided to run away from it, the other to clutch it to her heart. Both know the how and the that; the decision has been made, and all mystery has been stripped off. With the mystery gone, every thought and every act is bathed in the merciless light of simple acquaintance. Alcestis and Admetus are familiar with death; and that is why Euripides has introduced the personification, the Demon Death with his well-known traditional gestures and his brutal directness. It is true that, just before she dies, Alcestis shrinks from the irreversible

step. Her horror at the vision of death introduces a note of strangeness and wonder, suggesting that perhaps things have been taken
too much for granted. But this sense of uncertainty is short-lived. The
mood of familiarity and colloquial simplicity which marks the other
scenes is extraordinary even for Euripides, who, as we know from
Aristophanes, prided himself on having freed tragedy from its
shackles of symbolic ambiguity and rhetorical pomp. It would be fruitless in this play to look for elevated thematic images or significant
vocabulary clusters. Even the choral songs, all except the Ode to Necessity (962) for whose Aeschylean color there is a special reason, have
a minimum of pathos and lyric texture. The chorus is drawn straight
into the middle of an action which is realistic, humane, unmysteri-
ous; from the very beginning, the choristers share in the conversa-
tional and unwondering mood of the drama.

But can there be a tragedy without wonder? The truth is, to
answer the first of the two questions raised above, that the *Alcestis* is
not a tragedy. Tragedy dramatizes men's emotions, their victories
and defeats in the struggle for values and principles. Tragedy does
not deal with the natural necessities such as eating and drinking or
sleeping or dying. Because this is a play about death as a natural fact,
its tone is light and its machinery derives from the happy optimism
of the folk tale on which it draws. Dante's *Commedia* shows us that
the natural order of the world requires a nontragic exposition. We
may also remember the words of David when Bathsheba's child had
died:

> While the child was yet alive, I fasted and wept; for I said,
> Who can tell whether God will be gracious to me, that the
> child may live? But now he is dead, wherefore should I
> fast? can I bring him back again? I shall go to him, but he
> shall not return to me.

We know that Euripides did not conceive of his play as a tragedy
even in the more neutral Greek sense of the word. This is clear from
the fact that the *Alcestis* was performed as the last part of a tetralogy.
We do not have the first three plays but we have the titles and we know

what the plays were about. In all three of them Euripides seems to have emphasized the monstrosity of human instincts, the shabbiness of personal relations, and the impenetrability of the moral order. The subjects were depressing and even revolting, and one of the plays, the *Telephus,* came to be a by-word for the type of naturalism from which the Greeks on the whole shied away. There were, then, three statements of negation, or at best of painful disillusionment. At the end, in the position where ordinarily we should expect a satyr play, Euripides on this occasion put yet another drama dealing with men, and inglorious men at that. But the fourth play eventually turns out to voice a ringing "Yea," a vote of confidence calculated to compensate for the horrors which precede it. For in some peculiar way which we shall have to study, the sorry men and women of the *Alcestis* are also noble and perhaps even admirable. Apparently Euripides felt that a traditional satyr play, with the accent on amoral vitality and animal vigor, would have been less effective in counterbalancing the human futility of the first three plays than this lighthearted confrontation of natural necessity with the common feelings of fear and jealousy and love.

iii

The lightheartedness of much of the action, as of the antecedents, is unmistakable. It all started with Apollo, who served the Furies strong drink, "tricking and tripping them, like a professional" (33), to get Admetus off. This is part of the familiar tale; nevertheless the emphasis on drink at this early stage is significant. Drink is part of the structure of human necessities and temptations which lend themselves to comic treatment. Drink is predictable, it raises few questions, and it can be funny. Of all this Hercules will be the living proof, later in the play. In the Prologue on the stage, the language of the conversation between Apollo and Death shows that though they are gods they have nothing godly about them. They argue like business competitors. Fortunately for the conception of the play the word for "death" in Greek is masculine, hence the personification of death is male. If Death were female as she is in Latin and the Romance languages, no such robust negotiating at the conference table would have been possible. For an audience of men, the femininity of Death would endow her with mystic dimensions which the hopelessly masculine Death of the *Alcestis* does not possess. In his greeting to Death, Apollo gives us a taste of what is to be expected (26):

> He's come on the dot of the hour!

The bourgeois quality of the remark, both complimentary and a little resentful at the fact that trains are running on time, sets the tone for what follows. This is a well-regulated world in which men know all the answers; occasionally they wish there were a few they did not know.

Death is surprised and suspicious at seeing Apollo. Apollo tries to allay his suspicions (38):

> APOLLO: Fairness and persuasion are my tools.
> DEATH: If so, what is the purpose of that bow? *(points)*
> APOLLO: What bow? Oh, that! It's just a habit of mine to carry it.
> DEATH: Ah! Just as you patronize the rich?

The joke about the bow is characteristic. The god carries the bow by the same unreflected necessity by which we eat and drink and sleep. We go through the motions without contemplating their meaning. When they are brought to our attention we are embarrassed, for we like to think of ourselves as living fully conscious and purposeful lives.

The negotiating starts in earnest (54):

> APOLLO: A death is a death; why not accept another?
> DEATH: No deal; I like to bag them young and green.

In the sequel, Death voices the suspicion that Apollo has been bribed, and condemns bribery with all the sham dignity of a public orator. A good democrat, he despises Apollo for being on the side of the rich. He lives by the letter of the law; Apollo, he suggests, tries to set himself above it. Apollo's position is indeed peculiar. He had arranged for the death of Alcestis; now he tries to rescind the arrangement. In the eyes of Death, Apollo is an incurably unrealistic humanitarian who fights the windmills of natural necessity, the despair of the practical law-abiding bureaucrats who have their feet on the ground and loathe sentimentality. Death does not pretend to be a free agent; he has his work cut out for him, for he is a servant of the nether gods. He does not control or understand, nor does he wish to; his job is to act. At first blush this would seem to put him on the same level as Hercules, that other slave who acts rather than reflects. But Hercules' servitude is that of a Stoic king; he is a man so attuned to the natural world that the choice of action and the exercise of what little freedom he has become as congenial to him as the ties which bind him to necessity. Death is a real slave, a clockwork machine which has renounced all freedom. He is a tool of necessity.

Is the humor of the scene between Apollo and Death appropriate to the plot of the *Alcestis*? A woman courts death, virtually commits suicide, because she feels she can help her husband by sacrificing herself. Her husband knows about her intention and does nothing to stop her because, through a deficiency in his imaginative powers, he thinks life to be the highest good. In the end, faced with the fact of her death, he comes to his senses. This is the plot of the *Alcestis*. It is by no means funny, nor is it outlandish or contrived. Stalinism and Hitlerism provided many occasions for its re-enactment, and some years back films about lifeboats with too many occupants in them were very popular. In the political experience of fifth-century Athens, also, the institution of the scapegoat was well enough known. Why, then, does Euripides present us with, for the most part, a genial fairy tale, rather than a bitter drama of conflict and betrayal? Because, for one thing, the fairy tale consolidates the impression of necessity. All great drama, as everyone would agree, needs to generate the feeling that the plot is exactly as it had to be, and could not have been otherwise. For the building of this assurance the fairy-tale formulation does exceedingly well. Furthermore, the fairy tale allows beauty to coexist along with violence and necessity. And third, the fairy tale makes it possible for Euripides to write his *commedia*. The theme itself is not funny; but the fable frame allows the modicum of humor and playfulness which the author wants for his major design, which is the exploration of human character and ordinary behavior in the face of the fact of death. Character, as we know from the end of the *Symposium* and from the *Characters* of Theophrastus, can be studied best in an atmosphere of pleasantry and gentle detachment. High seriousness and a preoccupation with unnerving issues do not favor the development of those minor but trenchant insights whereby character is anatomized and revealed.

The action is designed not to engage our fear or pity. The Prologue, through the mouth of Apollo, tells us what is going to happen. We know, and the gods know; only the actors do not realize that everything is going to come out all right, that Hercules will be the *deus ex machina.* Thus the plot comes to be insulated against our emotions; it turns into an object for amusement, and perhaps for reflection, but not for empathy. We admire what we see on the stage very much in the way we admire and applaud a clever orator. We recognize his subtlety, his ability to make things come alive in our imagination, the verisimilitude of his fictions. But we cannot possibly feel anxiety, much less horror, at the visions he conjures up. And just as the orator knows that we know, and allows this knowledge to color his speech, so also the speeches of the *Alcestis* have about them an air, however faint, of posing. It is as if the characters were at one and the same time trying to rouse our emotions and apologizing for doing just that. And yet this touch of mockery is so slight that most of the time we are not even conscious of it; certainly it never endangers the simplicity of the action, or the credibility of the main characters.

The *Alcestis* presents us with a rhetoric of death. But rhetoric does not exclude realism. Knowing as we do the conventions of the Greek theater we do not expect a photographic type of realism. The speech consists of polished trimeters, and the action proceeds with a swiftness which defies the snail's pace of life. But in a larger sense the play comes as close to a successful realism as a Greek drama can be. There is no villain, but there is no hero either. Everybody is decent and well-meaning within his lights even if motivated by his special interests and grudges. Even Pheres is kind enough to play the mourner for Alcestis, and while he does so he is not necessarily insincere. What the play does tell us is this, that people often make each other intensely unhappy by their virtues. According to Plato, each action releases one or more effects, and each of these effects becomes itself a cause which releases new effects, which are no longer controlled or calculated so far as the original cause is concerned. This errant cause, as Plato calls it, is chiefly responsible for the various dislocations in the life of the world, and ultimately for the existence of evil. Life is a nexus of ill-connected events.

Euripides likewise teaches that by their very virtues men may contribute to the wrong in this world. The only figures on the stage not caught up in the concatenation of human causes are Apollo, Death, and the unerrant Hercules. But though they are not enmeshed in the tissue of failure and error as the others are, they are themselves sufficiently naturalized not to disturb the effect of realism. The gruff, puritan, class-conscious Death, the guzzling but tempestuously generous Hercules, the ineffectual and bow-ridden but well-intentioned Apollo fit well into the scheme of things. The mythological apparatus is gauged to further the ends of psychological realism. At the same time the presence of the gods, and the fairy-tale base, prevent the realism from turning sour and becoming a naturalism of indignity and ugliness. And in the figure of Hercules, Euripides shows us a man who, whatever his shortcomings—and the servant thinks he is more beast than man—has the power to act without causing unhappiness, except to Death. If there is a hero it is Hercules; in spite of—or because of?—his patent lack of discretion and intellect, he is the only one who can cope with necessity without hurting either himself or others. Decency, necessity, and death: these are the elements out of which Euripides composes this gentle anatomy of the unheroic soul.

iv

How does an ordinary human being protect himself against too keen an awareness of the weight of necessity? How does he manage to save his self-respect in the face of predictability? By embracing the conventions, if we are to believe the *Alcestis*. Conventions are man-made, they give an illusion of human mastery, they afford a fixed point, a dignified rest in the toss of the errant cause. The instrument which Euripides employs to dramatize man's reliance on the conventions is, naturally, the chorus. Throughout the repertory of Greek drama the chorus has the role of affirming conventional morality and conventional perspectives in the face of heroic deviations from the norm. Often its conventionality appears to us more like triteness or stupidity. But its traditional stand provides an ever-present internal rectification of the heroic imbalance, a constant therapy of the heroic madness. In the *Alcestis* there are no heroes who deviate from the norm, there is no inkling of the grand madness or intransigence which we associate with the character of a Medea or an Ajax. Still, the chorus delivers its sermons. But now these pledges to convention do not have their usual counteractive force. Rather, they give us the essence of the chorus, and through them the essence of all men.

As soon as the choristers enter, they ask, in effect (79): "Are we to grieve or not? Somebody please tell us whether Alcestis has died or not!" For the people, it requires a ceremonial to cope with necessity. Their reaction to the fact of death is a matter of timing and ritual observance. Their mourning need not be any less heartfelt for being mechanized; but they guard well against its being spontaneous. The question of the chorus: What shall we do? is a nontragic distortion of the tragic dilemma expressed in the words: What am I to do? In the *Alcestis,* the question really means: What does etiquette require us to do? Or better: How soon may we fall back on the regulations of etiquette? This is how the comedy of manners reformulates the question of how one behaves in the presence of death. The men of the chorus make no bones about it—they would be more comfortable if the Queen were already dead. They would rather practice the ceremonial than wait for it. At the moment they are waiting for the conventional signs of mourning, for the groaning and lamenting and beating of hands on breasts (86). In their mind's eye they contemplate the vision of a beautifully appointed funeral, complete with bowl of water and curl of hair (96). They want Alcestis dead so they can go through the apotropaic motions of the ritual. But, being decent and generous, they are ashamed of their secret expectations; they catch themselves and sing (90):

> Healer God, appear and soothe
> the wave of disaster!

as if Apollo had anything to say in the matter. But then again, later, they turn to the servant girl and ask with an unhealthy but quite natural eagerness (146),

> You're sure there is no hope she will be saved?

And again (150),

> Her death will make her famous!

In the eyes of the chorus, at any rate, Alcestis' death *is* a fact, and they are impatient to get on with it.

Eventually, when the Queen has deigned to give up the ghost, they remark, quite literally (416):

> You must, Admetus, try to bear this sorrow.
> You're not the first, nor will you be the last,
> to lose a worthy wife. After all, we must
> all of us go at one time or another.

This reminds us of nothing so much as of the Marx Brothers in *Room Service* exclaiming pious inanities at a fictitious deathbed. Would the effect in Greek be similarly funny? Perhaps not; it is the traditional function of the chorus to express collective wisdom. What seems silly to us, appears in many instances to have been intended as a serious contribution to the soothing of distress. Yet I for one cannot see Euripides writing these lines without tongue in cheek. For the chorus to say to Admetus "We've all got to go!" is comical in any language. The chorus relies on its stable conventions to see them through the present unhappiness, and they wish to let others share in this protection. They do not seem to realize that their age-old comfort cannot possibly be a comfort to their king.

A second characteristic of the chorus spotlighted by Euripides is their strong sense of masculine prerogative. Apart from an initial reference (82) to "Alcestis, child of Pelias," the chorus refuses to consider the Queen in her own right, preferring to think of her as the wife of Admetus. At one point (220) they pray to Apollo to save Admetus from being hurt through her death. What matters is not her sacrifice but her husband's suffering (cf. 144, 199, 226, 241). Alcestis must die, that is her obligation and her fate; any feeling that may be provoked by this fate is to be poured into sympathy with the lonely survivor. It is his loss, not hers, which feeds the compassion of the chorus. In the eyes of the servant girl, on the other hand, it is Alcestis who merits the greater share of the grief; as for Admetus, he could have prevented the unhappiness (197):

> If he had died, that would be all. But since
> he ran from death, he'll have his torture with him
> always.

The chorus, manly and middle-aged, cannot appreciate the greatness of the Queen's decision or, later, the violence of her suffering; they can speak and feel only with other men. They are too old-fashioned to put themselves in the place of a woman, too simple to look at the situation from two points of view. As in the original folk tale, Alcestis is for them little more than a means to an end, a willing instrument to ensure the survival of the King. For the slave girl, Alcestis is a heroine, and Admetus a coward.

Euripides is playing fast and loose with traditional morality. Tyrtaeus, the spokesman of masculine virtue, had said: "The man who deserts his post will lead an outcast's life, and in the end he is going to die anyway; hence, face death, for so you will live gloriously, or earn glory in death." In our play this creed is, with but one significant change—eternal pain instead of eternal shame—enunciated by the slave girl, while the brave men of the chorus, loyal supporters and spiritual companions of the King, throw the dictates of heroism to the winds. They seem to think that the privileges of their sex and the continued survival of masculine power should cancel out the claims of manly courage and *arete*.

What kind of a person is this man who is willing to sacrifice his wife? First of all let us look at the tradition. An ancient drinking song advises as follows:

> Friend, learn the rule of Admetus and keep distinguished company.
> Keep away from the mob; there is no grace in them.

In the old songs, apparently, Admetus was the ideal aristocrat, gracious, class-conscious, cultured to his finger tips, the kind of prince whose self-righteousness is unshaken by irrelevant notions of charity or brotherly love. In the folk tale on which the play is based, his superior standing guaranteed him a hero's rank, and he achieved the hero's supreme authentication by, for a time, overcoming death. That his wife got lost in the shuffle was unfortunate and regrettable but justified by the results. He was invincible, and she was one of his means of defense. In retrospect the victor has a right to expend fortifications. The brilliance of his position induces us to regard the death of Alcestis a mere incident and to forget it.

In Euripides' play Admetus is still the gracious and refined gentleman, but though his royal power is great (588), his personal distance from his subjects is much reduced. Like most of Euripides' kings, he is actually a man of the people, more sensitive perhaps than the rest, but a little confused and not entirely happy in the elevated position in which fortune has placed him. More important, Euripides shifts the emphasis of the ancient tale; he concentrates less on the deed itself than on the implications and consequences of the deed. He asks the question: What happened to the wife, and could the King really stand by and see his wife die for him without a stir of embarrassment? It is as if a dramatist were to take up the story of Hansel and Gretel and ask: What precisely was the position of the witch? Did she suffer? Could the children who caused her death sleep the sleep of the innocent thereafter?

Because of the new light thrown on Alcestis, we are now made to see Admetus from a radically different angle. It is the servant girl who supplies us with the fresh perspective: Admetus is a fugitive from justice, with Apollo, the god of blue-blooded honor and refinement, aiding and abetting him to turn tail. Worse yet, Admetus implores his wife not to "betray" him. He uses the word on more than one occasion (e.g., 250, 275). The servant girl copies the usage in her report (201):

> He weeps and clasps his lady in his arms
> and begs her: "Don't betray me," . . .

Admetus falls back on the same word to characterize his parents' unwillingness to die for him (659). It is a military term, taken straight from the spiritual arsenal of Tyrtaeus and other writers of patriotic poetry. Strictly speaking, it is applicable only to Admetus himself and no one else. We wince to hear it used of one who is a very much better soldier than he. But as a piece of psychological portraiture it is perfect. Admetus has transferred his fate to the shoulders of Alcestis; she is about to die, there is nothing now he can do to head off the event, and he is beginning to resent this infraction of his freedom to will and act. At the peak of his frustration he persuades himself that she is dying of her own free choice, and that she rather than he is the one who could yet rectify the mistake. There is some justice in this. The whole dramatic treatment does conspire to make Alcestis appear a freer agent than her husband. Admetus expressed a wish, and the gods acted; Alcestis had no gods assisting her to facilitate or direct her choice. Hence Admetus blames Alcestis for not revoking her decision.

The absurdity and the violence of his entreaties suggest that he is not without his share of tenderness. A coarser man might have commiserated with the woman, and yet taken the situation in his stride. He is vulnerable, hence he suffers. Again and again he assures Alcestis of his love and his concern. When he says to her (277): "If you die, we [he includes the children] shall die too," he means what he says, however preposterous the sentiment. He treats his wife as an equal, as a cherished partner in life. He wished to escape death, and he allowed Alcestis to substitute for him. But all that, Euripides wisely saw to it, is part of the antecedents, part of the folk tale rather than the drama. The facts are fixed, the drama cannot change them, it can only study the consequences of the facts. Seen from this vantage point, the sorrow of Admetus is not an ignoble thing. When the chorus, prior to the actual death of Alcestis, pity Admetus and voice their fear (328) that his suffering might drive him to suicide, we are at first inclined to feel that their compassion is misdirected. But they are right; his suffering is intense, and he knows that death might well have been better than the prospect that is now before him.

His personal embarrassment is that he cannot translate wish or thought into action. His life is a prime example of the ordinary man's incapacity to live the life which Aristotle recommends, the life of choice and commitment, the heroic life. He recognizes the sordidness of his existence, but he cannot lift himself above it. We are tempted to look down on him, but we should know that the figure of Admetus is a mirror in which we may recognize ourselves. The image is not repulsive, but it leaves little scope for pride or moral satisfaction, in spite of the honesty with which Admetus comes in the end to admit his inadequacies. The *Alcestis* inspires little pity, and less fear, but, in spite of the humor, a humiliating sense of solidarity.

V

Admetus is the unheroic hero of the people, warm, passionate, quick to trust and love and hate. Alcestis, his wife and adversary, is an entirely different character. We learn that she is well beloved by her servants. Both the slave girl and the steward who waits on Hercules clearly prefer her to her husband, from whose tempers she has often protected them (770). Toward her inferiors, in public, she has always been kind and considerate. But what about her private personality? Of her innermost nature we learn next to nothing. By stipulating that the decision to die lies in the past, by making her death a fact rather than a matter for doubt and choice, Euripides has deprived himself of the opportunity, fully exploited in other plays, of exposing the psychological piquancy of a moment of resolution. We are not permitted a glimpse into her soul at a time when she is not yet sure of herself. There is some partial compensation for this lack in the scene when she beholds the angel of death and flinches from the vision. But the experience is clinical rather than something that touches the spirit, a momentary weakening of resolve rather than a grappling with the dilemma of life and death. On the whole, her mind is made up, and she exhibits the serene, not to say the chilly, composure of a woman sure and proud of her purpose.

Obviously Euripides is interested in setting up a significant contrast between a struggling, ineffectual Admetus and a stoically proud Alcestis. The servant describes how the Queen went through all the ritual procedures preliminary to death (173)

> without a tear shed or a sigh, nor did
> she blanch in contemplation of her fate.

Unlike her husband, Alcestis sets a remarkable example of the heroic posture of endurance. But while Admetus is a whole person, and has a consistent attitude of weakness toward death, Alcestis faces death on two planes, in public and privately. After she has gone through the premortuary rites with the gravity of a marble statue, she goes home to uncoil her stored-up passion. Through the eyes of the servant girl we gain admission to the spectacle of her domestic extravagancies. We watch as she flings herself on her bed, only to hurl herself from the bed to the floor, all the time sobbing out her story of bitterness and frustration. The story required that she offer herself in sacrifice, not that she do so with pleasure. She is a queen; true to her standing she inspires her public subjects with an image of tranquility and resolution. But in the quiet of her bedchamber she abandons the role her people expect her to play, and gives full vent to a benefactor's pique. Alcestis has naturally come to despise the man who caused her to commit herself. She must also repent the rashness which prompted her to give her promise, and to wish her promise undone. The strength which drove her to offer herself in the first place now asserts itself as an urge to live, a tenacity which curses the unreasonableness of what is demanded of her. Euripides has caught the mixture of competing passions in the heart of Alcestis wonderfully well. But the subtlest stroke is this, that her grief is witnessed only by the children and the domestics. To her husband she presents her stoical front.

There is no doubt that her soul is breaking in two, as it is put in the Prologue (20, 143). But she is not going to give Admetus the satisfaction of meeting him on the common ground of human weakness and love of life.

I have referred to the play as embodying a rhetoric of death. Alcestis is death's chief rhetorician. To begin with, immediately upon her entrance, she intones an address to the Sun, the Clouds, and the Earth (244). As in the first utterance of Prometheus, the apostrophe to the cosmic powers marks her loneliness and her elevation. She is half-abstracted, and the presence of her husband means nothing to her. Then there follows a succession of two scenes whose order is to be explained as a Greek dramatic convention; first the exposition of her passions, in the form of an aria (252), then a set speech voicing her concurrent thoughts (280; cf. the same arrangement later for Admetus, 861, 935). First we behold Alcestis beside herself with the agonies of the vision of death; then abruptly she launches into a reasoned discourse on the meaning and implications of her action. A modern reader will perhaps find this sudden break neither realistic nor aesthetically satisfying. In fact, however, the two scenes are not to be understood as following one another in empirical sequence. They present two sides of one and the same experience which, because of the exigencies of literary formulation, have to be developed independently. Alcestis' response to the fact of death is at least twofold: the prospect engages her passions and her anxiety, but also her reasoning powers. In life, the two modes of reaction are bound together and simultaneous; in writing, they have to be separated unless the author tries to recapture the unity by some surrealistic measures such as those used occasionally by Eugene O'Neill. The Greek method, sanctioned and appreciated, it appears, by the Greek audiences, was to savor each mode by itself, to feature the response of the passions first and the commentary of the intellect second. This is a distortion of what happens in "real life." But to the extent that it catches the total experience more fully than would an emphasis on one or the other of the two modes, the convention may be said to make for a higher kind of realism. Certainly this solution of the difficulty seems to adapt itself more easily to an essentially realistic design than do other devices that have been tried for catching the fullness of the soul's life on the stage. Further, there is the old belief that a person on the threshold of death has a clearer understanding of the truth than other men, and that a deathbed speech is likely to carry the marks of a pure intelligence. There are thus sufficient reasons why the very last utterance of the hero or heroine should be a specimen of rational speech.

At any rate, first Alcestis has her tug of war with Charon. I like to think that Charon actually appears on the stage. Both the folk tale associations of the play, and its position in lieu of a satyr play, would encourage the utilization of the grotesque. One may assume that the mask of Death in the Prologue was designed to clash extravagantly with the mask and costume of the virtuous Apollo. The vision of Charon should indeed be hair-raising. As he grabs the Queen, she fails to maintain her public pose of calm resolution; her protests against forcible abduction spring straight from a desperate heart. Her position is not enviable, but it is not without a touch of the ridiculous. Her frantic shouts "Let me go!" alternating between the singular and the plural imperative, make it appear that she is being pulled in opposite directions, with Charon at one end and her family and attendants at the other. For the moment, the family wins out and Charon retires. In reality, of course, it is not the family that prevails but the dramatic convention that requires her to follow up her moment of passion with a speech. Charon withdraws so that Alcestis can give her husband a piece of her mind.

It is a most unpleasant speech (280). She begins by asserting that she might have been a merry widow, that her youth and attractiveness had promised to realize her every claim to happiness, but that she had decided otherwise. She reminds him that his parents had failed to do their duty by him; insists that her children remain motherless after she is gone; and finally, asks Admetus to concede that he may well be proud of calling such a wife his own. These are the four main points of her speech. For Admetus they become the theses of a creed which promises to rule and almost ruin his life henceforth. With these points, developed with the deadening authority of a master lawyer, Alcestis attempts to make sure that Admetus will never be a happy man again. She wants him to forswear all enjoyment of life, she asks him to deny his parents, she desires the children to remain orphans and remember her always and damn their father always; she expects him to be overcome with a continual awareness of his loss and with a never-ceasing contrition. Her language is in character (300):

> Permit me to ask a favor; not, of course,
> one matching mine, what I have done for you,
> for nothing is more precious than a life;
> but still, you will admit, you owe a favor.

This is the speech of a regal, a self-possessed, a purposeful woman, a heroine, if you wish. Yet imagine a play in which Alcestis' last speech was noble, self-effacing, warm, happy in the consciousness of her sacrifice. Such things are not unknown, especially in the classicistic tradition. But neither Euripides nor anyone else in fifth-century Athens was interested in this sort of romantic sweetening. He did not intend to portray a noble woman finding fulfillment in the act of self-immolation. Christian charity, the bliss of martyrdom, the happiness of a woman dying for a cause, are not the kind of subjects which appealed to his analytic mind. This is an essay in character, not a flight of utopian spirits. Alcestis speaks as a woman cheated out of her rightful legacy as mother, wife, and queen. At the moment of her death she despises her husband and twists the knife in his wound. We find her speech cruel and vindictive, but we also sense that her cause is just.

Admetus' speech in answer to Alcestis' harsh testament is a plausible mixture of self-pity, bravado, resentment, and daydreaming (328). Briefly the points of his reply are as follows. He promises never to marry another woman (330); to hate his parents (338); to organize a public mourning and to maintain private grieving in perpetuity (343); to have a statue of Alcestis made, to honor and embrace (348); to have his children bury him beside her when he dies

(365). What is more, he wishes he could descend into Hades and sing for her release (357). This catalogue of promises and wishes is an extraordinary thing, especially in the light of what is to follow. He says he will never remarry; the final scene of the play, when Hercules tries to force the veiled woman upon his attentions, is designed to demonstrate that Admetus had meant what he said. But the audience knows that his resolve is unnecessary and abortive, and the fervor with which he stresses the point may well arouse the suspicion that he protests too much. He promises to hate his parents; and yet, as we shall see later, the consummation of this hatred leads indirectly to the salvation of Admetus as a moral being. There will be perpetual public mourning; how can a king presume to mortgage the joys and affections of his subjects in payment for a personal debt? He would descend into the underworld and appeal to the king of the dead—with music, like Orpheus, not by force of muscle or character, in the way of Hercules! The children will put him beside her when he dies; when, or if? What is this mention of his own death in the hour when ostensibly he is surrendering his mortality? Is this his way of turning his back upon the agreement, or at least of making his own share in it easier to bear?

The crowning touch in this tissue of dreams and self-delusions is the provision for the statue (348):

> A likeness of your shape, made by the hand
> of skillful artists, will be stretched on our
> great bed, for me to kneel before and fondle.

"Stretched": Admetus chooses a word which in its specific corporeality denotes either the stiffness of death or the posture of sex. He cannot live without her; even in death her concrete body must continue to support him. His love and his feeling of guilt conspire to realize a fantasy which borders on the abnormal, not to raise the issue of good taste. But first, pedantically, let us ask whether the artists whom Admetus has in mind are stone masons or carvers in wood? The term used normally means "carpenter," but I suspect that he is thinking of a statue in marble, a cold substitute for a chillier reality. Admetus

loves his wife. He senses, as he must, that there is little loyalty and less
affection in the giving of the gift, but he is awed by the enormity of
the offering, and the warmth of his love is not diminished in the
hubbub of his conflicting responses. Hence the wish for the statue.
Frigid as the conceit may appear to us, it should be read as an attempt to express his love in the most forceful terms available. The
nature of the material is irrelevant—divine images may be made of
stone or of wood—as are the exact qualifications of the artists. All
that matters is Admetus' desire that Alcestis survive in some fashion or
other. This use of a statue, as a memento and by way of deification,
is found elsewhere in Greek mythology; Laodamia seems to have
consoled herself with an image of her husband, Protesilaus, who died
at Troy. Xenophon of Ephesus tells of an old fisherman who kept
his mummified wife at his side, a scene intended to touch us, not to disgust. Likewise the notion of Admetus is designed to testify to his
ardor, not to indicate a sickness. But it helps to round out the portrait of a desperate man.

After Alcestis and Admetus have both spoken, Alcestis appoints the
children to be witnesses of her husband's promises (371):

> Children, your ears are witnesses to this
> pledge of your father's; not to wed again
> and give you a second mother, but to honor me.

A social worker, Athenian or otherwise, would demur at this; we
are free to assume that Eumelus grew up to be a juvenile delinquent.
But by making the children watchdogs of their father, by implicating
them in the sorry existence which she has mapped out for him, Alcestis gives us the full measure of her hardness. She has made the
expected gesture; now she hits back at the person who is to benefit
from it, and she does so by establishing a relation between father
and children which is bound to lead to friction and disaster. If
Euripides felt that he was faced with the danger that Alcestis might
turn out to be the heroine who receives the sympathy of the audience,
he has avoided that danger expertly. Admetus, the passive, contemplative man, plays the traditional role of women or choruses. Alcestis

is active, or at any rate she is earning the fruits of her past action. Her singleness of purpose might easily distract our attention from the figure of Admetus; but it is he who chiefly interests Euripides, and around whom the play is principally written. So the author moves to prevent Alcestis from usurping the part of the central character. What he gives us is a sort of goddess, a woman who, publicly at least, is superior to the ordinary human emotions. Even so, he manages to make this goddess interesting and believable, because he endows her with the coldness of contained fury rather than the torpor of insensibility. Hers is the kind of impassioned frigidity which, though not so moving as the irresolution of Admetus, helps us to understand better the suffering through which he passes.

The final exchange is the climax of this interplay of energies. On the part of Alcestis, assurance, asperity, malice, contempt; on the part of Admetus, contrition, self-justification, regrets. Then Alcestis dies, and with the song of the child there is heard, for the first time, the voice of unadulterated grief. It is not a lifelike sorrow; musical sorrow never is, and in this case the terms of the grief are not childish.

> Father, your marriage has turned out
> stale and wasted!

is not the sort of thing a preadolescent would think up, no matter what the provocation (411). Prior to the fourth century, as we know especially from vase paintings, Greek art did not represent children as different in kind from adults. In drama, too, children speak the language of grown men in miniature. At the death of Alcestis, pure grief is voiced not so much by the child as through the child. The scholars who have studied Greek stage technique tell us that in all likelihood an aria such as this was sung by one of the adult actors, perhaps by the actor who played the part of Alcestis, now lying motionless on her bier behind the gesticulating child. The distress is mature; it is the quintessence of mourning felt or meant to be felt at the final sealing of the Queen's fate. But Euripides has it issue from the mouth of the child because all other characters on the stage are too rigidly caught up in their own interests and complexities to respond with the proper candor and simplicity.

This is especially true of Admetus. In spite of the depth and genuineness of his anguish he does not permit it to interfere with his duties as ex-husband and king. As he organizes the funeral cortege and announces the regulations for the official mourning (422), he takes refuge in the social conventions which make his sorrow bearable. Surprisingly it is the chorus that comes closest to echoing the unrefracted grief intoned by the child. But perhaps that is not so surprising after all. Now that Alcestis is dead the men can relax and play the role for which they had been preparing themselves, without thinking primarily, as they had hitherto, of the King's affliction or of the prerogatives of men. In a stately, ringing processional they turn, for the first time, to address Alcestis in her own right, in the second person, wishing her a happy sojourn among the dead, and promising her renown for many generations and in many cities of Greece. Even their blunt and naïve (473)

> I wish I had a wife like that!

is to be taken as an expression of unreserved appreciation. There is no longer any need for the note of urgency which characterized their earlier utterances. Alcestis is dead, and they have nothing to lose by paying her the traditional honor of retrospective acclaim, or even by interpreting her death as a loss. Their feelings on this score are almost disinterested; but they are not, for all that, contrary to their best interests. For their massive eulogy helps to fix the event, and to establish Alcestis firmly in her grave. If it were up to them, the song seems to say, no Hercules would come and restore her to life and bring back the old uncertainty.

The funeral ode, then, is in the nature of a confirmation. In this capacity it also serves to terminate the first part of the play. What follows is the beginning of the reversal which in the end will undo everything that had seemed safe and irrevocable. Appropriately, therefore, in the final section of the ode, the chorus put aside their role as

participants and turn, impersonally, to sum up some of the themes
which dominate the first movement; the specious hope that Alcestis
might be brought back from Hades, the gallant query of why the
parents did not die instead, the regret at the prospect of the King's
pledged celibacy. The emphasis on family tension, on deprivation
and death, is compressed within a very few lines to epitomize once
and for all the sense of inadequacy, of spiritual poverty which can
now be recognized as the hallmark of the first movement. Alcestis
has died; but her death has not produced the relief or the contentment
which comes from mutual understanding and trust. The chorus may
be moderately satisfied with the outcome; Admetus is not.

vi

In T. S. Eliot's *Cocktail Party* the Stranger
says to Edward:

> Most of the time we take ourselves for granted,
> As we have to, and live on a little knowledge
> About ourselves as we were. Who are you now?
> You don't know any more than I do,
> But rather less. You are nothing but a set
> Of obsolete responses. The one thing to do
> Is to do nothing. Wait.

Admetus has waited because he took himself for granted. But this
cannot go on in the light of the new fact, the emptiness where
formerly he could count on a life beside him. We expect the recoil.
But before we come to the awakening of Admetus, Euripides transforms the whole mood of the action by the introduction of a new
character. Again let me quote from the *Cocktail Party:*

> Just when she'd arranged a cocktail party.
> She'd gone when I came in, this afternoon.

Whereupon the unidentified guest says:

> This is an occasion.
> May I take another drink?

Before very long we shall see Hercules take that drink. Now he arrives, and his fast-paced interview with the chorus completely cuts off our preoccupation with death and frustration. This is the start of something new, a breath of fresh air admitted into the dank prison house of blindness and inaction and, above all, of pretended purposefulness.

Hercules happens to pass by on his way to perform his eighth labor, the taming of the fierce horses of Diomedes. He has recently completed the seventh, the overcoming of the Cretan bull. He has no exalted view of his duty; unlike Admetus he does not regard his position in life as a basis for speculation and bargaining. As the slave of Eurystheus he has a certain job to do, and that is that. Though a servant, he faces death repeatedly, as Admetus, the master of Apollo, cannot. Hercules is content to risk death even in a matter which is of no concern to him. From the manner of his talk about the horses of Diomedes it is quite apparent that he has no interest in them either as adversaries or as commercial value. What is more, he has not been briefed about them. Admetus, homo contemplativus, has all the insight and acumen he needs to appraise his situation properly, but he tries to shut the knowledge out until it can no longer be blinked. Hercules, homo activus, is truly uninformed; he undertakes each labor as if it were a business requiring nothing more than mechanical action. His matter-of-factness leaves no room for insights or fears or beliefs. The greatest hero of Greek fairy tales—and here Euripides once more has his fun with us—is not imaginative enough to believe in fairy tales. The man who is going to take the personal existence of Death seriously enough to wrestle with him and choke his windpipe, refuses to credit the existence of supernatural things. When the chorus suggest that it will not be easy to tame the horses of Diomedes, he replies tolerantly (493):

Surely they don't breathe fire from their nostrils?

Of course every child in the audience knew that that was precisely what the wild Thracian horses did do. Hercules just has a good laugh at the notion and goes about his business, pretending not to like it (499),

> Just my tough luck! I always get the worst breaks!

but eager enough to carry out the mission all the same. Hercules is not involved in the tragedy of inaction which plagues Admetus and his people. Nor is his role in life dependent on the support and comforts extended by fellow men. Admetus, even at the moment of his self-discovery and conversion, could not cope with his lot unless he knew himself to be a member of the group, sharing with them his anxieties and his dreams. Hercules stands alone; his simple strength and uncomplicated outlook operate best without the softening influence of human bonds. Nor again is he weighed down by conventions; being a successful man of action he has no need for them. He is in every way uninvolved. And the absence of involvement is dramatized visually through a break with the traditions of the Greek theater: his scene with the steward is played on an empty stage, with the chorus gone to attend the funeral.

Hercules is not entangled in the meshes of the errant cause; his cause is freedom, the freedom of spirit and freedom of action. Freedom is the theme of a drinking song which he bawls out, much to the pious horror of the steward. As corroborated in the speech which follows, the theme is pedestrian and untragic: Drink and be merry, for tomorrow you will die (782). With the Herculean labors freshly engraved in our minds, there is considerable humor in the spectacle of the Stoic saint preaching the philosophy of Omar Khayyám. Surely he is the one man in the world who does not pursue a hedonistic career. And yet, the man of action easily turns into the clown; Hercules' freedom from involvement also places him beyond the restrictions of a meaningful commitment. He does not need to be sensitive or tactful or morally obligated; he stands by himself, above the claims of society. It is perhaps worth noting that Euripides is here engineering a clever scheme of deflection. In the literary tradition it is Admetus who was associated with the philosophy now offered by Hercules.

A poem by Bacchylides, who lived a generation or so before Euripides, contains these lines:

> The lord Apollo
> . . . spoke to the son of Pheres:
> "You are mortal; hence you shall foster
> two thoughts, that you will see no more
> than the light of tomorrow's sun,
> or that you will draw out and complete
> a deep-treasured life of fifty years to come.
> Then, do what is right and enjoy yourself;
> that is the greatest of all profits."

In Euripides' version Admetus cannot take life so lightly; his friend Hercules can, and he can exemplify the finer qualities of Admetus to boot: warmth, generosity, tolerance.

Unlike the chorus, Hercules sees only kindness, not extravagance, in the fact that Admetus entertained him without informing him of the true conditions. In spite of his servile status he can admire a good act without envy or resentment (855):

> He took me into his house, he did not drive
> me away, despite the fierce weight of his sorrow;
> he hid it, in his kindliness and with
> his usual tact. Is there in Thessaly,
> or Greece, a man more liberal than he?

Hercules is a man without bitterness, without aggressions; he has no privileges to safeguard, no fancied status to maintain. His eye is free and unclouded, his heart ready to be moved by the actions of his friends. He may be somewhat lacking in imagination, but his capacity to love and admire is unlimited.

Why does Admetus deceive Hercules? For one thing, to admit that Alcestis had died would have meant provoking awkward questions. Hercules knows of Alcestis' promise, but the accomplished fact would force him to regard Admetus in a different light. Hercules does not believe that she will die—he does not believe in fairy tales—and so Admetus feels himself safe from his contempt. To this extent Ad-

metus' silence is selfish, a further token of his lack of fiber. The chorus
are appalled at his silence, but for another reason. In their eyes, ad-
mitting Hercules into the house is a breach of the conventions, or
rather the breach of one convention in the interest of another, and
they doubt that the duty of hospitality could ever take precedence over
the duty of mourning. But that is exactly what Admetus seems to
feel; a true Thessalian, raised in the traditions of the frontier and
the wide-open spaces, he regards the duty of entertaining a guest as
canceling all other obligations.

But that is not all; in effect, Admetus is trying to take the easy
way out. Upon Hercules' question whether his wife has died (518),
he answers: she has, and she has not. The whole passage which follows is riddling, and Hercules has a point when he remarks: "You
are talking mysteries!" Riddling is a kind of ritual; by reducing the
status of Alcestis and his own lamentable part in the affair to the
terms of a conundrum, Admetus hopes to be able to live with his
guilt more easily. Hercules is less subtle, he has no taste for puzzles,
and asks to be excused (544): "Let me go!" he says, using the words
which Alcestis had used at the moment of her vision of Charon. Admetus allowed Alcestis to leave him; he cannot now allow Hercules
to do likewise. Hospitality is easier to exercise than marital obligation.
It is a beneficent convention, ordered to measure to help you forget the
sting of personal defeat. Admetus craves to salvage what is left of
his pride, by clinging to the embarrassed guest. The tenacity with
which he presses him is an index of his desperation. It leads him to
renounce even the last shred of his moral integrity (541):

The dead are dead; come, go into the house!

Coming from the delicate Admetus, this is indeed a callous pronounce-
ment. He is attempting to escape, both from his own remorse and
from the painful memory of his wife's last actions. But the escape
into the role of host, even if momentarily effective, cannot last. The
time must come when Admetus will recognize his delusion and struggle to rid himself of it.

At this point the chorus, apparently forgetful of their earlier criticism of Admetus' conduct, sing their second great choral ode, a hymn to hospitality (569), in rhythms usually reserved for the extolling of victorious kings or athletes. The ode, with its praise of Apollo—an earlier guest who should never have come in the first place, and who stayed too long when he did—is designed to create an impression of security and contentment. The language is pastoral; the emphasis is on peace, stability, simple pleasure, the happy life. The song starts with an address to the house, then turns to call upon Apollo, who is pictured, like Orpheus, attracting the animals with his lyre (thus adding to the number of the house guests), and settles down to describe the wealth and liberality of Admetus. These three—the house, Apollo, and Admetus—form a compound image in which the meaning of hospitality takes concrete shape. True hospitality is the willed expression of a life that is full, happy, relaxed. At least it should be that. But often it becomes a gadget employed to make it appear *as if* the life which occasions it were unimpaired. In our play, hospitality is the most impressive manifestation of the code which is the ordinary man's support in the stream of life, and which marks its practitioner as a civilized person. But there is no doubt that it is mainly for the weak. They are the hosts; the strong are guests.

Hospitality, Admetus briefly hopes, will allow him to find his moorings. But the record of the convention as it pertains to this tale does not leave much room for confidence. The hospitality tendered by Admetus to Apollo initiated the loss of Alcestis. Admetus entertains Hercules, wrongly in most people's eyes, but the *faux pas* starts her recovery. Finally Admetus tries to shake off his weakness and proposes to deny hospitality to the mystery woman, and almost loses his wife once more. Thus the code, in its conflict with genuine sorrow and genuine involvement, makes for some difficult situations. But nothing better can be expected from the slipshod tactics of the civilized man who lives by rules rather than by instinct. Once the manipulation of the code has been substituted for the life of courage and conviction, the control must slip from the hands of the agent.

vii

There is a man in the play whose instincts, it seems, are as simple and straightforward, though not so generous, as those of Hercules: Pheres. It is true that when he comes on the stage he has a perfectly respectable little speech, full of pious and acceptable sentiments. One might almost believe that he is not an interested party, and that the reports about him put out by Alcestis were not entirely accurate. But this impression is at once wiped out when we come to the last two lines of his opening remarks, where he reveals his real feelings with singular coarseness (627):

> This is the sort of marriage that turns to profit;
> otherwise marriage is not worth a straw.

The method is characteristically Euripidean; neither Aeschylus nor the pre-Euripidean Sophocles has it (though Homer does): a man betraying his secret thoughts in an unexpected final disclosure, an epigrammatic revelation of the self, as if the pretended sentiments got to be too burdensome for the speaker to maintain. His remark immediately puts us out of sympathy with him, and makes us accept the position of Admetus in the scene which follows with less revulsion than might otherwise have been the case. And yet we cannot help but admire the old man; unlike his son he has not talked himself into believing his own fictions. He can take or leave the code as it fits his purposes, his true instincts always being on hand to run their consistently unsentimental course.

Admetus, to be sure, behaves like a cad. He calls his father a coward (642, 717), apparently forgetting his own inglorious role. Taking a leaf from his father's book he addresses him in terms of law rather than affection, as if the relationship between father and son were little more than a legal contract which might be revoked at the signer's discretion. The effect of his inaction has been to destroy his judgment and to atrophy his humaneness; for a brief interval he dispenses with his gentlemanly ideals of kindness and good will. His father repays him in kind. From legalistic charges and countercharges—I disown you, I have a new father and mother! . . . What crime have I committed? Have I stolen from you?—the quarrel degenerates into a battle of insults, into the most vitriolic enactment of the war of generations in Greek drama. No punches are pulled as the young calls the old superannuated, and the old, with equal justification, sneers at the softness and the dishonesty of the young.

Pheres says that he has no understanding of the nature of Alcestis' sacrifice (728):

> *She's* pure and blameless, yes; but does she have sense?

While Admetus decries his parents for the purpose of magnifying Alcestis, Pheres cannot see any point to her deed. He prides himself on being levelheaded, unromantic, unconfused; he does not mind being coarse in the bargain so long as the truth as he sees it comes out into the open. His coarseness is painful but it has a function. For it exercises on Admetus a peculiar spell which helps us to understand him further, and which eventually helps him to understand himself. Goaded by the memory of his wife's not-so-silent reproaches, angered by his father's brutal cynicism, the gentle Admetus turns savage and fanatical. The explosion is as terrible as it is unexpected. It must lead either to destruction or to catharsis. And this gives us a clue concerning the role of Pheres in the plot. His own character is drawn vividly enough; but his appearance in the play is due chiefly to the fact that Euripides is interested in the soul of Admetus, in the experience which a good man undergoes when faced with the fact of a loved one's death.

One barb which Pheres uses in his scolding is particularly sharp; he calls Admetus *sophos*—clever, or ingenious (699). Admetus is that. To say that you expect your parents to die for you is immorally clever; to consider such a statement natural, as Admetus in his violence does, is downright sophistical. But "cleverness" does not quite meet the situation, for Admetus is, at this stage, too confused to merit the tag. In reality his *sophia* is fantasy, self-delusion. A good son is made bad, his filial responses are distorted, by a good deed which put him to shame. The explosion helps to untwist the responses and to transmute the fantasy into a *sophia* proper, into an insight into his true self. Pheres functions as a kind of psychotherapist to assist Admetus in his recovery from the wound which Alcestis has dealt. That is not to say that Pheres thinks of himself as a healer; he is too old and too crude to think of anyone's welfare but his own. But he operates as one nonetheless. His refusal to participate in the fiction which his son has elaborated for himself shocks Admetus into first compounding and then surrendering his fantasy, into turning from delusion to knowledge. Pheres is little more than an instrument, a tool of conversion. After the scene between father and son, there is no further mention of Pheres; he has done the job he was designed to do. And when Admetus comes back from the funeral he is a different person.

Not so the chorus; they have changed very little, continuing to rely on their double props of convention and masculinity (892): it happens all the time, you are not the first one to lose a wife, and so forth. They do not understand the new single-mindedness of Admetus' grief, and on one occasion they offer a veiled criticism (903):

> I had a kinsman
> who lost a son, an only son;
> his death was bitter
> cause for tears. Nevertheless,
> he bore the loss well, though childless now,
> and graying of hair,
> and closing in on the eve of life.

In other words: too much fuss over a dead wife. But Admetus can no longer, after the set-to with Pheres, take shelter in externalizing or ritualizing his guilt. He begins by addressing the house, once the symbol of fullness and contentment. Now he is reluctant to enter it because it reminds him of the emptiness in his life and the draining away of his own self (861):

> Hated entrance way, hated sight
> of an empty home! Where am I
> to walk, where to stand? . . .
> I have been ill-starred from birth.

Apollo has enriched the house, now he has impoverished it; and Admetus has begun to realize that he is not separate from the house; as the house goes, so goes he. He had been blind to believe that life, domestic and political—as the second choral ode shows, the house symbolizes both—could go on much as before; that, with Alcestis gone from his side, he could continue to exercise his function as father and king. The delusion is gone, and Admetus recognizes his guilt.

In his speech after the musical exchange which marks the second entry of the chorus, Admetus openly confesses himself at fault. He does so by using the only formulation then readily available to a man and citizen. He imagines outsiders and personal enemies pointing their fingers at him and whispering (955):

> There goes the man who lives in shame, who did
> not dare to die, who bought a coward's life
> with his own wife's death . . .
> who hates his parents for his own panic!

And the capping humiliation:

> Is he a man?

The formulation is in terms of what anthropologists call shame rather than guilt; the language of guilt was not yet easily handled by Euripides or his audience. But the self-questioning of Admetus clearly is a pregnant dramatization of the dawning of guilt upon a soul in the process of conversion. "He has turned tail before Hades; is he a man?" Greek tragedy of the grand genre, the tragedy of Oedipus or Medea or Prometheus, does not allow for a learning from experience or a wisdom through suffering. But Greek melodrama, or tragicomedy, or the sort of drama we have here, occasionally does show us a hero who recognizes his faults and suffers for them and learns from them. Conversion is not a tragic business, it does not rouse the emotions of which Aristotle speaks. But for an author who is interested in character and character development, conversion is an eminently desirable theme. In the story of Admetus, Euripides gently guides us through the career of a man who, though initially self-deceived, proves his worth by permitting himself to be shocked into an admission of his cowardice. He now sees himself with the eyes of Pheres; and that is the beginning of his restoration to favor with the audience.

viii

Immediately after Admetus' condemnation of himself, the chorus sings a great ode to Fate or Necessity (962). It is a stately hymn, majestic and serious, with touches of Aeschylean grandeur unusual in the choral passages of Euripides. One may wonder how this announced submission to Necessity tallies with the obvious cancellation of necessity in the scene which is about to follow. It would obviously be a mistake to interpret the devout utterance of the chorus as documenting a philosophy which Euripides himself held and wished to broadcast. That is not the way in which the ancient dramatists proceed; in any case, being a dramatist Euripides would never accept a trust in the power of necessity as a pertinent philosophical creed. In his plays, even more than in those of Aeschylus and Sophocles, man is what he makes of himself, in spite of the unseen powers which rule beyond the scene of action. Hence the poignancy of Admetus' suffering; it would be uninteresting if Fate or Necessity was responsible for what happened to his soul.

Does the ode, then, tell us something of the beliefs of the chorus? Perhaps, for they are ordinary people, with ordinary and rather limited ideas, quick to grasp the simplest, most traditional formulation and to turn their backs on the prospect of personal responsibility. But if this were all, it would be awkward, to say the least. The play is almost over, and this is not the proper time to introduce new information about the inclinations of the chorus. As a matter of fact, the ode is not meant to add to our knowledge of character at all. The study of character has come to an end. The conversion has happened, the anatomy of the soul is complete, and Euripides must tackle the difficult task of bringing the play to a satisfactory ending. This is where the Hymn to Necessity comes in. With it the author accomplishes the revalidation of Admetus. The stress on Fate seems, but only seems, to diminish his culpability in retrospect. The scene which Euripides has just put on the stage, the conversion of Admetus, holds a danger. The danger is that the audience, who had to a certain extent shared in the delusion of the hero and the chorus, will now see him with *his* eyes, see him as a coward only. Psychological realism disenchants; the anatomy of an unheroic soul shows up a dynamic vacuum which may become intolerable. This will not do, either morally or aesthetically. Aesthetically the play can be concluded satisfactorily only if at the conclusion Admetus can once more be regarded with a modicum of respect and appreciation. Morally, our initial feelings about him were not so far wrong after all. He is a good man, a worthy man caught in circumstance, and his admission of guilt should, with the enlightened in the audience, enhance his ethical standing. That is why, by an act of artistic legerdemain, the audience is induced to focus on the government of Fate, thus to take Admetus back more willingly into the fold of their sympathy. As so often in Greek drama, the chorus is used to shape the feelings of the audience; under the guidance of the ode the spectators dispense with cold logic and submit themselves to the irrational demands of the play.

Toward the end of the Hymn to Necessity the chorus re-emphasize the deadness of Alcestis; they vow to extend to her almost divine honors. As before, there is in the song of the chorus a characteristic insistence on the fact of her admission to Hades. While Admetus asks (897), "Why could not I have died?" the chorus sings about the inescapable bonds of death which will keep Alcestis safely and beneficially underground (985, 992, 1002):

> She died for her husband; now
> she lives as a blessed goddess.
> Hail, mistress, and give us your blessings!

The song of worship is also a binding charm.

Enter Hercules, with a veiled lady. The audience knows who she is, the actors do not; a masquerade. Hercules starts out with emphatic reproaches (1012): "You never told me!" This is surprising, for when he first found out, in his conversation with the steward, that Admetus had not been completely frank with him, his impulse was to admire Admetus for his thoughtfulness (855). Only now does he take stock of what was due him as a friend and guest. But now he is about to make Admetus happy again. Are his reproaches playful? Are they the result of his recent bout with Death, a working off of the strain on the nearest bystander? The latter would not be without precedent. In the *Iliad* heroes snarl at their closest friends and relatives for no other reason than that they are under pressure and must vent their strain where it will do the least harm. But whatever the psychological motivation—and perhaps none is needed now—Hercules' criticism is artistically useful. His air of discontent keeps Admetus off balance until it is time to show his hand in earnest. To secure the fullest effect of the happy ending which is to come, the long ascent from apparent displeasure to ultimate benefaction is the most satisfying.

Hercules proposes to leave the lady with Admetus; Admetus objects. Do his remonstrances give us the picture of a man who is tempted to break faith with his promises but shrinks back because he does not wish to be censured? True, this is the fear he voices, but again it is a matter of terminology rather than substance. He states in terms of shame what we would expect to see stated in terms of guilt. His question (1057), "What will the people say?" really means the same as, "How can I square such an act with my self-respect?" The man who says he fears the censure of the people and of the dead Alcestis is not an inhibited libertine or a prurient ascetic, but one who is no longer interested in women, and for whom even the duty of hospitality has lost its meaning. The author wants no further dissection of Admetus' character. The last scene is pure fairy tale, to finish the play satisfactorily. Realistic portraiture and clinical psychology are left far behind. Euripides has said what he wanted to say by the time the closing scene opens. The scene is not without its subtleties, of course —witness the silence of Alcestis—but its purpose is resolution rather than further exploration. True, Admetus shows signs of a reawakening capacity for enjoyment; he says to the woman (1062):

You have the same measurements as Alcestis.

True, Hercules and Admetus between them strike just the right note of courteous hesitation and gentle urgency. There is humor and there is irony. But there is no further interest in the consequences of the fact of death.

Why does Alcestis not move or speak? Hercules' explanation, perhaps not entirely satisfactory to all of us, has a substantial kernel of wisdom and truth. It is an explanation on the level of ritual, appealing to the instincts operative during a religious festival such as the Dionysian festival at which the play was performed. Alcestis is to be purified before she may speak; she must readjust herself to the ways of life before she can be trusted to participate in life once more. But for once the ritual reinforces the dramaturgy. Earlier in the play Alcestis had stood under the shadow of death. Now she returns, alive, and that is awkward in itself. For the plot she was needed to die, not to come back. She must come back so that Admetus will be happy, or at least so that we shall not worry about the future of the hero. But that is all; for the rest her dramatic appearance must be pruned to zero. A single word from her and we should be put in mind of the whole complex of frustration and inadequacy which the final scene is designed to make us forget.

The last scene, then, is as clear an indication as one may wish of Euripides' pervasive conviction that the stage is not to offer solutions to moral or psychological problems. It is the author's task, after presenting the conflicts and the suffering which constitute the plot proper, to terminate the drama with a close which is not philosophically meaningful but artistically and psychologically satisfying. Mostly he does this by creating a compelling illusion of having cut the knot, by employing a *deus ex machina*. Hercules is no such august divinity lowered from the skies, but his role as the restorer of Alcestis is analogous to the intervention of a god. But there is a difference between this kind of conclusion and the ending of a true tragedy. In the *Medea* or the *Hippolytus* or the *Bacchae* the coming of the god serves as a public avowal that the situation witnessed on the stage is insoluble by purely human standards. The *deus ex machina* underscores the hopelessness of the human predicament. In the *Alcestis,* on the other hand, the action had come to a proper end before Hercules returns. With the conversion of Admetus the air has been cleared, and human dignity and intelligence have been, if not vindicated, certainly salvaged from utter loss. Hercules does not come back to solve a difficulty or to supply a spurious answer; he returns to bring back Alcestis. After all, the Queen had been sent off to Hades only so that we could see what happened to her husband under the peculiar circumstances of her death. We have seen what happened; now that Admetus has shown the signs of a moral recovery, why not liberate both of them from the forced conditions required by the experiment? It would be wasteful to leave Alcestis in Hades now that Admetus will be a much better husband to her. The masquerade is long-drawn-out; Euripides wants the audience to enjoy the fun. The emphasis is on relaxation, on happiness and sport. The spirit of the exordium augurs well for the future of the reunited couple.

When Admetus is first told who the veiled lady is, he thinks he is dreaming (1127). But the restoration of Alcestis suggests that it is not the present but the past which was the dream. In retrospect the events of the play have a chimerical quality about them, not only because they derive from a fairy tale, but because matters which are usually covered up have been exposed with a nightmarish precision. Now Admetus is emerging from the dream; his slowness in realizing who the veiled stranger is, shows the difficulty he has in putting it all behind him. It takes some time for the head to be cleared. The dream had helped to rid him of an immoral fantasy; now, for the sake of the audience, the dream itself must be exorcised. But what does the dream mean? Here Artemidorus, a writer of the second century A.D., may be of some help, for he knew more about the dream images of the Greeks and their feelings about them than we shall ever know. Here are a few scattered passages from his book. "A wedding and a death have the same meaning, for the things that go with them are the same." "For the unmarried man to dream of death means that he will marry; for death equals a wedding. Both have the same events linked with them, namely, a procession of men and women and garlands and incense and myrrh and a plate collection." "To dream that one descends into Hades and sees the things which are supposed to be in Hades, this has one meaning for those in good circumstances and another for the depressed. For the former, for those who live as they have chosen [and that disqualifies Admetus] the dream indicates bad circumstances and harm. For the others, those who are overcareful and worried and dejected, the dream foretells a release from these worries and cares; for the people in Hades are without cares and beyond all worrying."

Thus Artemidorus. To be sure, it is Alcestis who has descended into Hades, not Admetus. But the vision, the purifying fright, are his, and ours. The ending of the play suggests that henceforth he will be a better man, a more appreciative husband, a married man rather than an island to himself. And we share in the broadening of the perspective. The plot which Euripides has sketched for us, and the character of Admetus as he suffers and squirms and finally breaks free, have the sharply incised quality of a dream. It is, however, a benevolent dream which stops short of turning into unrelieved nightmare. There is nothing obsessive about the limpid naturalness of the action and the relations between Admetus and his household. The men and women in the play are not machines, nor are they monsters which are simply machines gone wild. They are the likely and, on the whole, likable characters of everyday life, forced to grapple with the natural necessities and trying hard to preserve their small portion of culture and dignity as they do so. In his entanglement with the fact of death Admetus takes on the outlines of Everyman. But not an Everyman stripped of all that does not bear on his entanglement. Rather an Everyman of flesh and blood, with the gestures and the foibles and the luxury of good will which makes him into one of Euripides' most successful characters, vastly more successful than the heroes and heroines of true tragedy, the outrageous Medeas and the tortured Pentheuses, who were of course never meant to be characters in quite the same sense. For a tragedy deals with issues or causes beyond the reach of ordinary men, issues that can be realized effectively only in the test-tube environment of extraordinary souls. Only a nontragic drama such as the *Alcestis* may venture to undertake the study of character for its own sake. This does not mean supplying reasons, or tracing origins; behavior is not studied as a fruit of the past, but as a pattern interesting and authentic in itself. Admetus appeals to us not for what made him act as he acts, nor for what he hopes to accomplish—that would be the tragic dimension—but simply for the way he acts when confronted with a situation which, in spite of its fairy-tale base, is perfectly natural. A play of this type requires very little interpretation; all that the audience is asked to do is to listen to what the characters have to say, and recognize themselves in them. We can do no more, and no less.